Oxford Modern English Grammar

Bas Aarts is Professor of English Linguistics and Director of the Survey of English Usage at University College London. His previous books include *Small Clauses in English: The Nonverbal Types* (Mouton de Gruyter, 1992); *The Verb in Contemporary English*, co-edited with Charles F. Meyer (Cambridge University Press, 1995); *English Syntax and Argumentation* (Palgrave, 1997, 2001, 2008); *Investigating Natural Language: Working with the British Component of the International Corpus of English*, co-authored with Gerald Nelson and Sean Wallis (John Benjamins, 2002); *Fuzzy Grammar: A Reader*, co-edited with David Denison, Evelien Keizer, and Gergana Popova (Oxford University Press, 2004); *The Handbook of English Linguistics*, co-edited with April McMahon (Blackwell, 2006); and *Syntactic Gradience: The Nature of Grammatical Indeterminacy* (Oxford University Press, 2007). He is one of the founding editors of the journal *English Language and Linguistics*.

Oxford Modern English Grammar

Bas Aarts
Department of English Language and Literature
University College London

OXFORD
UNIVERSITY PRESS

OXFORD
UNIVERSITY PRESS

Great Clarendon Street, Oxford ox2 6DP

Oxford University Press is a department of the University of Oxford.
It furthers the University's objective of excellence in research, scholarship,
and education by publishing worldwide in

Oxford New York

Auckland Cape Town Dar es Salaam Hong Kong Karachi
Kuala Lumpur Madrid Melbourne Mexico City Nairobi
New Delhi Shanghai Taipei Toronto

With offices in

Argentina Austria Brazil Chile Czech Republic France Greece
Guatemala Hungary Italy Japan Poland Portugal Singapore
South Korea Switzerland Thailand Turkey Ukraine Vietnam

Oxford is a registered trade mark of Oxford University Press
in the UK and in certain other countries

Published in the United States
by Oxford University Press Inc., New York

© Oxford University Press 2011

The moral rights of the author have been asserted
Database right Oxford University Press (maker)

First published 2011

British Library Cataloguing in Publication Data
Data available

Library of Congress Cataloging-in-Publication Data
Data available

Typeset by Glyph International, Bangalore, India
Printed in Great Britain
on acid-free paper by
Clays Ltd., St Ives plc

ISBN 978–0–19–953319–0

1 3 5 7 9 10 8 6 4 2

In memory of my mother Sjé Aarts-Postmes
(1934–2008)

Contents

List of figures

List of tables

Preface

The aim of this grammar is to offer a modern, concise, but nevertheless wide-ranging description of the structure of contemporary standard British and American English. The book is intended for anyone who is interested in English grammar, and has been written without an assumption on my part that the reader has any previous knowledge of grammatical concepts.

The account of grammar presented in this book is descriptive, not prescriptive: it describes the language as it is used today. Readers hoping to find confirmation that the so-called *split infinitive* is an odious manifestation of the decline of the English language—to give but one example of a common usage shibboleth—will be disappointed. The view taken here is that the English language is not a static entity, but is continually subject to inevitable change, which is reflected in its lexis and grammar.

It is not possible to write a book like this without acknowledging previous work on English grammar. The framework adopted here relies heavily on the two most complete and in-depth accounts of English grammar currently available, namely Randolph Quirk, Sidney Greenbaum, Geoffrey Leech, and Jan Svartvik's *Comprehensive Grammar of the English Language* (1985) and Rodney Huddleston and Geoffrey Pullum *et al.*'s *Cambridge Grammar of the English Language* (2002). These grammars offer sophisticated and detailed descriptions of English that go far beyond the scope of the present book. It should be noted, however, that I have not in all cases followed the grammatical analyses presented in these books. The major points of divergence are discussed in the *Notes and further reading* section.

I owe an enormous debt of gratitude to Flor Aarts, Peter Collins, Rodney Huddleston, and Geoffrey Leech (in alphabetical order) for reading the entire manuscript and commenting on it in great detail. I am very fortunate to have received this tremendously valuable feedback from such eminent grammarians, and their input has made this a much better book than it would otherwise have been. I'm also grateful to my editors at Oxford University Press, Ben Harris, Vicky Donald, Rebecca Lane and Clare Jenkins. For their help during the editing stage I would like to thank Jill Bowie for her superb copy-editing, Helen Liebeck for proofreading, and Phil Aslett for compiling the subject index.

BAS AARTS

University College London
April 2010

Notational conventions and abbreviations

Notational conventions

*	An asterisk indicates an impossible structure, i.e. a structure that does not conform to the grammatical rules of English. Example: *They likes to read*. In this example the third person <u>plural</u> Subject *they* is followed by a verb with a third person <u>singular</u> inflectional ending.
Ø	This symbol is used to indicate an implicit Subject. Example: *I want [Ø to read it]*.
Ø$_{rel.}$	This is used to indicate an implicit relativized element. Example: *The power [that Ø$_{rel.}$ enables this union] Coleridge categorized as the imagination*.
Ø$_{sub}$	This is used to indicate a missing subordinating conjunction *that*. Example: *They think [Ø$_{sub}$ they are funny]*.
¤	This symbol is used where the form label can be of different kinds (that is, where the function can be realized by different kinds of forms).
arrows	These indicate movement, e.g. passivization, extraposition, or raising. Example: *She seems ＿ to enjoy cricket.*

The underscore symbol is explained below.

brackets [...]	Brackets are used: (1) to indicate words that together form a constituent phrase, clause, etc. A *labelled bracketing* includes a subscript indicator of the syntactic status of the constituent. Example: [$_{NP}$ *Cats*] [$_{VP}$ *eat* [$_{NP}$ *fish*]]; (2) to indicate that a lexical item, usually a verb, is followed by a Complement which contains a particular word. Example: HAVE [*to*] indicates that the verb HAVE is followed by a Complement that contains the word *to*, e.g. *I have <u>to</u> leave*.
capitals	These are used: (1) to indicate functional grammatical labels, e.g. Subject, Direct Object; (2) semantic roles, e.g. Agent, Patient.

coindexing | Items that are coreferential can be coindexed, i.e. bear the same subscript letter, usually an 'i'. Example: *He$_i$ shaves himself$_i$ twice every day.*

italics | These are used:
(1) to indicate the first time a particular technical term is used;
(2) to cite words, sentences, etc. as linguistic forms;
(3) to indicate words, phrases, etc. that require highlighting.
For underlined italics, see below.

SMALL CAPS | These indicate lexemes (i.e. dictionary words). Example: the forms *laugh, laughs, laughed,* and *laughing* are inflectional forms belonging to the lexeme LAUGH. The small caps notation will be used for verbs throughout, and for other word classes whenever relevant.

<u>*underlined italics*</u> | Within italicized technical terms, underlining is used to distinguish citations of particular words (or other elements), e.g. *existential <u>there</u>, <u>–ing</u> participle clauses.*

underscore ('_') | This symbol indicates a 'gap' in the clause with which a displaced element is associated. Examples: in *What did you see _?* the *wh*-word (see below) functions as the Direct Object of the verb SEE and has been fronted to form an interrogative structure; in the passive clause *The flight was booked _ by me* the gap indicates the position from which the Direct Object of the verb BOOK was moved.

wh-words | This term is used for a set of words most of which begin with the letters *wh*-, e.g. *what, who,* but which also includes *how.*

Abbreviations

A	Adjunct
Adj/AdjP	adjective/adjective phrase
Adv/AdvP	adverb/adverb phrase
CC	Complement Clause
Comp	Complement
D/DP	determinative/determinative phrase
DET	Determiner
DO	Direct Object
EXT-A	External Adjunct
H	Head
ICE-GB	The British component of the *International Corpus of English*
ind	indicative
IO	Indirect Object
MC	matrix clause
N/NP	noun/noun phrase
NICE	An acronym for Negation, Inversion, Code, Emphasis properties
P/PP	preposition/prepositional phrase
PPi/PPt	prepositional phrase headed by an intransitive/transitive preposition
PC	Predicative Complement
PCR	Predicator
PPC	Prepositional Phrase as Complement
Pred	Predicate
Predet	Predeterminer
pres.	present
ps.	person
sing.	singular
Subj	Subject
subjve	subjunctive
V -*ing*	-*ing* participle form of a verb
V -*ed*/-*en*	past participle form of a verb
V/VP	verb/verb phrase

Part I: The basics

Chapter 1
An overview of English grammar

1.1 Grammar and grammar writing

Grammar is concerned with the structure of words (*morphology*), and of phrases and clauses (*syntax*). There is a long tradition of grammar writing, starting with the ancient Greeks and leading up to the present day. This tradition has had a lasting influence on how languages—not just English—have been described. The book in front of you is no exception: it will describe the structure of English relying heavily on this tradition in many different ways, not least in terms of the terminology adopted. However, it is important to stress that it does not exclusively base itself on the classical tradition, because it has long been accepted that we should not assume that the grammar of the classical languages, especially Latin, should serve as a model for the description of English. Many grammars of English were written in Latin up to the middle of the eighteenth century, though William Bullokar's *Pamphlet for Grammar* (1586), the first grammar of English to be written in English, is an exception. After 1750 grammarians increasingly recognized that the differences between Latin and English are too great to be ignored. As an example of the mismatch between English and Latin grammar, consider the word *the*, the most frequent word in the English language. In English this word belongs to the class of *determinatives* (see section 1.3), but in Latin this word class did not exist, and so it had to be introduced into grammatical descriptions of English. It is generally acknowledged that the playwright Ben Jonson was the first person to do so (though he used the more familiar label *article*).

In the history of grammar writing a number of different types of grammar can be distinguished. *School grammars* aim to teach basic and often simplified grammatical patterns. Very often they have a prescriptive outlook, rather than a purely descriptive one—that is, they tell their readers what to do and what not to do when speaking or writing in English. They were used very widely in the eighteenth and nineteenth centuries. One of the best known examples was Lindley Murray's wonderfully entitled *English Grammar, Adapted to the Different Classes of Learners. With an Appendix, Containing Rules and Observations for Promoting Perspicuity in Speaking and Writing* (1795). Stemming from this tradition, but more up to date and modern, are *pedagogical grammars*, used in a variety of educational settings. *Traditional grammars* are detailed scholarly works which belong to the nineteenth and early twentieth centuries. They are characterized by their length, usually several weighty volumes, and their extensive use of literary examples. Principal among them is Otto Jespersen's *A Modern English Grammar on Historical Principles* (1909–1949). The aim of *theoretical grammar* is to discover the (abstract) rules and principles underlying the structure (and sometimes use) of language. There are many different types of theoretical approaches to grammar. The best known is probably the theory of the American linguist Noam Chomsky which aims to arrive at a blueprint for a mentally encoded *Universal Grammar* that all human beings are genetically endowed with.

Although the present book has been influenced by ideas in theoretical work, its outlook is the same as that found in modern *descriptive reference grammars*. Such grammars describe the language as it is used today by its speakers, and do not aim to legislate in matters of 'correct grammar'. Thus, while you may find a description of the so-called *split infinitive* (*to cheerfully sing in the bath*) in a reference grammar, you will not be told to avoid this construction on the grounds that it is 'bad English'. Naturally, this does not mean that everything uttered by a speaker of English will be regarded as acceptable. If someone describes a painting as 'executed brilliant with also vividly colours', then they are violating the grammatical rule system of English. You may be wondering at this point whether the use of the split infinitive—or indeed my use of the pronoun *they* in the preceding sentence—does not also violate the rules of English. The answer is 'no', and the reason is that the use of the split infinitive and the use of the plural pronoun *they* with a non-specific singular antecedent are sanctioned by widespread current usage, the former more so than the latter. The thinking underlying these observations is that the grammar of a language is shaped over time by the speakers of that language, not by self-appointed individuals or learned bodies. The efforts of those who have tried in the past to influence how the language should be used have generally failed. Jonathan Swift, who proposed setting up an Academy in his 1712 pamphlet entitled 'A Proposal for Correcting, Improving and Ascertaining the English Tongue', was unsuccessful, and even the lexicographer Samuel Johnson, who thought he could improve the English language when he began his magisterial *Dictionary of the English Language* (published in 1755), had to give up on that idea. Joseph Priestley was opposed to setting up an Academy, and his attitude to usage, expressed in his *Rudiments of English Grammar* (1761), foreshadowed modern thinking when he wrote that the only standard we need to admit is that of custom.

Allowing the language to run its own course means that a previously frowned-upon usage can become normal. For different speakers this will happen at a different pace. Thus, while the *interrogative tag innit*, as in *He left the country, innit?*, used in London and southeast Britain, is not part of standard English at present, over time it may well become acceptable in the same way that *n'est-ce pas* in French is acceptable as a generalized tag. (See section 4.1.1.8 for an explanation of the term interrogative tag.) A less contentious example of usage that is slowly making its way into English is a particular way that the so-called *progressive construction* is used. This construction involves the verb BE followed by another verb that ends in *-ing*, as in *I'm watching television*. In the present tense its typical use is to express that a situation began in the past and is continuing beyond the present moment. Recently it has been possible to hear people say, for example, *I'm wanting to learn about grammar*, where the more established pattern is *I want to learn about grammar*. This novel use of the progressive construction is also found in the slogan *I'm loving it!*, coined by a popular purveyor of fast food. While usage matters will play a role in this grammar, they will not be the main focus of attention.

Instead of following the classical tradition too closely I will be describing the grammar of standard English as a system in its own right, making use of the insights of modern linguistics. As noted in the Preface, the descriptive framework adopted here is influenced by two major grammars of English, namely Quirk *et al.*'s *Comprehensive Grammar of the English Language* (1985) and Huddleston and Pullum *et al.*'s *Cambridge Grammar of the English Language* (2002). The description will focus on the two main standard varieties of English: British English and American English. Throughout, I will use authentic (occasionally adapted) written and spoken language data taken from two kinds of sources to illustrate grammatical points. The primary source is the British component of the *International Corpus of English* (ICE-GB), based at the Survey of English Usage, University College London. This is a collection of 500 'texts' (passages of 2,000 words) of grammatically analysed spoken and written English selected from various types of categories of language use. The structure of the ICE-GB corpus is outlined in Appendix 2. The second kind of source of examples includes online broadsheet newspapers, news channels such as BBC News, and the like. The sources of the examples are listed at the back of the book. As we saw above, traditional grammars often used literary examples, while more modern texts on grammar often use made-up examples. Using authentic examples is preferable because they offer an insight into how language is used naturally in real situations.

The grammar of English is a complex system in which all the components interact. In order to help readers get a grip on this system the remainder of this chapter will consist of an overview of the basic components of grammar. The section numbers correspond to the chapter numbers. Parts II, III, and IV of the book will then offer a detailed elaboration of this system. It is important to mention from the outset that the grammar of English is by no means fixed and agreed upon, and no description of it can in any way be regarded as definitive. To guide readers in understanding the differences in the treatment of particular grammatical phenomena in other frameworks, I will include brief discussions of other treatments in the *Notes and further reading* section at the end of the book.

1.2   Word structure and word-formation

We start with a discussion of words. Consider (1) below:

1 The very noisy visitor continually insulted the receptionist and the care-taker in the library.

Trivially, this structure contains fourteen *orthographic words*, that is, words as they appear in writing separated by blank spaces. In speech all the words are strung together without pauses, and someone who does not know English will not know where the word boundaries are. As for the meanings of the words in (1), if you did not know a particular word, you would consult a dictionary. In all cases, except for *insulted*, you would look for the word in the dictionary under the form in which it appears in (1). Thus, in the case of *noisy* you would look under NOISY; in the case of *receptionist* you would look under RECEPTIONIST; but in the case of *insulted* you would look under INSULT. Words which can act as dictionary entries are called *lexemes* (indicated above in SMALL CAPS), whereas words which perform a particular grammatical role (e.g. 'present tense form') are called *inflectional forms* (or *grammatical words*). The inflectional forms associated with the lexeme INSULT are: *insult, insults, insulted,* and *insulting*. Notice that *insulted* in (1) is an orthographic word as well as an inflectional form (namely the past tense form of the verb INSULT), but not a lexeme. Many words, but not all, have an internal structure. For example, the word *insulted* ends in *-ed* which is called a *past tense inflection*. This word thus communicates at least two things: the meaning 'offend verbally', and 'pastness'. The internal structure of words will be discussed in Chapter 2, as well as *word-formation* processes such as derivation, compounding, and conversion.

1.3   Word classes and simple phrases

Traditionally words are categorized into *parts of speech* which are also called *word classes*. English has the following word classes: *noun, determinative, adjective, verb, preposition, adverb, conjunction,* and *interjection*. The word class labels are referred to as *form labels*.

You will have come across the notion of a *noun* as a naming word, that is, a word that names a person, place, or thing. In (1) the words *visitor, receptionist, caretaker,* and *library* are nouns. In front of *visitor* we have three items. First we have the word *the* which is an example of a *determinative,* though you may be more familiar with the term *definite article* (the *indefinite article* is *a*). We also have *noisy* which is a descriptive word that tells you more about the person that the noun *visitor* refers to. We call such words *adjectives.* The adjective *noisy* is itself modified by *very* which belongs to the word class of *adverbs.* Next, we have *continually.* This is also an adverb, but this time it modifies the inflectional form *insulted,* which we called a verb. We will see in Chapter 3 that adverbs can modify items from more than one type of word class. Linking the phrases *the receptionist* and *the caretaker* we have the word *and,* which is a *conjunction,* more specifically a *coordinating conjunction.* We will need to distinguish such conjunctions from *subordinating conjunctions.* The latter are words like *that, whether,* and *if* which can introduce a *subordinate clause,* as in (2).

2 I think [$_{clause}$ *that he sings with a choir*].

A clause is a grammatical structure that exemplifies a *Subject–Predicate relationship,* that is, a structure where 'something is said about' ('predicated of') a Subject. Simple sentences like (1) contain only one clause, whereas (2) contains two clauses, namely the structure as a whole, and the string *that he sings with a choir.* Finally, we will say that in (1) the word *in,* which here carries a spatial meaning, is a *preposition.* We refer to the sequence enclosed in square brackets in (2) as a *labelled bracketing.* The brackets indicate that the string of words is a *constituent* (section 1.4) whose grammatical status is indicated by the subscript label.

Words are grouped together into *phrases.* Examples of *noun phrases* (NPs) in (1) are *the very noisy visitor, the receptionist, the caretaker,* and *the library.* The string *very noisy* is an *adjective phrase* (AdjP). As we have seen, the words *very* and *continually* are adverbs, but they are also *adverb phrases* (AdvPs). In Chapter 3 we will see that a word on its own can also be a phrase. The sequence *in the library* in (1) is a *prepositional phrase* (PP). A final type of phrase is the *verb phrase* (VP). In Chapter 3 we will see that the *verb phrase* in (1) does not consist only of the verb *insulted*, but also includes the phrases *continually, the receptionist and the caretaker*, and *in the library*. Every phrase has an element that functions as its *Head*. This is the most prominent element which the phrase as a whole is a 'kind of'. Thus in the phrase *the noisy visitor* the element *visitor* is the Head, and this is because a noisy visitor is a kind of visitor. Noun phrases are headed by nouns, adjective phrases are headed by adjectives, verb phrases are headed by verbs, and so on.

1.4 Grammatical functions, semantic roles, and tree diagrams

Consider (3) below.

3 The receptionist and the caretaker continually insulted the very noisy visitor in the library.

Here we have the same words as in (1), but in a different order. This results in a radically different meaning. How can we account for this? In order to explain why we can have the same words and yet a different meaning in (1) and (3), we need to appeal to a few further grammatical concepts, namely *grammatical functions*. In (1) we say that the *Subject* is the string of words *the very noisy visitor*, while *the receptionist and the caretaker* taken as a unit functions as the *Direct Object*. (Notice that I've used capital letters at the beginning of words that are function terms.) We furthermore say that the verb *insulted* functions as a *Predicator* and the string *continually insulted the receptionist and the caretaker in the library* functions as *Predicate*. The Predicator function is always *realized* by a verb, while the Predicate is easily identified as everything excluding the Subject. In (3) *the receptionist and the caretaker* is the Subject, while *the very noisy visitor* is the Direct Object.

What are Subjects, and what are Direct Objects? As a preliminary definition we will say that in the simplest clauses expressing actions the Subject refers to the person who carries out the action expressed by the verb (the 'Agent'), while the referent of the Direct Object undergoes the action expressed by the verb (the 'Patient'). The notions 'Agent' and 'Patient' are called *semantic roles* (also indicated by capital letters). We can now say that (1) and (3) do not mean the same because the action denoted by the verb *insulted* is carried out by different individuals in the two examples, and furthermore the undergoer of the assault in the two cases is a different person (or persons). What about *continually* and *in the library*? These phrases supply circumstantial information, and we will say that they function as *Adjuncts*.

The structure of phrases and clauses can be represented in so-called *tree diagrams*. A simple noun phrase like *the receptionist* can be represented using the tree diagram in (4).

4

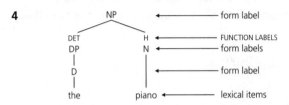

NP=noun phrase; DET=Determiner; DP=determinative phrase;
D=determinative; H=Head; N=noun

In (4) the function and form labels are indicated just above the lexical items. Tree diagrams will be discussed in Chapter 4, as will the notion of *constituent*, defined as a string of words that can be shown to behave as a unit of syntactic structure.

1.5   Complex phrases and coordination

Simple phrases were introduced in section 1.3 above. In Chapter 5 of this grammar more complex phrasal structures will be dealt with, exemplified by the noun phrases shown below.

5 *our* reviews

6 *our* <u>favourable</u> reviews

7 *our* <u>favourable</u> reviews <u>of the market</u>

8 *our* <u>favourable</u> reviews <u>of the market</u> <u>that were published last week</u>

9 *all* our <u>favourable</u> reviews <u>of the market</u> <u>that were published last week</u>

10 perhaps *all* our <u>favourable</u> reviews <u>of the market</u> <u>that were published last week</u>

Within phrases we distinguish the following functions: Head (in **bold**), Complement (<u><u>doubly underlined</u></u>), Adjunct (<u>underlined</u>), and, in noun phrases only, Determiner (*italics*), Predeterminer (*italics* + <u>underline</u>), and External Adjunct (**bold** + <u>underline</u>). The motivation for assigning different function labels to the highlighted strings will be discussed in detail. In this chapter we will also look at coordinated structures, that is, phrases and clauses linked by a coordinating conjunction.

1.6 Clause types and negation

Language can be used to *do* a wide range of things. For example, if I say *Paul lives in London*, then I'm using a *declarative clause* to make a statement. I can also use an *interrogative clause* to ask a question (*Does Paul live in London? What did they buy?*), an *imperative clause* to issue an order (*Leave the house at once*), or an *exclamative clause* to utter an exclamation (*What a nice house you live in!*). These particular structures are called *clause types*. What is interesting is that the various clause types do not have a one-to-one relationship with the uses that can be made of them. For example, if someone asks you 'Are you sure that your children are safely in bed?' they may be asking a simple question, but in a situation in which a person wishes to intimidate another person, it could be construed as a threat. These examples show that language must be studied *situationally* because the meaning of expressions in particular contexts often depends on circumstances. We will see how this works in Chapter 6, which will also discuss negation.

1.7 Finite subordinate clauses

In section 1.3 above we defined simple clauses as grammatical structures that instantiate a Subject–Predicate relationship. As we have seen, the example in (2) contains two clauses, each of which expresses its own Subject–Predicate relationship. On the one hand we have the *matrix clause*, which spans the entire structure. Within this clause there is a *subordinate clause*, namely the string of words introduced by *that*. We will say that this clause is *finite* by virtue of its lexical verb carrying a present tense inflection. The forms and functions of finite subordinate clauses will be discussed in Chapter 7.

1.8 Non-finite and verbless subordinate clauses

Here are some further examples of structures containing subordinate clauses.

11 I just want [*you to alter the scenario very slightly*].

12 I suppose in a way that gave them something in common, and perhaps made him [*feel protective towards her*].

13 We are [*training more of our young people*].

14 I have [*benefitted from this*].

In these cases the bracketed constituents are *non-finite clauses*. We distinguish four types of non-finite clause, namely *to-infinitive clauses* (exemplified in (11)), *bare infinitive clauses* ((12)), *-ing participle clauses* ((13)), and *past participle clauses* ((14)). Such clauses do not carry tense. The forms and functions of non-finite subordinate clauses will be discussed in Chapter 8, as will clauses without a verb.

I turn now to the chapters in Part IV of the book which deal with the interaction of grammar and meaning (semantics) in English.

1.9 Tense and aspect

Time is a real-world semantic concept that structures our existence. Languages characteristically use the grammatical system of *tense* to express time. Thus, as we saw above, the verb form *insulted* in (1) grammatically encodes that the event reported occurred at some point in the past. There is no further specification of when the verbal abuse took place, though it could easily be supplied, for example by adding the phrase *last week* or *yesterday*. English has only two grammatically encoded tenses, the *present tense* and the *past tense*.

As users of English we often need a grammatical device to make reference to the way a particular event *unfolds* in time. This is called *aspect*. For example, if we wish to express that an event took place in the past, but has relevance at the present time, we can use the English *present perfect construction* exemplified in (15):

15 We *have pursued* a limited war for limited objectives.

Compare (15) to (16):

16 We *pursued* a limited war for limited objectives.

The difference between (15) and (16) is that we view the event in (15) as being in some way still relevant at the moment of speaking (for example as an explanation of the reason why the troops can return home tomorrow). This is called *perfect aspect*. An example like (16) is likely to be used when pursuance of the war is viewed as being wholly in the past, that is, over and done with. Notice that we can add a phrase like *since last week* to (15), but not to (16). Conversely, we can add *years ago* to (16), but not to (15).

English also has *progressive aspect*, which is used to present an event as being in progress over a certain time span, as in (17).

17 She *was squinting*.

What this means is that at some point in the past the person referred to as *she* started squinting and this continued for a while. The beginning and end points are not specified, though they could be, for example by adding 'while we were in the meeting between 8 and 9 a.m. yesterday'. Aspect is a grammatical notion, which refers to the way the associated semantic notion of aspectuality is implemented linguistically.

1.10   Mood

Much of the time, language is used to communicate straightforward statements of fact. However, we often need to talk about situations which have not happened yet, or are hypothetical, uncertain, desirable, or necessary, as in the following examples.

18 You may be left out of it because you are a freelancer.

19 You must keep them moist.

20 I will leave the decision up to you.

In (18) the speaker is expressing a 'possibility'; in (19) an 'obligation' is imposed; while in (20) a 'resolve' is expressed. These are three of a number of concepts that belong to the realm of *modality*. This is a semantic notion (just like 'time' and 'aspectuality'), which is implemented in language by means of *mood*. In many languages mood is indicated by verb endings, but in English modality is principally expressed by a group of verbs called *modal auxiliaries*, namely CAN/*could*, MAY/*might*, SHALL/*should*, WILL/*would*, and MUST. These will be discussed in Chapter 10, along with other ways of expressing modality.

1.11　Information structuring

The words in (1) all add up to express a meaning, namely the proposition that there was some individual, namely a visitor to a library, who on some occasion in the past verbally offended a receptionist and a caretaker. As far as their meaning is concerned, the words in (1) each have a contribution to make, but they are not equal in this regard. Thus, while it is easy to say what the meaning of a word like *visitor* is, you would be hard put to say what *the* means. What about the meaning of the structure as a whole? Although the words individually contribute meanings, it should be obvious that the words by themselves are not enough. In other words, it is not enough to say that the meaning of (1) is simply the sum total of the meanings of its parts. The reason is that if we use exactly the same words, but in a different order, as in (3), repeated here as (21), the meaning changes.

21 The receptionist and the caretaker continually insulted the very noisy visitor in the library.

However, it is important to see that a change in order does not always result in a change of meaning, as (22), a variant of (1), shows.

22 The receptionist and the caretaker were continually insulted by the very noisy visitor in the library.

This is the *passive* version of (1). Notice that (1) and (22) mean exactly the same in terms of what happens to whom. We will say that they have the same *propositional meaning*. This raises the question of why users of English have a choice between these two structures. The answer is that (1) and (22) present the information contained in them in slightly different ways. Thus, (1) can be said to have the noisy visitor as its topic of interest, while (22) has the receptionist and the caretaker as its topic. Speakers very frequently vary the structure of their utterances, which gives their addressees important (subconscious) clues as to what requires their attention. In the case of the passive, changing the order of the various constituents does not result in a change of propositional meaning, merely in a change of highlighting. Further examples of variations in constituent order which affect the way information is presented will be explored in Chapter 11.

Part II: Form and function

Chapter 2

Word structure and word-formation

In this chapter we will take a look *inside* words to see how they are structured. Word structure is studied under the heading of *morphology* in linguistics. This term is generally thought to have been introduced in the nineteenth century by the German author Goethe. It is used not only in linguistics, but also in the geological and biological sciences, and means 'the study of form'; compare *biology, psychology, criminology*, and so on. Diagrammatically, we can represent the field of morphology as in Figure 2.1:

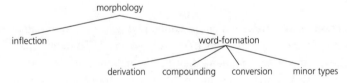

Figure 2.1 The field of morphology

2.1   Morphology

Recall from the previous chapter that we can distinguish between the following types of words:

- *Orthographic words* are words that appear on a page or screen, separated by blank spaces.

- In a dictionary we look up the meaning of a word (or of words grammatically related to it) under an entry called a *lexeme* or *dictionary word* (written in SMALL CAPITALS in this book). Thus, we look up the word *there* (which has no variants) under THERE, *cats* under CAT, and the verb forms *work, works, worked*, and *working* under WORK.

- *Inflectional forms* (also called *grammatical words*) are words that play a particular grammatical role: for example, *cats* is the plural of the noun CAT; *worked* is the past tense form of the verb WORK.

Inflection is concerned with the forms lexemes can take. For example, the forms of the noun lexeme CAT are *cat* and *cats*, and the forms of the verb lexeme WORK are *work, works, worked*, and *working*. The endings on these words (*-s, -ed, -ing*) are called *affixes*. More specifically, they are *inflectional suffixes*. They will be discussed in section 2.2.

Consider next *pre-* in PREHEAT and *un-* in UNHAPPY. These are *derivational affixes*. By adding these to a *lexical base* (an element to which affixes can be appended) we derive a new lexeme. Derivational affixes can be prefixes or suffixes. As the diagram above shows, *derivation* is one type of *word-formation*, a branch of morphology that deals with the creation of new lexemes, along with *compounding, conversion*, and a few minor types. Word-formation processes will be discussed in section 2.3.

2.2 Inflection

Inflection is a notion which is concerned with the alternative forms, called *inflectional forms*, that lexemes can take, as determined by the syntactic environment they occur in. Inflection is a *morphosyntactic* notion, which means that it is a phenomenon that is relevant both to syntax and morphology. Inflections are typically realized by different suffixes. As we have seen, we can add a plural suffix to *cat* resulting in *cats*. In the clause *Cats are independent animals* the plural form of the noun <u>cat</u> requires the verb BE also to be in the plural form. This is a matter of syntax. The *shape* of particular inflectional forms (spelling and pronunciation) is a matter of morphology.

2.2.1 Verb inflections

2.2.1.1 The person system in English

The person system of grammar can be shown as in Table 2.1.

	Singular	Plural
1st person	I	we
2nd person	you	you
3rd person	he, she, it, the cat, Paul, etc.	they, the cats, etc.

Table 2.1: The person system

The first person singular refers to the speaker. In the plural *we* refers to a group of people which includes the speaker. The second person refers to the person addressed, either one person (singular) or a group (plural). The third person singular typically refers to a person other than the speaker or the person being addressed. Apart from *he*, *she*, and *it*, referential expressions like *the cat*, *the church*, and *Paul* are also third person singular. In the plural *they* typically refers to a group of people other than the speaker and addressee. Noun phrases headed by plural nouns (e.g. *the cats*) are also third person plural.

2.2.1.2 Tensed and non-tensed verb forms

Consider the following example.

1 His refusal to resign, compounded by his re-election, *insults* everyone who truly holds English cricket dear.

The -*s* ending on the verb is a *verbal inflectional affix*, and *insults* is an inflectional form of the lexical verb INSULT. It is a matter of syntax in (1) that the verb ends in -*s* because all lexical verbs with third person singular Subjects (see section 1.4) take this ending in the present tense. However, it is a matter of morphology that we can speak of an ending on the verb (an affix) with the shape -*s*.

We can display all the forms for English verbs in a grid like the one shown in Table 2.2 for the verb INSULT.

Tensed			Non-tensed		
Present tense 3rd ps. sing. form	Plain present form	Past tense form	Participle *-ing*	past	Plain form
insults	insult	insulted	insulting	insulted	insult

Table 2.2: The paradigm for the regular verb INSULT

Such grids are called *paradigms*, which some readers may be familiar with from learning foreign languages. In many languages the verbal paradigms display different forms for each person in the singular and plural, but English does not have a rich verbal inflectional system, as Table 2.2 illustrates.

Verbal inflectional forms can be tensed or non-tensed. As their names suggest, present tense forms and past tense forms are tensed. The present tense forms of regular lexical verbs occur in two shapes: with the ending *-s* for third person singular Subjects (*-es* for some verbs, e.g. DO/*does*, GO/*goes*, SNATCH/*snatches*, HURRY/*hurries*), and in the *plain present form* for other persons. *Regular verbs* have past tense forms ending in *-ed*, whereas *irregular verbs* typically form their past tenses (and past participles, see below) by means of a vowel modification (called *ablaut*), as the paradigm for BREAK in Table 2.3 shows.

	Tensed		Non-tensed		
Present tense 3rd ps. sing. form	Plain present form	Past tense form	Participle *-ing*	past	Plain form
breaks	break	broke	breaking	broken	break

Table 2.3: The paradigm for the irregular verb BREAK

See Appendix 1 for a full list of irregular verbs.

We will say that lexical verbs *agree* with their Subjects in the present tense for person and number, although the agreement is only visible on the third person singular form of the verb. There is no agreement between Subjects and verbs in the past tense, because the inflectional forms are identical for all Subjects. However, the verb BE is an exception: its past tense forms do agree with their Subject. We have *was* for the first and third person singular, *were* elsewhere.

The non-tensed forms are the *participle* and the *plain form* of the verb. We distinguish *-ing participles* from *past participles*. The former end in *-ing*, as their name suggests, whereas the latter end in *-ed* in the case of regular verbs, and in *-en* (and a number of other shapes) in the case of irregular verbs. Participles occur as the italicized items in the constructions exemplified in Table 2.4.

The progressive construction: BE + *-ing* participle form of a verb (*V -ing*)
Example (a): British supermarkets <u>are</u> *selling* sushi, but not as the Japanese know it.
The perfect construction: perfect HAVE + past participle form of a verb (*V -ed/-en*)
Example (b): The rhetoric <u>has</u> *changed*.
The passive construction: passive BE + past participle form of a verb (*V -ed/-en*) (*by* NP)
Example (c): Mr Forty <u>was</u> *reported* for careless driving.

Table 2.4: The progressive, perfect, and passive constructions

The progressive construction expresses an ongoing situation, while the present perfect construction in the example above is used to signal that the event in question took place in the past and has present results. (Other perfect constructions will be discussed in sections 3.6.3.3 and 9.3.1.) The passive construction is used as a means of highlighting a particular unit in a clause. The constructions in Table 2.4 and their meanings will be discussed and exemplified further in chapters 4, 8, 9, and 11.

The non-tensed plain form of the verb is used in *infinitive, subjunctive*, and *imperative* clauses. The *infinitive* exemplified in (2) is preceded by the word *to*. We call this the <u>*to*</u>-*infinitive*.

2 I wouldn't want him to *leave* her for me, but when I met him she'd already left him.

When the infinitive occurs after modal verbs (see section 1.10), as in (3), and after a few other verbs, it is called the *bare infinitive*.

3 These methods may *mean* very little to you.

Infinitives can occur in a wider range of structures. These will be discussed in Chapter 8.

Notice that the shape of the inflectional forms for the past tense and past participles is the same for regular verbs (e.g. *insulted/insulted*). We nevertheless distinguish two inflectional forms here because irregular verbs in English often have two different shapes for these inflectional forms (e.g. *broke/broken*).

The plain present and the plain form of lexical verbs also have the same shape, as (4) and (5) show.

4 They *insult* us whenever they can.

5 They will *insult* us, I'm sure of it.

In the former we have a plain present form of the verb INSULT, while the latter has a plain form. Again, we regard these as being two different inflectional forms. The reason for this is that there is at least one verb in English, namely BE, which has a wider range of shapes for its present tense forms. It has three forms in the present tense singular, and one form, namely *are*, for the plural (see Table 2.5). The plain form is *be*. It is because the verb BE has a plain form which does not share its shape with any of the present tense forms that we need to distinguish the plain form as a distinct inflectional form. And if we do so for BE we should do so for all verbs.

Person	Present tense		Plain form
	Singular	Plural	
1st	am	are	be
2nd	are	are	
3rd	is	are	

Table 2.5: The present tense forms of the verb BE

Notice that the plain present form is always tensed, whereas the plain form is always non-tensed.

2.2.1.3 On so-called 'subjunctive verb forms'

Readers may have noticed that I have made no mention of the 'subjunctive verb', a term traditionally used for the underlined verb in the bracketed portion in (6).

6 His friends should demand [that he get justice].

A bracketed clause like the one in (6) is used in a situation in which a speaker is talking about a state of affairs that he *wants* to obtain, but which does not obtain at the moment of speaking. In a situation in which someone utters (6), the person referred to as *he* has not received justice. It is important to stress that many speakers would opt to use the third person singular form *gets* instead, as in (7), especially in British English.

7 His friends should demand that he *gets* justice.

This is perfectly acceptable, and there is no difference in meaning.

The verb in the highlighted clause in (6) is traditionally called a *present subjunctive verb*, a label which we will not be using. The reason is that the inflectional forms of the so-called 'present subjunctive' are the same for each person. There is no distinct inflectional form for it. When this happens we speak of *syncretism*. The inflectional form in (6) is the plain form, and we call the bracketed clause in (6) a *subjunctive clause*. The notion of subjunctive clause is useful, because for the third person singular the form that occurs in a subjunctive clause differs from the form that appears in a non-subjunctive clause with which it can be contrasted, such as the *that*-clause in (7), where the verb ends in -*s*. In addition, compare (8) and (9).

8 His friends should demand [that he *not be* arrested].

9 His friends should demand [that he *is not* arrested].

In the negated subjunctive *that*-clause in (8) the negative word *not* precedes a form of BE, whereas it follows one in (9), which does not involve a subjunctive subordinate clause, but an ordinary *declarative clause* (sections 1.6 and 6.1).

Contrast (6) with (10).

10 I wish we *had* more of that sort of competition in the family of nations.

In traditional grammar the verb *had* is called a *past subjunctive verb* whose appearance is triggered by the verb WISH. However, in English, 'past subjunctive' forms are indistinguishable from past tense forms.

We will therefore say that English does not have a past subjunctive verb inflection. Unlike with the 'present subjunctive', in this case we will not recognize *past subjunctive clauses* in English. The reason is that we cannot contrast a clause containing a 'past subjunctive verb' with a clause containing a past tense form of the verb, in the way that we contrasted (6) and (7), because the inflectional forms are identical.

What about the verb form *were* in (11)?

11 I rather think you wish [it *were* true].

This form of the verb BE, in the first or third person singular, can be seen as a relic of the past subjunctive. Notice that subjunctive clauses can be main clauses (*Heaven forbid, God save the Queen*), but again only as fossilized constructions.

2.2.1.4 The traditional moods indicative, subjunctive, and imperative

Some readers may be familiar with the notions *indicative, subjunctive*, and *imperative*, and think of them as the *moods* of English, as in traditional grammar. Recall from Chapter 1 that mood is the grammatical implementation of the semantic notion of modality which is concerned with a range of meanings in English such as 'possibility', 'obligation', 'intention', 'necessity', and the like. The labels indicative, subjunctive, and imperative were applied to verb forms in traditional grammars, such that they recognized 'indicative verb forms', 'subjunctive verb forms', and 'imperative verb forms'. Indicative verb forms were said to be typically used in clauses that make statements believed to be true by the speaker ('unmodalized' statements); subjunctive verb forms, as in (6) and (10), were said to be used in clauses that express the speaker's attitude or opinion towards what was being said; and imperative verb forms were said to be used in clauses expressing commands. From what has been said above it will be clear that it is better to regard mood as a non-inflectional notion. (The one exception to this is the verb *were*, used in examples like (11).) English principally grammatically implements mood through the use of clause types or modal auxiliary verbs. For example, rather than say that speakers use indicative verb forms to make assertions, we will say that they typically use declarative clauses to do so. Thus, if I utter

(12) I'm saying something about a state of affairs in the world which I believe to be true.

12 Everyone likes flattery.

The labels 'subjunctive' and 'imperative' likewise do not apply to inflections, as we have already seen, but to clausal constructions. Although there is no 'subjunctive clause type', we do recognize an 'imperative clause type'. (Note that by 'clausal construction' I mean a string of words that form a clause, whereas 'clause type' is a grammatical term which will be discussed in Chapter 6.) The concepts of mood and modality will be discussed further in Chapter 10.

2.2.1.5   The concepts finite and non-finite

We now turn to the concepts *finite* and *non-finite*. The term *finite* means 'finished' (from the Latin *finitus*) or 'limited'. Traditionally, 'finiteness' is concerned with variation for person and number, and is applied to verbs, in that they take on different inflectional forms depending on the person and number of their Subjects. However, in present-day English it makes much more sense to speak of finite and non-finite *clauses* (or constructions), since the verbal paradigms contain almost no forms with distinct endings. As a generalization we can say that any clause that is tensed is also finite. However, not all finite clauses are tensed. Specifically, subjunctive clauses (cf. the bracketed portion in (6)) and imperative clauses (e.g. *Open the door*; see section 6.3) are finite, but not tensed. Despite not containing a tensed verb, subjunctive clauses can be considered to be finite because they alternate with tensed clauses (cf. (7)), and because they resemble the structure of typical tensed clauses in two respects: they must have a Subject, and they take the same subordinator as some tensed clauses do, namely *that*. Imperative clauses are less clearly finite, but we can consider them as such because they always occur as main clauses, though note that the fact that they typically lack a Subject detracts from this observation.

Non-finite clauses are clauses that do not contain a tensed verb, and are always subordinate (section 1.3). As we saw in section 1.8, we recognize four types, shown in Table 2.6 with examples.

Type of non-finite clause	Example
to-infinitive clause	(a) Would anybody like *to eat?*
bare infinitive clause	(b) They can *stop at any point.*
-ing participle clause	(c) We are *selling them.*
past participle clause	Perfect:
	(d) So we have *played our part in the history of cricket.*
	Passive:
	(e) She was *delayed by train difficulties.*

Table 2.6: Non-finite clauses

Structures containing non-finite clauses will be discussed in detail in Chapter 8.

2.2.2   Noun inflections

English nouns display two kinds of inflections, namely those for *number* (singular/plural) and for *case* (nominative/accusative/genitive).

2.2.2.1   Number: plurals

Table 2.7 shows ways of forming the plural in English. The lists are not exhaustive.

Regular plural in *-s* or *-es*
group–groups; idea–ideas; theme–themes; bus–buses; class–classes; potato–potatoes
With a change of vowel
foot–feet; man–men; tooth–teeth
With a modification of the base-final vowel (*-y* > *-ies*)
activity–activities; body–bodies (but not if *-y* is preceded by a vowel: *boy* > *boys*)
With a change or doubling of the base-final consonant
knife–knives; life–lives; wife–wives; quiz–quizzes
Singular is the same as the plural
aircraft, bison, deer, series, sheep, trout
Plurals without formal marking
cattle, people, police

Plurals with irregular suffixes
brother–brethren; child–children; ox–oxen
Foreign plurals
alumnus–alumni; antenna–antennae (also *antennas*); *criterion–criteria; datum–data* (plural also used as a singular); *index–indices; kibbutz–kibbutzim; mafioso–mafiosi; tableau–tableaux; thesis–theses*

Table 2.7: Plural-formation

Some English nouns occur only in the plural. These are the so-called *pluralia tantum*. Among them are: *auspices, binoculars, jeans, scissors, trousers, valuables*.

2.2.2.2 Case: nominative, accusative, and genitive

Old English had an extensive case system, but in Modern English the system is much less rich. *Nominative case* and *accusative case* show up only on *pronouns*, which also have special genitive forms, as Table 2.8 shows for personal pronouns.

	Nominative	Accusative	Genitive	
			Dependent	Independent
1st person singular	I	me	my	mine
2nd person singular	you	you	your	yours
3rd person singular	he/she/it	him/her/it	his/her/its	his/hers/its
1st person plural	we	us	our	ours
2nd person plural	you	you	your	yours
3rd person plural	they	them	their	theirs

Table 2.8: The case forms of personal pronouns

Nominative case is typically used for pronouns in Subject position, while accusative case is typically used for Indirect Objects, Direct Objects, and Complements of prepositions (see section 1.4 and chapters 4 and 5), as the following examples make clear.

13 *I* (Subject) like *her* (Direct Object).

14 *They* (Subject) like *us* (Direct Object).

15 *She* (Subject) gave *him* (Indirect Object) *a lift* (Direct Object).

16 *I* (Subject) gave *the folder* (Direct Object) to *him* (Complement of a preposition).

Notice that *you* and *it* do not distinguish nominative and accusative case.

The genitive of nouns is formed by adding the suffix *-'s* to a regular noun, or simply an inaudible apostrophe (*-'*) if the noun already ends in an *-s*, cf. (17)–(20).

17 the book's cover

18 those books' covers

19 Peter's house

20 Jesus' (or Jesus's) mother

We will see in Chapter 3 that it is more accurate to say that the genitive ending is attached to noun phrases. The genitive forms are *dependent* when they occur in non-final position inside noun phrases, as in *my house*, or *independent*, as in *The house is mine, Mine is a modern house,* or *this house of mine* (see sections 3.2.2.1.1 and 5.2.1.2). The basic meaning expressed by the genitive is 'possession'. The case forms of other types of pronouns will be discussed in Chapter 3.

2.2.3 Adjective and adverb inflections

Adjectives and adverbs can inflect for comparison. The *plain form* of adjectives is used to describe the referents of nouns (for example, *the clean house/the house is clean*). Constructions containing the *comparative form* or *superlative form* indicate that the property denoted by the adjective applies to different degrees (for example *My house is cleaner than yours/My house is the cleanest house in the street*). The comparative forms are formed by adding *-er* to a base. The superlative forms are formed by adding *-est*. Similar considerations apply to adverbs, except that they do not generally modify nouns, as we have seen. Table 2.9 shows that there are a number of irregular items whose comparative and superlative forms are morphologically unrelated, a phenomenon that is called *suppletion*.

	Plain form	Comparative form	Superlative form
Adjectives	clean	cleaner	cleanest
	bad	worse	worst
	good/well (as in *I am well*)	better	best
Adverbs	fast (as in *She runs fast*)	faster	fastest
	badly	worse	worst
	well (as in *He writes well*)	better	best
	much	more	most

Table 2.9: The inflectional forms of adjectives and adverbs

Adjectives and adverbs that have two or more syllables usually do not form their comparative and superlative forms inflectionally, but *analytically*, that is by using *more* and *most*, as with *incongruous– more incongruous–most incongruous*. Adverbs that end in *-ly* never take inflections.

2.3 Word-formation

Under this heading we will discuss derivation, compounding, conversion, and a number of minor word-formation types.

2.3.1 Derivation

In this grammar we will regard derivation as a word-formation process involving suffixation or prefixation.

2.3.1.1 Suffixation

Consider again (21), taken from Chapter 1:

21 The very noisy visitor continually insulted the receptionist and the caretaker in the library.

Here the word *receptionist* is a noun which is formed from the noun *reception* by adding *-ist*. Notice that we have formed one lexeme from another through a process of suffixation, and that the suffix *-ist* is a *class-maintaining suffix*, because both the input and output forms are nouns. Consider next the adverb *continually*. This lexeme is formed from the word *continual* by adding *-ly*. Here too we have suffixation, but this time it is a *class-changing* process (adjective > adverb). Here are some further examples of suffixation:

22 *address* > *addressee* (class-maintaining: noun)

23 *furious* > *furiously* (class-changing: adjective to adverb)

24 *happy* > *happiness* (class-changing: adjective to noun)

25 *regular* > *regularize /-ise* (class-changing: adjective to verb)

26 *relate* > *relation* (class-changing: verb to noun)

27 *spite* > *spiteful* (class-changing: noun to adjective)

28 *work* > *workable* (class-changing: verb to adjective)

29 *yellow* > *yellowish* (class-maintaining: adjective)

In Table 2.10 a number of common derivational suffixes are shown.

-able	-ess	-ion	-most	-sion	-ways
-ance	-fold	-ish	-ness	-some	-wise
-ation	-ful	-ism	-nik	-ty	
-ee	-gate	-ize/-ise	-or	-uous	
-eme	-ible	-less	-ory	-ville	
-en	-ic	-like	-ous	-vore	
-er	-ical	-ly	-ship	-wards	

Table 2.10: Some common derivational suffixes

British English spelling prefers suffixes in *-ise/-isation*, while in American English the preference is for *-ize/-ization*, though this distinction between the two varieties of English is fading, the more common spelling being *-ize/-ization*.

2.3.1.2 Prefixation

We can also create lexemes through prefixation. This process is mostly class-maintaining. Here are some examples of prefixation:

30 *historical* > *ahistorical* (class-maintaining: adjective)

31 *edit* > *co-edit* (class-maintaining: verb)

32 *watt > kilowatt* (class-maintaining: noun)

33 *list > enlist* (class-changing: noun to verb)

34 *bus > minibus* (class-maintaining: noun)

35 *earth > unearth* (class-changing: noun to verb)

36 *wit > outwit* (class-changing: noun to verb)

37 *offend > reoffend* (class-maintaining: verb)

Table 2.11 shows some common prefixes.

a(n)-	bi-	ex-	maxi-	post-	sur-
ab-	circum-	fore-	mid-	pre-	trans-
ad-	co-	geo-	mini-	quasi-	un-
after-	counter-	in-	mis-	re-	under-
ante-	de-	inter-	non-	step-	
anti-	eco-	intra-	out-	sub-	
arch-	en-	kilo-	over-	super-	

Table 2.11: Some common derivational prefixes

2.3.2 Compounding

Compounds can be defined as formations that involve, in the majority of cases, combinations of two bases, which can manifest themselves in various shapes. Examples are *caretaker*, *boyfriend*, and *operations chief*. Compounds can also involve phrases, as in *off-road route*. English allows a great variety of compounds, as shown by Tables 2.12–16. Readers should be aware that not everyone agrees exactly on how to delimit the class of compounds.

It should be borne in mind that some of the items in the tables can have dual classifications. Thus, DOWN-AND-OUT in the NP *down-and-out tramp* is a phrasal adjectival compound, but in *These down-and-outs are here most of the day* it is a noun (witness the *-s* plural inflection). Similarly, MAKE-BELIEVE is a compound noun in *the strategy of make-believe*, but an adjectival compound in *make-believe allegations*.

There are a number of issues in the study of compounds which we do not have the space to discuss here. Among them is the question of

Compound noun/pronoun types	Examples
noun + noun	bedtime, city-dweller, girlfriend, goldfish, nutcracker, place name, she-wolf, shoemaker, singer-songwriter, table-top, window-cleaner
noun + verb/noun	fleabite, footstep, handshake, nosebleed, sunshine, waterfall
noun + preposition	hanger-on, looker-on, passer-by
determinative + noun	
any-series	anybody, anyone, anything, anywhere
every-series	everybody, everyone, everything, everywhere
no-series	nobody, no one, nothing, nowhere
some-series	somebody, someone, something, somewhere
verb + verb	make-believe
verb + noun	blowtorch, breakfast, call girl, copycat, glow-worm, pickpocket, push-button, spoilsport, swearword, workman
verb + preposition	breakthrough, cop-out, drawback, fallout, runabout, stand-off, summing-up, take-off
adjective + noun	blackboard, blacksmith, busybody, fast food, free-thinker, grandmother, handyman, hotbed, tightrope, wet nurse
preposition + noun	after-effect, bystander, in-crowd, off-chance, onlooker, outpost
preposition + verb	after-ski, downturn, offshoot, underlay, upkeep
adverb + noun	twice-winner (of a prize)
phrasal	down-and-out, jack-in-the-box, son-in-law, writer-in-residence

Table 2.12: Compound nouns

Compound verb types	Examples
verb + verb	blow-dry, dare say, drink-drive, freeze-dry, make do, stir-fry
noun + noun	handcuff, stonewall
noun + verb	babysit, brainwash, carbon date, colour code, hand-wash, proofread
adjective + noun	bad-mouth, blindfold, deep-fry, fast-track, short-change
adjective + verb	cold-call, dry-clean, whitewash
preposition + noun/verb	upstage, background, overbook, overrun, underestimate

Table 2.13: Compound verbs

Compound adjective types	Examples
adjective + adjective	bitter-sweet, blue-black, dark-red, icy-cold, deaf-mute, squeaky-clean
adjective + noun	broad-brush (assessment), white-collar (staff)
adjective/adverb + verb	clean-shaven, easy-going, hard-working, high-rise, long-suffering, plain-spoken, quick-change, well-behaved, well-travelled
noun + verb	awe-inspiring, drug-related, hair-raising, home-made, newborn, thought-provoking
noun + adjective	accident-prone, ankle-deep, bone-dry, camera-shy, capital-intensive, dirt-cheap, germ-resistant, head-strong, oil-rich, razor-sharp, self-conscious, sky-high, sugar-free
verb + noun	roll-neck (sweater)
verb + verb	go-go (dancer)
verb + adjective	fail-safe
verb + preposition	see-through (shirt)
preposition + adjective	over-qualified, overactive, uptight
phrasal	down-and-out (tramp), top-of-the-range, under-the-weather, up-to-the-minute

Table 2.14: Compound adjectives

Compound preposition types	Examples
preposition + preposition	hereat, hereby, herefrom, herein, hereof, hereon, hereto, herewith, into, onto, thereat, thereby, therefrom, therein, thereof, thereon, thereto, therewith, throughout, upon, within, whereat, whereby, wherefrom, wherein, whereof, whereon, whereto, wherewith, without
preposition + noun	downhill, downstairs, indoors, inside, overland, upstream

Table 2.15: Compound prepositions

Compound adverb types	Examples
determinative + adverb/adjective/noun	
al(l)-series	almost, already, also, altogether, always
any-series	anyhow, anyway
some-series	somehow, sometimes, somewhat
miscellaneous	forthwith, furthermore, indeed, maybe, meantime, meanwhile, moreover, nevertheless, nonetheless, nowadays, oftentimes

Table 2.16: Compound adverbs

how to distinguish a compound from a phrase. As a general rule the stress in compounds is on the first component, while in phrases the second component tends to be stressed. Compare **black**board ('a board fixed to the wall, used in schools for teaching') with black **board** ('a board which is black'), where in both cases the stress is indicated by the boldface type. Individual cases can remain tricky. For example, in Table 2.14 above, I have listed *white-collar* in *white-collar staff* as an Adj–N compound, but we might equally say that in this particular case the Head noun *staff* is modified by the NP *white collar*.

In addition to the compounds in the tables above English has a number of *neoclassical compounds*. These typically consist of two *combining forms* of classical origin: an *initial combining form* and a *final combining form*. A list of both kinds is given in Table 2.17.

Initial combining form	Final combining form
aer(o)-	-(a)emia
andr(o)-	-cephaly
anthrop(o)	-cide
astr(o)-	-crat
audio-	-ectomy
aut(o)-	-gamy
bibli(o)-	-geny
bio-	-gerous
cardi(a/o)-	-grade

(*Continued*)

Initial combining form	Final combining form
electr(o)-	-gram
giga-	-graph(y)
heter(o)-	-lithic
hom(o)-	-logy
hydr(o)-	-meric
hyper-	-merous
idio-	-morph
macro-	-morphous
mega-	-nomy
morph(o)-	-onym
neur(o)-	-opia
omn(i)-	-opsy
phil(o)-	-pathy
phot(o)-	-phil(e)
pseud(o)-	-phobe
psych(o)-	-phone
socio-	-saurus
tele(o)-	-stasia
the(o)-	-stat

The element '(o)' is inserted to link combining forms.

Table 2.17: Combining forms

Here are some examples of possible combinations of items from the two columns: *anthropology, autocrat, bibliophile, morphology.* Some of the combining forms that are in common use can occur on their own, for example *audio, homo.* In certain cases the initial or final combining forms combine with existing lexemes, as in *aeroplane, astrophysics, biodiversity, heterosexual, insecticide.*

2.3.3 Conversion

It is possible in English to create new lexemes from others through a process called *conversion*. In these cases the word class of the element in question changes. The resulting lexeme can display the inflectional forms that are appropriate for the word class it newly belongs to. The following conversions are possible.

N > V

Example: He *bagged* the goods. (BAG^N > BAG^V)

Other possibilities: *badger, bottle, bridge, butcher, can, eye, eyeball, finger, gesture, holiday, knife, mail, vacation, water*

V > N

Example: The *assault* was recorded on tape. (ASSAULT^V > ASSAULT^N)

Other possibilities: *abstract, attempt, cheat, coach, control, discount, guess, import, laugh, read, transfer, whisper*

Adj > N

Example: These Olympic *hopefuls* are not ready for action. (HOPEFUL^ADJ > HOPEFUL^N)

Other possibilities: *daily, intellectual, natural, original, regular, roast*

Adj > V

Example: They *emptied* the bath. (EMPTY^ADJ > EMPTY^V)

Other possibilities: *bare, better, blind, calm, dirty, faint, right, smooth, weary, wrong*

In the case of verb > adjective conversions it is the *-ing* participle or past participle form of the verb that is converted.

V > Adj

Example: These silly stories are not very *amusing* at all. (AMUSE^V > AMUSING^ADJ)

Other possibilities: *bored, boring, entertaining, missing, spoilt, stunning*

P > V

Example: He *downed* his drink. (DOWN^P > DOWN^V)

Other possibilities: *out, up*

2.3.4 Minor types of word-formation

In this section I exemplify a number of minor word-formation processes.

2.3.4.1 Abbreviations and acronyms

One type of abbreviation is made up of the first letters of a series of words, which, when spoken, are pronounced individually: *AMS* (American Meteorological Society), *BBC* (British Broadcasting Corporation), *BC* (Before Christ), *ETS* (Emissions Trading Scheme), *EU* (European Union), *NYPD* (New York Police Department), *WWW* (World Wide Web). These are called *initialisms*. Other abbreviations are less predictable in their composition: *etc., Ltd, viz.*

Acronyms, by contrast, are pronounceable abbreviations. Examples include *CAD* (computer aided design), *FAQ* (frequently asked question), *JPEG* (joint photographic experts group; pronounced 'jay peg'), *LAN* (local area network), *NATO* (North Atlantic Treaty Organization), *UNESCO* (United Nations Educational, Scientific, and Cultural Organization), and *WYSIWYG* (what you see is what you get). In some cases the acronyms have developed into words in their own right, as is the case for *laser* (light amplification by stimulated emission of radiation) and *radar* (radio detection and ranging).

2.3.4.2 Back-formation

Some words are formed by removing suffixes. A stock example of a back-formation is the creation of the verb *edit* from the noun *editor*. This process often takes place by analogy with other existing formations. Further examples of back-formations are: *headhunter > headhunt; television > televise; recycling > recycle; sculptor > sculpt.*

2.3.4.3 Blending

Blending occurs when two bases are combined into a new lexeme. Reduction of one or both of the bases may occur. Here are some examples.

channel + tunnel > chunnel

smoke + fog > smog

breakfast + lunch > brunch

breath + analyser > breathalyser

guess + estimate > guesstimate

gigantic + enormous > ginormous

motor + hotel > motel

stagnation + inflation > stagflation

2.3.4.4   Clippings

Clippings involve a number of ways in which words can be short-ened by removing syllables. Personal names are often shortened as well. Some examples are shown below.

advertisement > ad

doctor > doc

influenza > flu

laboratory > lab

Metropolitan Police > Met

Michael > Mike

omnibus > bus

Peter > Pete

radiator > rad

Sebastian > Seb

Chapter 3

Word classes and simple phrases

In the previous chapter we looked at the internal structure of words. In this chapter we look at words as wholes, and how they form phrases.

3.1 Word classes: distributional definitions

In English we can distinguish the *word classes*, also called *parts of speech*, shown in Table 3.1.

Word classes
noun
determinative
adjective
verb
preposition
adverb
conjunction
interjection

Table 3.1: Word classes

In my preliminary overview of the word classes in Chapter 1 I defined them mainly *notionally*, that is, in terms of their meaning. For example, I wrote that nouns are words that name a person, place, or thing. In many cases this definition will identify the nouns in a clause. However, it is not satisfactory if we wish to be more precise about nouns. For example, with regard to 'things', how do we establish what they are? A table is a thing, but what about *friendship, happiness, idea, intention, love, thought,* and *yesterday*? These words denote concepts, mental constructs, time spans, and the like. The problem is that we can only label something as a noun if we already know that it is a thing. A similar problem rears its head when we say that verbs are action-words. Not all the words that we would like to class as verbs denote actions. It is easy to think of verbs that do not, such as KNOW, POSSESS, RESEMBLE, and WANT. What's more, there are nouns that denote actions (e.g. *announcement, departure*). What we need is a definition of each of the various word classes that encompasses all members, or at least the typical members.

If we cannot (exclusively) appeal to meaning, how do we define the word classes? The answer is that we can do so on the basis of their behaviour in clauses. That is, we need to define the word classes by looking at the company words keep. This is called *distributional analysis*. In each of the sections below the word classes will be defined in terms of the way they behave syntactically in clauses. Where appropriate, meaning considerations will also be included. In addition to the word classes I will also discuss simple *phrases*, such as noun phrase and adjective phrase. Complex phrases will be discussed in Chapter 5.

3.2 Nouns and noun phrases

· ·

The word class of *nouns* includes words that denote concrete objects in the world around us, for example *bicycle, cat, house, door, planet, vase, pencil, screen*. The nouns listed here are *common nouns*. We also distinguish words like *he, she, his, her, who, what*, which are called *pronouns* (section 3.2.2), and *proper nouns* (section 3.2.3) such as *Peter, Leonard, Tim*.

3.2.1 Distributional properties of nouns

What are the distributional properties of nouns in English? The first thing to note is that a noun can function as the *Head* of a *noun phrase* (NP). A Head is the most prominent element of a string of words, and a noun phrase is a string of words whose Head is a noun. Here are some examples.

1 [NP the *house*]

2 [NP the big *house*]

3 [NP the big *house* with the red roof]

In each of these strings the word *house* is the Head, because it deter-mines what the string as a whole is a kind of. Thus *the big house* is a kind of house, as is *the big house with the red roof*. In each case the noun *house* is obligatory. Note that the Head can also occur on its own, as in the following example.

4 He buys [NP *houses*] for a living.

The unity of the words in the phrase has been indicated by the square brackets, with the opening bracket carrying the label NP. NPs can perform a variety of functions, such as Subject, Direct Object, and Indirect Object (see section 1.4 and Chapter 4). For example, in (4) the NP is a Direct Object.

A second property of many nouns is that they can take a plural inflection, as in (4) (see section 2.2.2.1).

Thirdly, nouns are words that can be preceded by the word *the*, as in *the cat*. That is, they can occur in the following frame:

the —

The dash indicates the position of the noun. Most nouns can also be preceded by *a*, but not all of them. Exceptions are so-called *uncountable nouns* like *salt* and *flour* which refer to a mass of some sort, and *pluralia tantum* (Latin for 'plural only'), such as *trousers*, *scissors*. Uncountable nouns cannot be pluralized by adding the inflectional suffix *-s*: *two salts, *three flours* (the asterisk indicates that a structure is impossible in English). We will see in section 3.3 that words like *the* and *a* belong to the class of *determinatives*.

Another characteristic of nouns is that they can be preceded by descriptive words, which we called adjectives in section 1.3: *the big house, the hungry cat, the final draft*, and so on (see also section 3.4). A few nouns can be followed by adjectives, as in set expressions like *governor general, president elect*.

Morphologically, a great many nouns end in suffixes that are typical of nouns. In Table 3.2 some common nominal suffixes are shown.

Finally, it is sometimes said that nouns are words that can take genitive case endings (see section 2.2.2.2), as in these examples: *the cat's paws, the teachers' reports*. However, the genitive ending is best analysed as attaching to a phrase, rather than to a noun, as becomes

Some common nominal suffixes				
-age	-eme	-ism	-nik	-ville
-al	-er	-ist	-or	-ware
-ant	-ery	-ity	-ory	
-archy	-gate	-mania	-ship	
-ation	-hood	-ment	-tion	
-ee	-ion	-ness	-ty	

Table 3.2: Some common nominal suffixes

clear when we consider noun phrases like the following: [*the President of France*]*'s statement*, [*the woman in the library*]*'s briefcase*. See also section 5.2.1.2.

The distributional characteristics of typical nouns are listed in Table 3.3.

Typical nouns...
• function as the Head of a noun phrase which can perform a variety of functions, such as Subject, Direct Object, Indirect Object;
• take plural forms;
• can occur in the frame *the —*;
• can be preceded by adjectives.

Table 3.3: The distributional properties of typical nouns

Typical nouns conform to all or most of these criteria. However, not all nouns do so. *Pronouns*, which we regard as forming a subset of the class of nouns, are a case in point. We turn to them next.

3.2.2 Pronouns

Pronouns belong to the class of nouns because they can head noun phrases that can function as Subject, Direct Object, Indirect Object, Complement of a preposition (see section 3.7), and Predicative Complement (see section 4.1.3.3). Compare (5) and (6): the full NPs in (5) are replaced by pronouns heading NPs in (6).

5 [NP Frank Rigby's wife] endures [NP working-class poverty] dutifully.

6 [NP She] endures [NP it] dutifully.

Example (6) shows that pronouns (heading NPs) can occur in typical noun phrase positions. For this reason we treat them as a subclass of nouns in this grammar.

In some grammars pronouns are regarded as a separate word class. There are a number of reasons for this. Among them are the following.

- Pronouns show a distinction between nominative, accusative, and genitive case, while common nouns do not. See section 3.2.2.1.1 below.

- Pronouns show a distinction for *person* (1st person, 2nd person, etc.; see section 2.2.1.1) and *gender* (*he/she*, *him/her*, etc.), but common nouns do not.

- Pronouns do not have inflectional plurals (see section 2.2.2.1) in Standard English (cf. *yous*, *hes*, etc.), though they do have singular vs plural person distinctions (e.g. *I* vs *we*). The pronoun *one* is an exception, cf. *I like those ones* (see section 3.2.2.1.4).

- Pronouns are much more limited than common nouns in their potential for taking dependents. For example, while we can have determinatives and adjectives in front of common nouns (as we saw in the preceding section), they cannot generally determine and modify pronouns. Thus we cannot say *The he left the meeting* or *Intelligent you did well in the exams*. There are some exceptions, of course, as when we say *I'm not the me I used to be* or *Silly old me left the gas on*. Nouns can be followed by prepositional phrases (see sections 1.3 and 3.7), as in *my cancellation of the reservation*; pronouns generally cannot.

- Noun phrases with common nouns as Head can have independent reference, while pronouns rely on the linguistic or extralinguistic context for their reference. Thus, if I say *I met the boss this morning* the NP *the boss* refers to a mutually identifiable individual. If I say *Katie married Harry because she loves him* then the most likely reading of this utterance is for *she* to refer to Katie and for *him* to refer to Harry.

Despite these observations we take the fact that pronouns can act as the Heads of phrases that can function as Subject, Direct Object,

Predicative Complement, and so on, as a sufficiently weighty reason for regarding them as nouns.

In English we recognize the types of pronouns listed in Table 3.4.

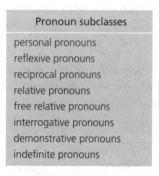

Pronoun subclasses
personal pronouns
reflexive pronouns
reciprocal pronouns
relative pronouns
free relative pronouns
interrogative pronouns
demonstrative pronouns
indefinite pronouns

Table 3.4: Pronoun subclasses

3.2.2.1 Personal pronouns

Personal pronouns depend for their reference on a preceding noun phrase (the *antecedent*), or their reference can be established from the context.

3.2.2.1.1 Case forms

Personal pronouns can carry nominative, accusative, and genitive case, as we saw in section 2.2.2.2, depending on their function in a clause. Thus we say *I love her*, not *Me loves she*, and we say *I sent the letter to them*, not *Me sent the letter to they*. The genitive pronouns typically indicate possession, as in *her glasses*. In this example the pronoun is placed before the Head noun. We call this the *dependent use* of the pronoun. The *independent* form is used in examples like the following: *the glasses are <u>hers</u>* and *these glasses of <u>hers</u>*.

The dependent genitive forms are often classed as determinatives by virtue of being positioned in front of nouns, but in this grammar we regard them as pronouns for two reasons. One is that determinatives do not take genitive inflections; another is that the dependent forms can occur in Subject position, as in (7), where determinatives cannot occur.

7 I actually find it quite difficult to remember very much about [clause *my* being very young].

Note that despite being a dependent form, the pronoun is not followed by a noun in this example. We will see in sections 3.2.2.3 and 3.2.2.5 that genitive *whose* in dependent pre-nominal position (e.g. *whose house*) is also a pronoun. See also sections 5.2.1.2 and 8.1.2.1.

3.2.2.1.2 It

The pronoun *it* occurs in various guises. We distinguish *referential it*, *dummy it*, *anticipatory it*, and *cleft it*. The first of these is used to refer to an entity that has already been introduced into a particular discourse, as in (8).

8 You gave *it* to her.

Dummy *it* is meaningless, and is used in Subject position when we talk about the weather or the environment in general.

9 *It* was raining.

10 *It*'s really hot in here.

It can also be used in Direct Object or prepositional Complement position in idiomatic expressions.

11 I interview people that have made *it* in some way.

12 Let them get on with *it*.

Anticipatory it is used to stand in for a clausal Subject or Object which has been *extraposed* (displaced) due to its 'heaviness', as in (13) and (14).

13 _ is quite clear <u>that farmers are very happy</u>.

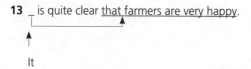

It

14 I find _ extremely difficult <u>to explain to anybody how it works</u>.

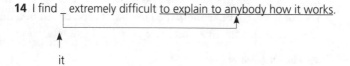

it

These examples will be discussed further in section 11.3.2.2. In a sense anticipatory *it* refers *forward* to the displaced clause, and could for that reason be regarded as being referential. However, unlike *it* in examples like (8), anticipatory *it* does not refer to an entity in the discourse, and can never occur on its own in a clause.

Finally, *cleft it* is used in so-called *cleft constructions*, exemplified in (15) and (16), to be discussed in detail in section 11.8.1.

15 *It* is Simioni who's gone down.

16 *It* was ancient history that attracted me.

3.2.2.1.3 There

The pronoun *there* in (17) is called *existential there* because it occurs in clauses which are concerned with the existence of a person, entity, or situation. It is regarded as a meaningless word that fills the obligatory Subject slot.

17 *There* are lots of windows.

In (18) below $there_1$ is an example of existential *there*, but $there_2$ is not. It is called *locative there* since it points out a location. Of the three instances of *it* in this passage it_1 and it_3 are referential, taking *the occasional shard of fruit* and *the chicken* as antecedents. It_2 is an example of anticipatory *it*, which substitutes for the extraposed Subject clause *to find the chicken*.

18 $There_1$ is more julienned carrot on the plate than anything else; when you do come across the occasional shard of fruit, it_1 is overripe and woolly; and it_2 takes a joint action from both sides of the table to find the chicken. $There_2$ it_3 is.

See section 11.6 for further discussion of existential constructions.

3.2.2.1.4 One

Like *it* and *there* the word *one* also occurs in several guises. In (19) it is a common noun, witness the fact that it is preceded by a determinative and an adjective, and has a plural inflection (section 2.2.2.1).

19 I like the sweet *ones*.

In (20) *one* is used as a personal pronoun in a formal manner to refer to the speaker, or to people in general.

20 *One* can't say that they get a good press.

When *one* substitutes for a full noun phrase, as in (21), where it stands in for *a photograph*, we also regard it as a pronoun. (22) is a special case: here *one* refers back to *part* of a noun phrase, namely the Head noun *cancellation*.

21 Have I shown you a photograph? I've got *one* somewhere.

22 This is her second cancellation. It's not just the first *one*.

One can also be used as a numeral; see section 3.2.4 below.

3.2.2.2 Reflexive and reciprocal pronouns

Reflexive pronouns are typically linked to a preceding antecedent in the shape of a noun phrase (underlined in the examples below), which refers to the same individual(s) or entity.

23 The goalkeeper committed *himself*.

24 The subjects of Byzantium were to call *themselves* Rhomaioi.

In these cases *himself* refers to *the goalkeeper* and *themselves* refers to *the subjects of Byzantium*. In both cases the reflexive pronouns function as the Heads of NPs which in turn function as Direct Objects.

A reflexive pronoun can occur without an overt antecedent, as in (25), though not in Subject position (cf. (26)).

25 Enjoy *yourself* lots.

26 *Myself* ordered a steak for dinner.

In (27) and (28) the reflexive pronouns are used emphatically.

27 She *herself* acquired a summer disposition after the trauma of her recent manner of life.

28 I'm not doing it *myself*.

Oneself, exemplified in (29), is rather formal.

29 It must be peculiarly disconcerting, don't you think, to be left for someone entirely different from *oneself*?

Increasingly, the pronoun *themself* is used as the reflexive form of the personal pronoun THEY with a singular antecedent. To illustrate, compare (30), in which *they* refers back to *someone*, with (31).

30 If someone doesn't wear appropriate footwear or develops muscle strength imbalances, *they* can get hurt.

31 Not everyone who is handed a scalpel considers *themself* a surgeon, and not everyone given a Steinway considers *themself* a concert pianist.

The principal reflexive pronouns occur in the forms shown in Table 3.5.

	Reflexive pronouns	
Singular	1st person	myself
	2nd person	yourself
	3rd person	himself/herself/itself
Plural	1st person	ourselves
	2nd person	yourselves
	3rd person	themselves

Table 3.5: Reflexive pronouns

The *reciprocal pronouns each other* and *one another* (Table 3.6) are used when the verb's meaning applies mutually between two or more people or groups of people, as in (32) and (33).

32 Anyhow, you and Harriet know *one another*.

33 That's a good way of trying to get to know *each other*.

In (32) there is an explicit mention of the antecedent that *one another* refers to. As (33) shows, an antecedent need not be present. Reciprocal pronouns are not only used for people, as (34) demonstrates.

34 The energy that makes the components of a muscle fibre slide along *each other* when the muscle exerts a pull is ultimately derived from the breakdown of ATP.

Like reflexive pronouns, reciprocal pronouns cannot occur as Subject:

35 *Each other* watched the movie.

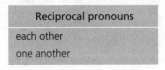

Table 3.6: Reciprocal pronouns

3.2.2.3 Relative pronouns

The *relative pronouns* in English are *who*, *whom*, *whose*, and *which* (Table 3.7).

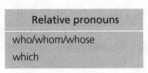

Table 3.7: Relative pronouns

These pronouns belong to a larger set of <u>wh</u>-*words* (that is, words that begin with the letters *wh*-), which additionally includes *what*, *where*, *when*, *why*, and *how*. (Although the latter does not begin with *wh*-, it behaves like the words that do, and is grouped with them for that reason.) Not all *wh*-words are pronouns, as we will see.

Relative pronouns occur inside a <u>wh</u>-*phrase* positioned at the beginning of a *relative clause*. Such clauses provide more information about a person or entity denoted by a preceding noun, called the *antecedent*. The pronouns *who* and *whom* carry nominative and accusative case, respectively, and typically have human antecedents. *Whose* carries genitive case, and can have human and non-human antecedents. *Which* is case-neutral, and usually has non-human antecedents. Here are some examples. The relative pronouns inside the bracketed relative clauses are underlined in each case; the antecedents are in boldface type.

36 Another **student** [[NP <u>*who*</u>] *wrote the same essay*] made the same mistake.

37 Lunch was served in the restaurant downstairs by the proprietor himself – a **Monsieur Savlon** [[NP <u>*whom*</u>] *we'd met _ briefly*].

38 I shall reread **Thomas Mann's Buddenbrooks** (Minerva), [[_{NP} *which*] *I read _ so long ago I've forgotten a lot of it*].

39 The **Family Practitioner Committee (FPC)** [[_{PP} *to* <u>*whom*</u>] *your form will be sent _*] may however check your claim at a later date.

40 In a report from Greenpeace last year, and still available online, retailers and canning companies were ranked in order of their tuna-fishing policies. Sainsbury, Co-op and Marks & Spencer came top; **Princes and John West** – [[_{NP} *most of* <u>*whose*</u>] *was from purse seiners*] – came bottom.

In (36)–(38) the *wh*-phrases are simple *wh*-NPs, headed by a relative pronoun, whereas in (39) and (40) the *wh*-phrases are complex. In (39) it is a prepositional phrase whose Head *to* takes an NP headed by the relative pronoun *whom* as its Complement. In (40) the relative pronoun occurs inside a PP which complements the Head of an NP (*most*). Complex *wh*-phrases will be discussed in section 7.3.3.1.

The symbol '_' in the examples above indicates a 'gap' in the clause with which the initial *wh*-phrase is associated. One way of viewing the association between the *wh*-phrase and the gap is to regard the former as having been *moved* from the gap position to a clause-initial position. There is no suggestion that this movement actually takes place in our minds; the term 'movement' is used merely as a convenient way to conceptualize the relation between the *wh*-phrase and the gap.

In formal writing *whom* is used when the relative pronoun functions as Direct Object or as the Complement of a preposition. Thus in (37) *whom* is the Direct Object of MEET, and in (39) it is the Complement of *to*. This rule is often relaxed, though less so after a preposition; *who* is then used instead.

In all the examples above the relative pronouns are used *independently*. Relative *whose* can only be used independently after a preposition, as in (40). It is used *dependently* before a noun in (41).

41 Apparently, Johnson still gets the odd "Morning, Boris" from sellers of The Big Issue magazine, [[_{NP} *whose cover*] he currently adorns _].

In (41) we use *whose cover* rather than the more complex *the cover of which*. We regard *whose* as a pronoun here, rather than as a determinative, because it carries genitive case. It functions as a Determiner inside the genitive NP headed by *cover*. (See also section 3.2.2.5 for the independent use of *whose* as an interrogative pronoun.)

In (42) *which* is a relative determinative.

42 But the results were inconclusive, [[PP *at which point*] its shares were suspended].

It is not a pronoun here because *which* before a noun can never take genitive case (cf. *The society, which's regulations were amended, was without a chair*). See section 3.3.5.

The word *that* in the bracketed relative clause in (43) is analysed in this grammar as a subordinating conjunction, not as a relative pronoun (see section 3.9).

43 It sounds like some kind of therapy [*that* you're doing].

I will return to relative clauses in section 7.3.3.

3.2.2.4 Free relative pronouns

The bracketed strings in the examples below are called *free relative clauses*, which typically occur in noun phrase positions.

44 [[NP *What*] you do _] is just to switch it off.

45 You have got the right to do [[NP *whatever*] you want _], think [NP [*whatever*] you want _] and say [NP [*whatever*] you want _]. Those rights were won by people who fought for us and died for us.

46 Is it worth complaining to [[NP *whoever*] was in charge]?

In these cases the free relative clauses are introduced by the italicized *free relative pronouns*, which function as the nominal Head of a *wh*-phrase. The most typical member of this class is *what*. Less typical are *who(m)*, *which*, *who(m)ever*, and *whatever*. They are said to be 'free' because they lack an antecedent. Within the clauses in (44) and (45) the italicized words are associated with the gaps indicated by '_', as before.

It is important to be aware of the fact that the words we have analysed as free relative pronouns above can also be assigned to other word classes, depending on the syntactic environment in which they occur. For example, *what* is an interrogative pronoun in

What did you eat? (section 3.2.2.5), and an interrogative determinative in *What films did you watch?* (section 3.3.4). Finally, in (47) *what* is a *free relative determinative*, to be discussed in section 3.3.5.

47 She had sent her [[NP *what money*] she could].

I will discuss free relative clauses in detail in section 7.3.3.5.

3.2.2.5   Interrogative pronouns

Interrogative pronouns (listed in Table 3.8) are *wh*-words that occur inside *wh*-phrases positioned at the beginning of *interrogative clauses*. These are characteristically used to ask questions (section 6.2). The forms *who, whom,* and *whose* refer to humans.

Interrogative pronouns	
who/whom	(occur only independently)
whose	(occurs independently and dependently)
which/what	(occur independently as pronouns, dependently as determinatives)

Table 3.8: Interrogative pronouns

48 [NP *Who*] needs more of these?

49 [NP *Whom*] did you beat _ in the final?

50 [PP To *whom*] are you accountable _?

51 [NP *Whom*] did you enjoy working with _ the most?

52 When there are competing rituals – stockings or pillowcases – [NP *whose*] do you jettison _?

Who is the nominative form used in Subject position, while *whom* is the accusative form associated with a Direct Object position or with a prepositional Complement position (indicated by '_'). *Whom* is formal, and more likely to occur in written language. Prepositional phrases containing interrogative pronouns can either be displaced as a whole, as in (50), or have only the Complement moved, as in (51). The word *whose* in (52) is an independent genitive form functioning as the Direct Object of the verb JETTISON. It can be contrasted with the dependent genitive interrogative pronoun inside an NP, exemplified in (53).

53 [NP *Whose home*] did you take her to _?

See also sections 3.2.2.3, 5.2.1.2, and 6.2.1.

The interrogative pronoun *which* can be used to ask questions about humans or non-humans.

54 [NP *Which* of these men] would you choose _ to babysit for you?

55 [NP *Which*] came first, the golden goose or the golden egg?

By contrast, the pronoun *what* can only be used to ask questions about non-humans.

56 *What* did you say _?

57 *What* is the time?

Notice that in (52) and (55), but not in (56), we have a sense that a noun is missing.

We will treat dependent *which* and *what* in (58) and (59) as interrogative determinatives.

58 [NP *Which* lane] was the debris found in _?

59 [NP *What* nationality] is he?

See section 5.2.1.2 for further discussion.

3.2.2.6 Demonstrative pronouns

English has four demonstrative pronouns, as shown in Table 3.9: *this* and *that*, and their plural forms *these* and *those*. *This* and *these* are used to refer to entities that are *proximal* (i.e. close by), whereas *that* and *those* refer to entities that are *distal* (i.e. further away).

Demonstrative pronouns		
	singular	plural
proximal	this	these
distal	that	those

Table 3.9: Demonstrative pronouns

Here are some examples.

60 *This* is a perfectly good conversation as far as I'm concerned.

61 *These* are peanutty.

62 *That*'s the challenge.

63 *Those* are defined in very broad terms to include the entire Jewish people.

It is important to be aware of the fact that when they occur before nouns, *this/these* (as in *this story/these stories*) and *that/those* (as in *that allegation/those allegations*) are determinatives (see section 3.3).

3.2.2.7 Indefinite pronouns

This category comprises pronouns which are 'indefinite' in the sense that they do not refer to individuals or entities that are identifiable to the addressee. For example, if someone says *I've eaten six cakes and I want another* the word *another* refers to any cake that can be chosen from a set of cakes. Table 3.10 lists the indefinite pronouns in English with examples. Some of these pronouns are simple in form (*all*, *many*, *some*), while others are compounds (*anyone*, *somebody*).

Indefinite pronouns	
additive	another
	(a) One example is the vertebrate immune system. *Another* is the learning system.
degree	few, fewer, less, little, many, more, most, much
	(b) *Few* have succeeded.
disjunctive	either, neither
	(c) *Neither* will be standing at the next general election.
distributive	each, every, everybody, everyone, everything, everywhere
	(d) *Everybody* questions the significance of the results.
existential	any, some, somebody, someone, something
	(e) *Somebody* had been in to talk to Pauline next door to borrow all her vases.
negative	nobody, no one, none, nothing
	(f) *Nothing* is put away and *nothing* really has a fixed place where it is kept.

(Continued)

Indefinite pronouns (*continued*)	
positive paucal	a few, a little, several
	(g) By combining *several* like this you can make a distribution list.
sufficiency	enough
	(h) *Enough* was *enough*.
universal	all, anybody, anyone, anything, both
	(i) Obviously *anyone* is entitled to come forward.

Table 3.10: Indefinite pronouns

Many of the items listed in the table can also belong to the word class of determinatives, to be discussed in section 3.3.

3.2.3 Proper nouns

Proper nouns are used for the names of people, places, animals, and so on, for example *Harry, Pete, James, Kelvin, Amsterdam, Japan, France, May, September*. Such nouns function as the Head of *proper names*. For example, in the simple clause *Harry likes Sally* both *Harry* and *Sally* are proper nouns which function as the Head of noun phrases which are proper names. We can represent the latter as follows using a labelled bracketing (section 1.3): [$_{NP}$ [$_N$ *Harry*]] and [$_{NP}$ [$_N$ *Sally*]]. We also regard as proper names multi-word expressions such as *The Hague, University College London*, and *the United Kingdom*. These may have a proper noun as Head (e.g. *New York*), but are sometimes headed by a common noun (*the Isles of Scilly*).

In a particular context of use proper nouns have a unique reference. Their modificational properties are limited, as with the pronouns. Thus, they cannot normally be pluralized (*Harries, *Toms, *Petes), or preceded by determinatives (*the Mary, *a Jeremy), though there are exceptions. For example, in a situation where several groups of people with the same name have gathered one might ask *Would all the Pauls go to room A, and all the Petes to room B?* In this case we have both a determinative in front of the noun, and pluralization. Modification by adjectives seems to be more freely allowed, as in *The lovely Roxanne kissed young Frank*.

3.2.4   Numerals

We distinguish between *cardinal numerals* and *ordinal numerals*. The former are nouns when they occur on their own, as in (64) and (65)—notice the plural endings in (65)—but determinatives (section 3.3) when they occur before nouns, as in (66).

64 He's *seventy-one*.

65 He took me to what he called a place round the corner, a kind of club where youngish men, all civilians, sat in *twos* and *threes* at little tables with drinks in front of them, talking in low voices.

66 I fell asleep for *two* hours.

Ordinal numerals (*first*, *second*, *third*, etc.) are adjectives, exemplified in (67).

67 Could we have a *second* question please?

3.3   Determinatives
. . . .

Words belonging to the class of *determinatives* function as the Heads of *determinative phrases* (DPs) which in turn principally function as Determiners inside noun phrases (see Chapter 5 for examples of DPs performing other functions). The meanings expressed by determinatives include 'definiteness', 'proximity/remoteness', 'number', 'gender', and 'quantification'. Table 3.11 lists the most common determinatives, with examples.

Distributionally, determinatives, as Heads of DPs, almost always precede nouns, either immediately (e.g. *the* story) or before other phrases such as adjective phrases (e.g. *the* unlikely story). Some determinatives can be modified, and can take inflections (e.g. [*very many*] *results*; [*almost every*] *comment*; [*these*] *results*), but they cannot take case, with the exception of the personal determinatives (cf. *us lawyers*). Table 3.12 summarizes the properties of determinatives.

Determinatives			
additive	another – (a) He's had [NP *another* chance].		
articles	indefinite	a – (b) Well that is [NP *a* point of view].	
	definite	the – (c) [NP *The* group] has stabilised at about ten people.	
degree	few, little, many, much – (d) [NP *Few* details of the Iranian initiative] have emerged.		

		singular	plural
demonstrative	proximal	this – (e) You don't know [NP *this* woman].	these – (f) I don't even like [NP *these* people].
	distal	that – (g) We could have dinner [*that* evening].	those – (h) [NP *Those* pictures] never appeared in the west.

disjunctive	either, neither – (i) [NP *Either* way], it's the end for the Sharptor mine.
distributive	each, every – (j) [NP *Every* day] she goes out at six in the morning.
existential	any, some – (k) I'll get [NP *some* salmon] from the stall.
interrogative	which – (l) [NP *Which* painters] are you talking about?
	what – (m) [NP *What* station]'s that?
	(NB: whose – in e.g. *Whose home did you take her to?* is a pronoun. See section 3.2.2.5.)
negative	no – (n) Philip has [NP *no* right] not to agree.
numeral (cardinal)	one, two, three,.... – (o) You only have to pay [NP *five* quid] for a coach trip.
personal	we/us, you – (p) But [NP *we* lawyers] never tire of them.
positive paucal	certain, a few, a little, several, various – (q) I've tried [NP *a few* times].
relative	which – (r) He'd be going to Moscow, Rome, Vienna and Verona, and coming back to London on Friday night, [clause [PP at [NP *which* point]] he just wanted somewhere slick and easy to go to sleep].
free relative	which – (s) You then choose [clause [NP *which* cheese] you prefer _] and whether you want onions, peppers or other toppings.
	what – (t) We ate [clause [NP *what* food] we had _ on the trees].
	whatever/whichever/whosever – (u) The Liberal Democrats would support [clause [NP *whichever* party] had the most seats] if there was a hung parliament.
sufficiency	enough, sufficient – (v) I haven't got [NP *enough* time].
universal	all, both – (w) [NP *Both* sides] were wrong.

Note that many of these items can also occur on their own, but are then analysed as pronouns rather than determinatives (see section 3.2.2). Cardinal numerals occurring on their own are nouns (section 3.2.4).

Table 3.11: Determinatives

Typical determinatives...
• function as the Heads of determinative phrases which in turn function as Determiners, principally in the leftmost position inside noun phrases;
• can be modified or inflected to a very limited extent (some cannot be modified at all);
• do not take case (with the exception of the personal determinatives).

Table 3.12: The distributional properties of typical determinatives

In what follows I will discuss the most important determinative types listed in Table 3.11. As noted, determinatives always function as the Heads of determinative phrases, though for clarity of exposition the DP level is not always mentioned or represented.

3.3.1   Articles

The word *a* is traditionally called an *indefinite article*, and can only be used in front of singular nouns, while *the* is referred to as a *definite article*, and can be used before singular and plural nouns. We use *a* in situations where we introduce an entity (or concept) that is not uniquely identifiable to the addressee (hence 'indefinite') into a discourse or text, as in the fragment in (68).

68 *A* new word is creeping into the world of banking: netting. *It* could make banking cheaper and safer.

The indefinite article *a* is used here because the new word in question has not been mentioned before in the context. On subsequent mention it is referred to by the pronoun *it*.

The determinative *the* is used when the noun in front of which it occurs has been used before, or is identifiable, as in (69) which is from a story in which flying has previously been mentioned.

69 *The* plane came down at night time on the narrow strip that juts across the bay.

In some cases *the* can be used in front of a noun that has not been mentioned previously. This happens in cases where the referent of the noun is known to the addressee. For example, in (70) the addressee will assume that the speaker is talking about the cat she keeps in her house.

70 It's nice and quiet. I've got it all to *the* cat and myself.

Similarly, consider (71).

71 I met a girl on *the* train today.

Even if (71) is uttered in a situation in which speaker and addressee do not know each other and have never met before, the addressee will construe a meaning for the phrase *the train*, such as 'the train on which the speaker travels to work'. Notice that if (71) had read *I met the girl on the train today*, this would have been odd without a girl having been mentioned previously.

3.3.2 Degree determinatives

We regard the items *few*, *little*, *many*, and *much* as degree determinatives, though it is worth pointing out that they share a number of properties with adjectives. If we take *many* as an example, consider first (72) and (73) below, where we have *more* and *most*, which are the comparative and superlative forms of MANY. Taking comparative and superlative forms is a property of adjectives (and adverbs, section 2.2.3), but not of determinatives.

72 [NP *More* people] were beginning to sit on chairs in the Ottoman world.

73 Women read [NP the *most* books]!

Next, *many* can be modified by the adverb *very*, which is typical of adjectives.

74 There are [NP *very many* basilica churches] built all over Byzantium in the first three centuries of Christianity.

We thus see that degree determinatives resemble adjectives in their distributional behaviour.

3.3.3 Demonstrative determinatives

The *demonstrative determinatives this/that* and *these/those* have a 'pointing' function: they serve to identify people or objects that are nearby (*proximal* determinatives) or further away (*distal* determinatives), either in the singular or in the plural. See also section 3.2.2.6.

3.3.4   Interrogative determinatives

The *interrogative determinatives* occur in interrogative clauses (see section 6.2), as in the following examples.

75 [_{NP} *Which* painters] are you talking about _?

76 [_{NP} *What* painters] are you talking about _?

The difference between these examples is that the former can be used when the speaker has a definite set of painters in mind, such as the Impressionist painters, whereas the choice can be from a non-specific set when *what* is used.

Note that interrogative *whose* occurring before a noun, as in (77), is an interrogative pronoun, not a determinative, as we saw in section 3.2.2.5. This is because it carries genitive case, which determinatives cannot do.

77 *Whose* idea was that?

3.3.5   Relative and free relative determinatives

The *relative determinative* <u>which</u> occurs before nouns in relative clauses (sections 3.2.2.3 and 7.3.3). It cannot occur as an independent element.

78 You won't get this letter till Monday [_{clause} [_{PP} by *which* time] I'll no doubt have spoken to you _].

As we saw in section 3.2.2.3, *whose* in (79) is a relative pronoun functioning as Determiner. It is not a determinative, by virtue of carrying genitive case.

79 I was encouraged to play the clarinet and was taught by a teacher [_{clause} [_{NP} *whose* claim to fame] was that he had taught Reginald Kell].

Free relative determinatives occur inside noun phrases that introduce *free relative clauses*, which were briefly discussed in section 3.2.2.4. What distinguishes them from relative determinatives is that they lack an antecedent noun. In the examples below, repeated from Table 3.11, the free relative clauses function as the Direct Object of the verbs CHOOSE, EAT, and SUPPORT. Within the free relative clauses themselves the NPs are associated with the positions indicated by '_'.

80 You then choose [clause [NP *which* cheese] you prefer _] and whether you want onions, peppers or other toppings.

81 We ate [clause [NP *what* food] we had _ on the trees].

82 The Liberal Democrats would support [clause [NP *whichever* party] had the most seats] if there was a hung parliament.

I will return to relative clauses in section 7.3.3 and to free relative clauses in section 7.3.3.5.

3.4   Adjectives and adjective phrases

An adjective is a word that functions as the Head of an *adjective phrase* (AdjP) and can describe the referent of a noun phrase in *attributive position* (i.e. in front of a noun).

83 He said [AdjP *bright*] pupils would be prevented from fulfilling their potential.

84 We've had a [AdjP very *interesting*] year.

Attributive adjectives can be *stacked*, that is, occur in sequence, without limitation (e.g. *the big green* box), though adding too many adjectives to an NP will obviously lead to problems of comprehension due to limitations on human memory. A number of adjectives occur exclusively in attributive position. Among them are *former, future, main,* and *utter.*

Adjectives functioning as Heads of adjective phrases can also occur in *predicative position* after so-called *linking verbs* like APPEAR, BE, BECOME, and SEEM (see section 3.6.1 below).

85 I was [AdjP *lucky*].

86 If anything, it seems [AdjP *lighter*].

Some adjectives can only occur in predicative position, for example *afraid, alive, alone, awake, aware.*

Thirdly, adjectives can be modified by such words as *completely, quite, really, so, too, very*.

87 The building will be [$_{AdjP}$ *completely* closed] for approximately one week during the religious holiday periods.

88 There are some [$_{AdjP}$ *really* nice] people there.

89 There are two types of gorilla, [$_{AdjP}$ *so* similar] that it takes a specialist to tell them apart.

90 It seems [$_{AdjP}$ *very* expensive].

Related to this is the property of *gradability*. This concerns the plain, comparative, and superlative forms of adjectives and their analytic forms with *more/most*, which were discussed in section 2.2.3.

Finally, a number of adjectives, but by no means all, can take the prefix *un-*: *(un)friendly, (un)helpful, (un)decided, (un)married*, and so on. Table 3.13 summarizes the properties of typical adjectives.

Typical adjectives can...
• act as the Head of an adjective phrase;
• modify the Head of a noun phrase (attributive position);
• occur after linking verbs (predicative position);
• be intensified;
• be graded;
• take the prefix *un-*.

Table 3.13: The distributional properties of typical adjectives

It is important to stress that adjectives that occur on their own are also adjective phrases. This is because they can usually be expanded to a phrase with more than one word. Compare (83) and (84) above.

3.5 The differences between determinatives and adjectives

In some grammars determinatives are analysed as adjectives, since both occur before nouns, as in the example *the brilliant explanation*. This cannot be correct for several reasons. The first point to note is that determinatives add a very different type of meaning to the phrases in which they occur. In the NP above the word *the* adds definiteness, which means that the explanation that is being referred to can be identified uniquely by the addressee. By contrast, the word *brilliant* adds descriptive meaning to the Head noun.

A second point to observe is that there are limits on the number of determinatives that can be added to NPs, and there are syntactic restrictions on their order. Adjectives can be stacked without limit in principle, and the ordering restrictions are semantic in nature. I will return to this point in section 5.2.4.1.

Finally, adjectives can take inflections and a range of modifiers, such as adverbs, whereas determinatives are much more restricted in this respect.

3.6 Verbs and verb phrases

Verbs are the most central elements of clauses. They can express actions, events, states of affairs, and the like. In this section we will expand on the initial notional characterization of verbs as 'action words' by describing their grammatical properties.

3.6.1 Intransitive, transitive, and linking verbs

Verbs can be inflected for tense, or occur in non-tensed forms (see section 2.2.1.2), with the exception of the modal verbs (section 3.6.3.2) which always carry tense. Verbs are typically positioned after a clause-initial noun phrase which functions as Subject. In (91) below the italicized verb stands on its own, and is said to be an *intransitive verb*.

91 Hence if you *smile*, you will feel happy.

Other intransitive verbs include ARRIVE, BLUSH, COLLAPSE, COME, DANCE, DIE, FAINT, FALL, JOKE, RELAX, and WALK.

Contrast (91) with (92) where the verb WANT requires a Direct Object to complete its meaning.

92 She just *wants* a change.

We cannot say *For lunch he wants* without specifying what it is he wants. Verbs that take a Direct Object are called *transitive verbs*.

In (93) the italicized verb is a *linking verb* which is followed by a *Predicative Complement* (underlined).

93 This *is* <u>a perfectly good conversation</u>.

Predicative Complements typically indicate a property that is ascribed to a Subject or Direct Object. In (93) the NP *a perfectly good conversation* is a *Subject-related Predicative Complement*. This grammatical function will be discussed in section 4.1.3.3, along with the function *Object-related Predicative Complement*. Other common linking verbs include BECOME, SEEM, and APPEAR.

3.6.2 Verb phrases

Verbs function as the Heads of *verb phrases* (VPs). We will say that the verb phrase in (91) comprises only the intransitive verb SMILE, as shown in (94).

94 Hence if you [vp [v *smile*]], you will feel happy.

Intransitive VPs can contain optional Adjuncts (section 1.4), as in (95), where the phrase *in June* supplies a time reference.

95 I'm [vp [v *graduating*] [pp in June]].

In (92) and (93) the VP consists of a verb and a following noun phrase taken together, as indicated in (96) and (97).

96 She just [vp [v *wants*] [np a change]].

97 This [vp [v *is*] [np a perfectly good conversation]].

As we have seen, in (96) the NP functions as Direct Object, whereas in (97) it functions as Subject-related Predicative Complement (to be discussed in section 4.1.3.3.1). In (98) the VP contains a verb, a noun phrase functioning as Direct Object, and a prepositional phrase functioning as Adjunct (see section 4.1.3.6). The latter is less closely related to the verb than the Direct Object.

98 She [vp [v *had*] [np a dog] [pp at her feet]].

Other Complements that can appear inside verb phrases will be discussed in section 5.4.1.

3.6.3 Lexical verbs and auxiliary verbs

Consider the set of examples below.

99 The agents <u>will</u> <u><u>book</u></u> the tickets.

100 A thick fog <u>has</u> <u><u>descended</u></u> on the city.

101 The teacher <u>is</u> <u><u>preparing</u></u> an outdoor lesson.

102 The crook <u>was</u> <u><u>apprehended</u></u>.

103 He <u>did</u> <u><u>agree</u></u>!

In each of these examples there is more than one verb. We will make a distinction between *lexical verbs* and *auxiliary verbs*: lexical verbs (doubly underlined) express the principal action or event in a clause, whereas auxiliary verbs (singly underlined) are traditionally said to 'help' lexical verbs in specifying additional meanings. For example, in (99) the auxiliary verb WILL expresses 'intention'. The class of auxiliary verbs can be divided into four categories: *modal auxiliaries, aspectual auxiliaries* (comprising *perfect* HAVE and *progressive* BE), the *passive auxiliary* BE, and *dummy* DO. Here's an overview of how English verbs can be subclassified.

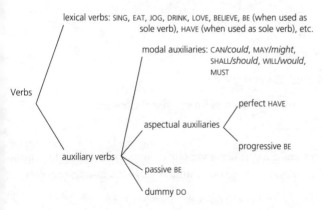

lexical verbs: SING, EAT, JOG, DRINK, LOVE, BELIEVE, BE (when used as sole verb), HAVE (when used as sole verb), etc.

modal auxiliaries: CAN/*could*, MAY/*might*, SHALL/*should*, WILL/*would*, MUST

aspectual auxiliaries
- perfect HAVE
- progressive BE

Verbs

auxiliary verbs
- passive BE
- dummy DO

Figure 3.1 The subclassification of English verbs

The syntactic properties of auxiliary verbs will be discussed in the next section.

3.6.3.1   The NICE properties

Auxiliary verbs share a number of distributional characteristics, collectively referred to as the NICE properties. NICE is an acronym that stands for <u>N</u>egation, <u>I</u>nversion, <u>C</u>ode, and <u>E</u>mphasis. Let us look at each of these in turn.

As regards negation, auxiliary verbs can be followed by *not* or take an ending in *-n't* as the following examples show. (This is rare for the verb MAY.)

104 The agents *will not/won't* book the tickets.

105 A thick fog *has not/hasn't* descended on the city.

106 The teacher *is not/isn't* preparing an outdoor lesson.

107 The crook *was not/wasn't* apprehended.

Lexical verbs cannot be negated by using *not*, and do not take the ending *-n't*, cf. *He agreed not/agreedn't*. Instead, as (108) shows, dummy DO (section 3.6.3.5) is used.

108 He *didn't* agree!

Auxiliary verbs can invert with their Subjects.

109 <u>Will</u> <u>the agents</u> book the tickets?

110 <u>Has</u> <u>a thick fog</u> descended on the city?

111 <u>Is</u> <u>the teacher</u> preparing an outdoor lesson?

112 <u>Was</u> <u>the crook</u> apprehended?

In (113) dummy DO is used to invert with the Subject.

113 <u>Did</u> <u>he</u> agree?

The term 'code' in the acronym NICE refers to the property of auxiliaries that allows them to be 'stranded', as in the examples below.

114 The agents will book the tickets, and so *will* the representatives.

115 A thick fog has descended on the city, and a gloomy atmosphere *has* too.

116 The teacher is preparing an outdoor lesson, but the lecturer *isn't*.

117 The crook was apprehended, and so *was* the solicitor.

118 He did agree, and so *did* she.

The italicized auxiliaries are a shorthand 'code' for the larger verbal constructions. Thus (116) is an elliptical version of *The teacher is preparing an outdoor lesson, but the lecturer isn't* [*preparing an outdoor lesson*]. In each of these cases an italicized auxiliary verb appears without a lexical verb accompanying it. This type of structure is not possible for lexical verbs:

119 *He agreed, and so agreed she.

The 'E' in NICE refers to prosodic emphasis (i.e. the force with which something is uttered), indicated by underlining in the following examples:

120 The agents <u>will</u> book the tickets.

121 A thick fog <u>has</u> descended on the city.

122 The teacher <u>is</u> preparing an outdoor lesson.

123 The crook <u>was</u> apprehended.

124 He <u>did</u> agree!

Lexical verbs do not allow such emphasis. For example, if I say *Jim didn't watch television last night*, it would not be possible for someone else to say *Jim <u>watched</u> television last night* with heavy stress on the verb *watched*. Instead, they would say *Jim <u>did</u> watch television last night*.

The lexical verbs BE and HAVE, exemplified in (125) and (126), also conform to the NICE properties, but we will not regard them as auxiliary verbs. The reason is that they can occur on their own in clauses, whereas auxiliaries can't.

125 I *was* lucky.

126 She *has* a huge range in her kitchen.

3.6.3.2 Modal auxiliaries

Modal auxiliaries (or 'modals' for short) are involved in expressing the following meanings, amongst others: 'ability', 'probability', 'possibility', 'prediction', 'obligation', 'necessity', 'intention', 'permission', 'logical conclusion'. As an example, consider the clause in (127), which involves a prediction about a future situation.

127 I *will* be really busy that night.

The English modal auxiliaries are shown in Table 3.14.

The modal auxiliaries	
present tense form	past tense form
will	*would*
can	*could*
may	*might*
shall	*should*
must	n/a

Table 3.14: The modal auxiliaries

There are a few morphosyntactic points to note about the modals. Firstly, they do not have third person singular present tense endings. Thus, while we have *he works*, *she paints*, and so on, we do not get *he mays*, *she cans*, and so on.

Secondly, they occur only in tensed forms (present or past), though notice that MUST does not have a past tense form.

Thirdly, except in 'code' structures (section 3.6.3.1), the modals are followed by a *bare infinitive* form of the verb (BE in (127)).

A more detailed description of the syntax and semantics of the modal auxiliaries follows in section 10.3.3. Chapter 10 will also discuss a number of marginal modals and modal idioms.

3.6.3.3 Aspectual auxiliaries

Aspectual auxiliaries and the lexical verbs that follow them are instrumental in expressing how an event is viewed in time. There are two aspectual constructions in English: the *perfect* and the *progressive*, which we already briefly discussed in section 2.2.1.

The perfect construction is realized by perfect HAVE + a past participle form of a verb (section 2.2.1.2), as shown in Table 3.15.

The perfect construction: perfect HAVE + past participle form of a verb (*V -ed/-en*)	
present perfect	*have/has + V -ed/-en*
past perfect	*had + V -ed/-en*
non-finite perfect	*have/having + V -ed/-en*

Table 3.15: The perfect construction

The present perfect construction concerns events that took place in the past, but have 'current relevance'. Thus, in (121), repeated here as (128), the event is viewed as having commenced in the past, and as being still relevant at the moment of speaking, for example because the fog is hampering the flow of traffic.

128 A thick fog <u>has</u> descended on the city.

Because the verb HAVE occurs in its third person singular present tense form, the structure above involves a *present perfect* construction. In (129) the verb HAVE occurs in the past tense. In this case the construction is called a *past perfect*.

129 By the time we arrived here, we *had* had enough of travelling.

The past perfect typically involves a reference point in the past, in relation to which a situation is located in time. For example, in (129) the reference point is the point in time when 'we' arrived, and the situation of 'our' having enough of travelling is temporally located in relation to that point. The perfect can also occur in non-finite clauses (section 2.2.1.5), as (130) and (131) show. In these examples the perfect construction expresses that the situations in the bracketed clauses took place in the past from the point of view of the moment of utterance.

130 Anyway it's nice [to *have met* her].

131 [*Having said* that], I can really only say how it was for me when I came to work.

In a progressive construction the progressive auxiliary BE is always followed by an *-ing* participle form of a verb, as shown in Table 3.16. This combination expresses that an event is ongoing or was ongoing.

The progressive construction: progressive BE + -*ing* participle form of a verb (*V* -*ing*)	
present progressive	*am/are/is* + *V* -*ing*
past progressive	*was/were* + *V* -*ing*
non-finite progressive	*be/been* + *V* -*ing*

Table 3.16: The progressive construction

Thus *The teacher is preparing an outdoor lesson* (a 'present progressive' construction) communicates the fact that the preparation is in progress. In *We were watching a film last night* (a 'past progressive' construction) the event of watching the film was in progress in the past. The progressive focuses on the unfolding of events, rather than on an event viewed as a whole with a beginning point and an end point.

As with the perfect, the progressive can also occur in non-finite structures, as in (132).

132 The class seems [*to be voting* with its feet].

The perfect and progressive constructions will be dealt with in greater detail in section 9.3.

3.6.3.4 Passive BE

The passive construction in English is formed by combining the passive auxiliary BE with the past participle form of a lexical verb, followed by an optional *by*-phrase, as shown in Table 3.17.

The passive construction: passive BE + past participle form of a lexical verb (V -*ed/-en*) (*by* NP)	
present passive	*am/is/are* + V -*ed/-en* (*by* NP)
past passive	*was/were* + V -*ed/-en* (*by* NP)

Table 3.17: The passive construction

Passive constructions containing a *by*-phrase can be related to *active* counterparts, such that a Direct Object, Indirect Object, or Object of a preposition of an active clause becomes the Subject of a passive clause. Here are some examples.

133 Present active: *They always ignore me.*

Present passive: *I am always ignored by them.*

134 Past active: *He downloaded the file.*

Past passive: *The file was downloaded by him.*

135 Past active: *She sent me an invoice.*

Past passive: *I was sent an invoice by her.*

136 Past active: *The hospital attended to their needs.*

Past passive: *Their needs were attended to by the hospital.*

In active constructions there is characteristically an agentive Subject, that is, the Subject refers to an animate instigator of an action denoted by the verb, whereas in passive clauses the Subject is typically a Patient ('Undergoer') of an action denoted by a verb. I will return to such notions as 'Agent' and 'Patient' in section 4.2.

A special type of passive construction involves the verb GET. Some examples are shown below.

137 I *got sent* home.

138 These temples *got abandoned* after medieval times, though the site was still used and inhabited by medieval people up to about the eighth century BC.

The GET-*passive construction* is less formal than the construction with BE, and is often used when the speaker wishes to impute some responsibility for the situation being expressed to the Subject of the clause. Thus in the case of (137) it is likely that the speaker in some way brought about his being sent home. The passive version with BE carries no such implication.

Passivization will be discussed further in sections 4.1 and 11.4.

3.6.3.5 Dummy DO

We already had cause to refer to dummy DO a number of times in the preceding sections. This verb has this name because it is meaningless.

It is inserted to allow lexical verbs to form negative, interrogative, 'code', and emphatic structures. This kind of insertion is called DO-*support*. To illustrate, consider the 'basic' clause *He reads a lot*, together with its negative, interrogative, 'code', and emphatic counterparts, in Table 3.18.

Uses of dummy DO	
'Basic' version:	He reads a lot.
Negated version:	He <u>doesn't</u> read a lot.
	*He readsn't a lot.
Inverted version:	<u>Does</u> he read a lot?
	*Reads he a lot?
'Code' version:	He reads a lot, and so <u>does</u> she.
	*He reads a lot, and so reads she.
Emphatic version:	He <u>does</u> read a lot.
	*He <u>reads</u> a lot. (The * pertains to the stress, not the structure per se.)

Table 3.18: Uses of dummy DO

It will be clear from these examples that dummy DO is required each time there is need for a negated, interrogative, 'code', or emphatic version of a clause which does not already contain an auxiliary verb.

In section 8.6 I will discuss combinations of two, three, or four auxiliary verbs.

3.7 Prepositions and prepositional phrases

Prepositions function as the Heads of *prepositional phrases* (PPs). They are uninflected, usually short words which often express spatial meanings which can be literal (<u>*in*</u> *the box*, <u>*near*</u> *the school*, <u>*on*</u> *the desk*) or figurative (<u>*in*</u> *love*, <u>*beyond*</u> *belief*, <u>*beneath*</u> *contempt*). Other meanings are non-spatial and abstract, as in the phrases <u>*for*</u> *your benefit*, *the first* <u>*of*</u> *July*. We distinguish *transitive prepositions* which take NPs or clauses as Complements, *intransitive prepositions* which do not take a Complement, *complex prepositions* which consist of more than one word, *postpositions* whose Complement precedes them, and *deverbal prepositions* which are derived from verbs.

3.7.1 Transitive prepositions

Prepositions can be transitive in which case they take a Complement. We distinguish two types of transitive preposition: *regular prepositions* which take an NP, AdjP, AdvP, or PP as Complement, and *conjunctive prepositions* which take a clause as Complement. Some prepositions belong to both classes. Conjunctive prepositions will be discussed in section 5.5.1.5.

Regular prepositions typically take an NP as a Complement, as in (139)–(143).

139 An extra facility [PP *in* [NP the area]] is therefore unnecessary.

140 Cats can go out [PP *through* [NP the cat flap]].

141 I will be away from the 17th August to the 9th of September so somehow if you want to be with me [PP *during* [NP that time]] I have to share this magic with you.

142 The dance world or the world that I was working in and studying in was [PP *in* [NP many ways]] very removed from the rest of life.

143 Tonight Emily has gone off [PP *with* [NP her Dad]].

When a noun phrase functioning as Complement of a preposition is headed by a pronoun that can have a case contrast (e.g. first and third person personal pronouns), the pronoun carries accusative case (section 3.2.2.1.1):

144 Why are you looking [PP *at* [NP me]]?

Less commonly prepositions take AdjPs, AdvPs, and PPs as Complements. These will be discussed in sections 5.5.1.2–5.5.1.4.

3.7.2 Intransitive prepositions

Intransitive prepositions can stand on their own as Heads of prepositional phrases which typically function as verbal Complements. Examples are shown below.

145 I shall probably look [$_{PP}$ [$_P$ *in*]] at the College.

146 We might go [$_{PP}$ [$_P$ *out*]] for a meal.

147 Presumably you've been [$_{PP}$ [$_P$ *inside*]]?

Structures like these will be discussed further in section 4.1.3.4. Table 3.19 lists common English prepositions.

Prepositions			
aboard$^{\pm NP}$	beforehand^{intr}	herefrom^{intr}	outside$^{\pm NP}$
about$^{\pm NP}$	behind$^{\pm NP}$	herein^{intr}	outward(s)^{intr}
above$^{\pm NP}$	below$^{\pm NP}$	hereof^{intr}	over$^{\pm NP}$
abreast^{intr}	beneath$^{\pm NP}$	hereon^{intr}	overboard^{intr}
abroad^{intr}	beside(s)	hereto^{intr}	overhead^{intr}
across$^{\pm NP}$	between	herewith^{intr}	overland^{intr}
adrift^{intr}	beyond$^{\pm NP}$	home^{intr}	overseas^{intr}
aft^{intr}	by	homeward(s)^{intr}	past$^{\pm NP}$
after	despite	in$^{\pm NP}$	plus
afterward(s)^{intr}	down$^{\pm NP}$	indoors^{intr}	round$^{\pm NP}$
against$^{\pm NP}$	downhill^{intr}	inside$^{\pm NP}$	rightward(s)^{intr}
aground^{intr}	downstage^{intr}	into	seaward(s)^{intr}
ahead^{intr}	downstairs^{intr}	inward(s)^{intr}	since
aloft^{intr}	downstream^{intr}	leftward(s)^{intr}	skyward(s)^{intr}
along$^{\pm NP}$	downward(s)^{intr}	like	southward(s)^{intr}
alongside$^{\pm NP}$	downwind^{intr}	minus	than
(a)mid(st)	during	near$^{\pm NP}$	then^{intr}
among(st)	eastward(s)^{intr}	next	thence^{intr}
apart^{intr}	except	northward(s)^{intr}	thenceforth^{intr}
around$^{\pm NP}$	for	notwithstanding$^{\pm NP}$	there^{intr}
as	forth^{intr}	now^{intr}	thereat^{intr}
ashore^{intr}	forwards^{intr}	of	thereby^{intr}
aside^{intr}	from	off$^{\pm NP}$	therefrom^{intr}
at	heavenward(s)^{intr}	on	therein^{intr}
away^{intr}	hence(forth)^{intr}	onward(s)^{intr}	thereof^{intr}
back^{intr}	here^{intr}	onto	thereon^{intr}
backward(s)^{intr}	hereat^{intr}	opposite$^{\pm NP}$	thereto^{intr}
before	hereby^{intr}	outdoors^{intr}	therewith^{intr}

(Continued)

Prepositions (*continued*)			
through	unlike	upwind[intr]	wherein[intr]
throughout[±NP]	until	via	whereof[intr]
to[±NP]	up[±NP]	westward(s)[intr]	whereon[intr]
together[intr]	uphill[intr]	when[intr]	whereto[intr]
toward(s)	upon	whence[intr]	wherewith[intr]
under[±NP]	upstage[intr]	where[intr]	with
underfoot[intr]	upstairs[intr]	whereat[intr]	within[±NP]
underground[intr]	upstream[intr]	whereby[intr]	without
underneath[±NP]	upward(s) [intr]	wherefrom[intr]	

Prepositions marked '[±NP]' occur with or without an NP Complement. Prepositions marked '[intr]' do not take a Complement. Prepositions without a superscript indicator occur only with an NP (or in some cases with another phrase type). Some of the prepositions listed in the table can also take other types of Complements (e.g. *after*, *before*, and *since* can take clausal complements); see section 5.5.1.

Table 3.19: Prepositions

3.7.3   Complex prepositions

The prepositions listed in Table 3.19 consist of one word with one or more syllables. English also possesses a number of *complex prepositions*. These are prepositions that consist of two or more words. Examples are shown below, and Table 3.20 provides a list.

148 Like most of us, I had assumed this meant a site in the middle of the village [PP *next to* [NP the church]] where there is a flat area big enough and ideal for the purpose.

149 I knew we'd be [PP *out of* [NP pocket]] over it, but I was blowed if we were going to have just that.

150 This pressure is maintained [PP *by means of* [NP water towers and gravity]].

Complex prepositions are transitive: they can license NPs or clauses as Complements. Those which license clauses are called *conjunctive complex prepositions*, and will be discussed in section 5.5.1.5.

Complex prepositions			
according to	by way of	in front of	next to
ahead of	close to	in lieu of	on account of
along with	due to	in line with	on behalf of
as for	far from	in place of	on the grounds of
as from	for (the) sake of	in quest of	on the part of
aside from	for/from want of	in relation to	on top of
as per	in accordance with	in/with respect to	out of
as to	in addition to	in return for	outside of
as well as	in between	in search of	owing to
at the expense of	in case	in terms of	prior to
at the hands of	in case of	in (the) light of	so [that]
at (the) risk of	in charge of	in the name of	subsequent to
at variance with	in compliance with	in spite of	such as
away from	in comparison with	instead of	up to
because of	in conformity with	in step with	up against
by dint of	in contact with	in touch with	with a view to
by means of	in exchange for	in view of	with the exception of
by virtue of	in favour of	near to	

Many of the prepositions listed in the table can also take clausal Complements; see section 5.5.1.5.

Table 3.20: Complex prepositions

3.7.4 Postpositions

Some transitive prepositions *follow* their Complements, and for that reason are best called *postpositions*. Examples are shown below, and Table 3.21 provides a list.

151 [PP [NP College work] *aside*], I have just ended this strange relationship with the girl we spoke about in Paris.

152 [PP [NP Seventeen years] *ago*] I met a young man called Nat David Schwartz.

153 To be fair to our Prime Minister, while seldom conducting charm offensives in Brussels, he has sedulously worked on his relationships with other European leaders, and this strategy, [PP [NP our aloofness from the eurozone] *notwithstanding*], has served him well at this time of crisis.

154 "I have been real lucky and everything went perfect [PP [NP all year] *through*]," he said.

Notice that these prepositions cannot precede their Complements, though *notwithstanding* is an exception. Thus in (153) *notwithstanding our aloofness from the eurozone* would also have been possible. *Through* can take an NP as Complement (e.g. *through the door*), but cannot precede *all year* in (154).

Postpositions
ago
apart
aside
notwithstanding
through

Table 3.21: Postpositions

3.7.5 Deverbal prepositions

Transitive prepositions that take the same form as -*ing* participles or -*ed* participles are called *deverbal prepositions*. See the examples below and the list in Table 3.22.

155 But to many Londoners, [PP *including* [NP some of the stars gathered here tonight]], these are dangerous times.

156 [PP *Regarding* [NP the issue of diagnosis]], Szasz raises two major criticisms concerning the analogy between physical and mental disease, implicit in the medical model.

157 You may even be thinking that [PP *given* [NP your studied ignorance on the matter], the democratic process will be far better off without your participation, no matter how close all our parliamentary institutions are to meltdown.

Deverbal prepositions		
according [to]	failing	pertaining [to]
allowing [for]	following	regarding
barring	given	respecting
concerning	gone	saving
counting	granted	touching
excepting	including	wanting
excluding	owing [to]	

Table 3.22: Deverbal prepositions

3.8   Adverbs and adverb phrases

Adverbs function as the Head of *Adverb Phrases* (AdvP) which modify verbs, adjectives, or other adverbs, as in the following examples.

158 Lansbury [$_{VP}$ [$_{AdvP}$ *cheerfully*] accepted his second imprisonment].

159 We had a [$_{AdjP}$ [$_{AdvP}$ *very*] good] turnout.

160 You're no doubt working [$_{AdvP}$ [$_{AdvP}$ *extremely*] hard].

The adverb in (161) below is a *clause adverb* because its meaning applies to an entire clause, as becomes clear when we paraphrase (161) as follows: 'It is probable that this tissue does not have any important function in adult human subjects.' It carries modal meaning (section 10.3.11.4).

161 This tissue [$_{AdvP}$ *probably*] does not have any important function in adult human subjects.

In (162), the adverb is orthographically placed within the second of the two clauses, though in actual fact it is syntactically quite detached from both, and merely has a linking function. Notice that when (162) is read aloud, there is a pause after *however*. We will call such adverbs *linking adverbs*. Others include *besides*, *finally*, *furthermore*, and *moreover*.

162 I don't quite know how to answer that one. [$_{AdvP}$ *However*], I will speak to you shortly.

See also section 4.1.3.6.3.

A large number of adverbs are homonymous with (i.e. have the same forms as) adjectives. Compare (163), where *hard* is an adjective, with (164), where it is an adverb.

163 They require a lot of *hard* work.

164 They'll have to work *hard* in the months ahead.

Other adverbs that are homonymous with adjectives include *clear, daily, deadly, free, likely, part-time, pretty, still, well, wrong.* The adjectives and adverbs do not necessarily have the same meaning. Thus *well* in *I am well* does not mean the same as *well* in *He did it well.*

3.8.1 Meanings expressed by adverbs

Adverbs can express a huge range of different types of meanings. For example, inside the VP in (158) the adverb expresses 'manner'. Such adverbs typically end in *-ly*. Other adverbs can express 'intensity' or 'degree' inside AdjPs and AdvPs, as in (159) and (160). Further meanings include 'direction' (*edgeways, sideways*), 'extent' (*completely, wholly*), 'frequency' (*always, often, seldom, weekly*), 'instrument' (*microscopically*), 'location' (*worldwide*), 'time' (*early, sometimes*), and 'modality' (*maybe, necessarily, perhaps, possibly, probably, surely*; see section 10.3.11.4).

3.9 Conjunctions

Conjunctions are linking words of which there are two types: *coordinating conjunctions* and *subordinating conjunctions*.

Coordinating conjunctions are words like *and, or,* and *but,* and a handful of other items, which are used to link phrases and clauses. The following examples show coordinated noun phrases, adjective phrases, and prepositional phrases.

165 I'm trained as [NP *a dancer*] and [NP *a creative artist*].

166 Well basically you're born with genes which say you're going to be [AdjP *small*] or [AdjP big].

167 We no longer talk [PP *of virtues*] but [PP *of values*].

Further examples will be discussed in section 5.7.

Subordinating conjunctions (also called *subordinators*) are linking words which serve to subordinate one clause to another (sections 1.3, 1.7, and 7.1). In the following example the verb THINK takes a clausal Direct Object which is introduced by the subordinating conjunction *that*.

168 I think [*that* this poem justifies his point].

We can represent the structure of (168) as follows.

main/matrix clause
subordinate clause

We refer to a clause in which a *subordinate clause* is *embedded* as a *matrix clause*. A matrix clause which is itself not embedded within any other clause is called a *main clause*. Thus in (168) the string *I think that this poem justifies his point* is a main clause and a matrix clause, whereas the string *that this poem justifies his point* is a subordinate clause.

The words *whether* and interrogative *if* are also subordinating conjunctions in English. They are illustrated in the examples below.

169 I don't know [clause *whether* I got your letter].

170 And she rang up the other day to ask [clause *if* I needed to see somebody].

Finally, we recognize *for* as a subordinating conjunction in clauses that do not carry tense, as in (171). This construction is more frequent in American English.

171 There is nothing I want [clause *for* you to say anyway].

Table 3.23 provides a list of subordinating conjunctions.

Note that the structure as a whole in (168) is also a *sentence*. As we briefly saw in Chapter 1, *sentences* are composed of clauses. Minimally a sentence contains one clause. However, we cannot equate the notion of 'sentence' with 'main clause', because a sentence can be composed of two main clauses, for example in a coordinated structure like (172).

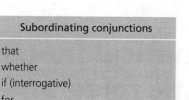

Subordinating conjunctions
that
whether
if (interrogative)
for

Table 3.23: Subordinating conjunctions

172 [sentence [main clause *It was a fourteenth or thirteenth century château*]
and [main clause *we just sort of wandered in*]].

In this grammar we will not have much use for the label 'sentence'.
Instead we focus on the structure of phrases and clauses, as well as
clause relationships. These topics will be discussed extensively in
Chapters 5, 6, 7, and 8.

3.10 Interjections

The class of *interjections* includes words like *ah, aha, cool, damn,
oh, mmm, ooh, ouch, uh, uhm, wow, yippee, yuck*. They are used
to express reactions, emotions, approval, disapproval, and so on,
but are very marginal to the grammar of English. Here are some
examples.

173 *Ah* that's nice of you.

174 *Oh*, I thought you got it from Bow.

175 *Uhm* besides that I've been phoning round the press.

176 *Mmm oh* you mean the pop group didn't like it?

Chapter 4

Grammatical functions, semantic roles, and tree diagrams

In the previous chapter we looked at the word classes in English, together with their associated phrases, at the *form level* of analysis. In this chapter we will turn to *grammatical functions*. Analysing English at this level entails considering the grammatical roles (Subject, Direct Object, etc.) that particular *constituents* (strings of words that behave as units) can play in a clause. A typical clause is defined as a grammatical structure in which 'something is said about' ('predicated of') a Subject. Within clauses we will recognize several *semantic roles* (Agent, Patient, etc.) that constituents can play from the point of view of meaning. These will be discussed in section 4.2. In the final section I will discuss a way in which we can use so-called *tree diagrams* to represent the structure of clauses graphically.

4.1   Grammatical functions

In English we distinguish the grammatical functions listed in Table 4.1.

Grammatical functions
• Subject (Subj)
• Predicate (Pred)
• Predicator (PCR)

(Continued)

Grammatical functions (*continued*)
• Complements:
▪ Object
◦ Direct Object (DO)
◦ Indirect Object (IO)
▪ Predicative Complement (PC)
◦ Subject-related
◦ Object-related
▪ PP as Complement (PPC)
▪ Complement Clause (CC)
• Adjunct (A)

Table 4.1: Grammatical functions

In what follows I will focus on the main grammatical characteristics of the various functions.

4.1.1   Subject (Subj)

In Chapter 1 we provisionally defined the Subject of a clause notionally as referring to the entity that carries out the action denoted by the verb. In a large number of cases this definition works very well. In the following examples the Subjects are italicized.

1 *Prosecutors* stopped the video.

2 *I* deleted it manually.

3 *A court in India* postponed the release of a film entitled Hari Puttar.

The referents of these Subjects can indeed be said to be carrying out an action: physical actions in the first two examples, and an act of a more abstract kind in the case of (3). However, in a large number of cases the referents of the Subjects do not engage in any kind of action at all, cf. (4) and (5).

4 *Tony* likes films with lots of gratuitous violence.

5 *I* assumed that I must've come through the questioning satisfactorily.

In addition, sometimes the Subject of a clause is itself a clause which cannot be said to carry out an action, as in (6).

6 [*That Moro felt certain he was being sacrificed*] is evident from his last letters.

Clauses functioning as Subjects will be discussed in Chapters 7 and 8.

Finally, the notional definition is problematic for passive clauses (sections 1.11 and 3.6.3.4) in which the Subject carries a Patient role (see section 4.2 below). This is made clear by example (7) in which Danny Maddox is the perpetrator of a foul undergone by the person that the Subject refers to.

7 He was fouled from behind by Danny Maddox.

In view of the above, we conclude that Subjects are best defined using grammatical criteria, to which we now turn.

4.1.1.1   Subjects are obligatory

The first thing to notice about Subjects is that they are *obligatory* in main clauses. Exceptions are imperative clauses (sections 1.6 and 6.3), short messages like those sent by mobile phone (e.g. *Will be late*), and diary entries (e.g. *Went to see a film last night*). None of the examples below is grammatical without a Subject.

8 *stopped the video.

9 *deleted it manually.

10 *postponed the release of a film entitled Hari Puttar.

11 *likes films with lots of gratuitous violence.

12 *assumed that I must've come through the questioning satisfactorily.

13 *is evident from his last letters.

4.1.1.2   Subjects are mostly realized as noun phrases

Subjects are overwhelmingly *realized* as noun phrases. When we speak of the realization of a particular function we are referring to the *form* (NP, AdjP, PP, clause, etc.) that the function in question can assume in English. In the ICE-GB corpus, which contains one million words, there are 107,531 Subjects, 99 per cent of which are NPs. Of these 64 per cent are headed by pronouns.

Prepositional phrases can function as Subject, though this is very rare. Two examples follow below.

14 [PP *Under the bed*] is where dust and childhood monsters lurk.

15 [PP *Between half and three-quarters of the farm*] is likely to be grassland.

Adverb phrases can only function as Subject in set expressions like the following, the last two of which are headlines.

16 Sheffield United could employ their usual tactic and try to get a few Arsenal players sent off early on. [AdvP *Carefully*] does it, though.

17 [AdvP *Gently*] does it.

18 [AdvP *Prudently*] does it as banker's banker sees off his inquisitors.

Finally, a small number of Subjects are realized as clauses. An example was given in (6) above. See Chapters 7 and 8 for further discussion.

4.1.1.3 Subjects characteristically occupy a clause-initial position in declarative clauses

Subjects generally occur at the beginning of *declarative clauses* (sections 1.6 and 6.1), as in all the examples we have looked at so far in this chapter. From the point of view of meaning they can often be said to express what the clause is about.

4.1.1.4 Pronouns heading NPs in the Subject position of finite clauses take nominative case

In finite clauses (section 2.2.1.5) pronouns which can show a case alternation (e.g. first and third person personal pronouns) heading NPs in Subject position occur in the nominative case (section 2.2.2.2). In non-finite subordinate clauses Subjects can also carry accusative or genitive case, as we will see in Chapter 8.

4.1.1.5 Subjects can be semantically 'empty'

Subjects can be realized by semantically 'empty' elements, like *it* and *there* (sections 3.2.2.1.2 and 3.2.2.1.3), as in the examples below.

19 *It* is absolutely boiling here.

20 *There* is a sense that nobody is left out of this group.

Empty *it* and *there* predominantly occur in Subject position, though they can also occur as 'raised Objects' (see section 8.1.3.3).

4.1.1.6 Subjects invert positions with verbs in interrogative main clauses

Subjects can exchange positions with auxiliary verbs or with the lexical verbs BE or HAVE (section 3.6.3) in main *interrogative clauses*, which are typically used to ask questions (sections 1.6 and 6.2). Each of the clauses in (21)–(24) displays *inversion* of the Subject and a verb.

21 <u>Could you</u> start again?

22 <u>Has she</u> booked in yet?

23 <u>Is this</u> coq au vin?

24 <u>Have you</u> a pen?

Interrogative clauses will be discussed in section 6.2, and in Chapters 7 and 8.

4.1.1.7 Verbs agree with their Subjects in the present tense

Verbs are said to *agree* with their Subjects in the present tense for person and number (section 2.2.1.2). In (25) the third person singular present tense inflection -*s* is obligatory. In (26) the agreement on the plain present form of the verb is not visible as a verb inflection.

25 Andy *hates* them.

26 I *like* the Catherine Cookson books.

In the past tense only the inflectional forms of BE agree with their Subject: we have *was* for the first and third person singular, and *were* elsewhere.

27 He *was* not amused.

28 They *were* interested in selling the business.

4.1.1.8 Subjects can be the antecedents of pronouns in interrogative tags

Subjects can act as the antecedents of pronouns in so-called *interrogative tags*. This property is illustrated by the examples in (29)–(34).

29 Prosecutors stopped the video, *didn't _they_*?

30 I deleted it manually, *didn't _I_*?

31 A court in India postponed the release of a film entitled Hari Puttar, *didn't _it_*?

32 Tony likes films with lots of gratuitous violence, *doesn't _he_*?

33 I assumed that I must've come through the questioning satisfactorily, *didn't _I_*?

34 That Moro felt certain he was being sacrificed is evident from his last letters, *isn't _it_*?

The italicized portions of these examples are interrogative tags, whose underlined pronouns have the Subjects of the matrix clauses as their antecedents. Notice that *it* is used in (34) to refer to the clausal Subject (*That Moro. . .sacrificed*).

The properties of Subjects are summarized in Table 4.2.

Typical Subjects...
• refer to a person or entity that instigates an action expressed by a verb in a declarative active clause (this is a notional property);
• are obligatory (except in imperatives, text messages, diary entries);
• occupy a clause-initial position in declarative clauses;
• are realized as noun phrases;
• carry nominative case in finite clauses (this only applies to pronouns that can alternate in case);
• invert with a verb in interrogative main clauses;
• induce agreement with a verb in the present tense and with BE in the past tense;
• can be the antecedents of pronouns in interrogative tags.

Table 4.2: The properties of typical Subjects

4.1.2 Predicate (Pred) and Predicator (PCR)

The function of *Predicate* applies quite simply to everything to the right of the Subject in a clause. You may recall that in section 3.6.2 we said that VPs consist of verbs together with any associated phrases. We can now say that VPs function as Predicates within clauses. Furthermore, within the Predicate the verb is the pivotal element, and functions as *Predicator*. In the examples below the Predicates appear in italics and the Predicators are underlined.

35 Prosecutors *<u>stopped</u> the video.*

36 I *<u>deleted</u> it manually.*

37 A court in India *<u>postponed</u> the release of a film entitled Hari Puttar.*

38 Tony *<u>likes</u> films with lots of gratuitous violence.*

39 I *<u>assumed</u> that I must've come through the questioning satisfactorily.*

40 That Moro felt certain he was being sacrificed *<u>is</u> evident from his last letters.*

In each of these cases the Predicate expresses the action, event, etc. with which the Subject is involved. Predicator and Predicate are functions that operate only at clause level.

4.1.3 Complements

We apply the functional label *Complement* to any constituent in English that is *licensed* by a particular Head (verb, noun, adjective, preposition, etc.). Licensing is a grammatical notion whereby a Head determines which type of phrase(s) or clause(s) complement it, subject to certain meaning restrictions. For example, inside a VP the verb DEVOUR licenses an NP Complement denoting something edible (*He devoured the carrot*), while PUT licenses two Complements, namely an NP and a PP, with the PP specifying a location (*We put the present in the bag*). Some Heads allow different Complements in different structures. For example, the verb BELIEVE can license an NP (*She believed the story*), or a clause (*She believed that he was telling the truth*). Heads belonging to other word classes can also license phrases or clauses as Complements. For example, the adjective *fond* licenses a PP (*Sam is fond of his cousin*), while the noun *idea* licenses a clause (*The idea that the world is flat was once commonplace*). The Complement-taking properties of lexical Heads are listed in the *lexicon*, that is, the mental word store or dictionary that a speaker of a language has access to.

Within verb phrases we recognize six types of Complements, namely *Direct Object* (DO), *Indirect Object* (IO), *Subject-related Predicative Complement*, *Object-related Predicative Complement*, *PP as Complement* (PPC), and *Complement Clause* (CC).

It is important to point out that Adjuncts are *not* licensed by verbs. This is because they supply additional information about a situation expressed. Nevertheless, Adjuncts *are* part of the verb phrase in a clause, though they are less closely related to the verb than any Complements that may be present, for the reason just mentioned.

4.1.3.1 Direct Objects

In chapter 1 we saw that the grammatical function of Direct Object is typically expressed by a phrase that refers to a person or entity that undergoes the action specified by the verb (see also section 4.2 below). Verbs that license a Direct Object are called *transitive verbs* because the verb + DO sequence expresses that something is transferred (e.g. an action) from one entity to another.

In our original set of examples below, the referents of the italicized DOs in (41) and (42) undergo the actions of 'stopping' and 'deleting', respectively. In a more abstract sense—in that no physical action is involved—this is also true for (43). However, in (44) clearly the films in question are in no sense affected by Tony's enjoyment of them.

41 Prosecutors stopped *the video*.

42 I deleted *it* manually.

43 A court in India postponed *the release of a film entitled Hari Puttar*.

44 Tony likes *films with lots of gratuitous violence*.

Given that the notional criterion of 'undergoing the verbal action' is not sufficient to characterize Direct Objects, we need to turn to a grammatical characterization.

4.1.3.1.1 Direct Objects form a close bond with a lexical verb

The first thing to observe is that in unmarked declarative clauses Direct Objects are positioned after a lexical verb, with which they form a close bond, as in (41)–(44) above. We cannot leave out the DOs, as examples (45)–(48) show.

45 *Prosecutors stopped. (This example is grammatical, but with a different meaning, namely 'brought themselves to a standstill'.)

46 *I deleted manually.

47 *A court in India postponed.

48 *Tony likes.

In other cases the DO can be omitted, but is implicit. Thus if I utter (49) the addressee will understand that I must be reading *something*.

49 I'm reading.

The bond between verbs and their Complements is also evident from the fact that they cannot generally be separated from each other.

50 *Prosecutors stopped *immediately* the video.

51 *I deleted *without reason* it manually.

52 *A court in India postponed *legally* the release of a film entitled Hari Puttar.

53 *Tony likes *very much* films with lots of gratuitous violence.

4.1.3.1.2 Direct Objects are mostly realized as noun phrases

In the one-million-word ICE-GB corpus there are 55,276 Direct Objects, the vast majority of which are NPs, namely 77 per cent. Of these just over 21 per cent are headed by pronouns. In the ICE-GB corpus the remaining Direct Objects are realized as clauses. See Chapters 5, 7, and 8 for discussion.

4.1.3.1.3 A subset of pronouns heading NPs in Direct Object position take accusative case

When an NP functioning as Direct Object is headed by a pronoun that can have a case contrast (e.g. first and third person personal pronouns, *who*), the pronoun carries accusative case (sections 2.2.2.2 and 3.2.2).

4.1.3.1.4 Direct Objects of active declarative clauses can generally become the Subjects of passive clauses

Direct Objects of active declarative clauses (section 1.6) can commonly become the Subjects of passive clauses. This process is called *passivization*, and was briefly discussed in section 3.6.3.4. It is further illustrated in the following set of examples.

54 *Prosecutors* stopped *the video*. > *The video* was stopped (by prosecutors).

55 I deleted *it* manually. > *It* was deleted manually (by me).

56 A court in India postponed the release of a film entitled Hari Puttar. > *The release of a film entitled Hari Puttar* was postponed (by a court in India).

In each of these pairs the first clause is referred to as having *active voice*; the second is its *passive* counterpart. Passivization involves the introduction of the passive auxiliary BE (section 3.6.3.4), and an optional *by*-phrase. Active and passive clauses mean the same, though they differ in the way that the information is presented to the hearer. (We will return to this issue in section 11.4.)

Not all verbs allow passivization to the same extent, as (57) shows.

57 Tony likes *films with lots of gratuitous violence*. >?*Films with lots of gratuitous violence* are liked (by Tony).

The NP following the verb in the active version of (57) cannot become the Subject of a passive clause. The same is true for the postverbal NPs in (58) and (59), which contain the verbs SUIT and COST.

58 That beret does not suit you, you know. > *You are not suited by that beret, you know.

59 Your private sight test costs £9. > *£9 is cost by your private eye test.

Notice also that certain types of Direct Object, for example NPs headed by reflexive pronouns, cannot become the Subjects of passive clauses.

60 He scarcely knew himself. > *Himself was scarcely known by him.

Table 4.3 summarizes the properties of typical DOs.

Typical Direct Objects...
• refer to a person or entity that undergoes an action (a notional property);
• form a close bond with a lexical verb;
• are realized as noun phrases;
• carry accusative case (this only applies to pronouns that can alternate in case);
• of active declarative clauses can become the Subjects of passive clauses.

Table 4.3: The properties of typical Direct Objects

Table 4.4 shows a selection of English transitive verbs.

A selection of transitive verbs		
ACCEPT	HEAR	PASS
AWAIT	HELP	PRODUCE
BEGIN	HAVE	READ
BELIEVE	INSPECT	RECEIVE
CALL	INVESTIGATE	REJECT
DISCUSS	KILL	SEE
EAT	MEET	SELL
FEEL	MIND	START
FIND	NEED	UNDERSTAND
GET	OPEN	WANT

Table 4.4: A selection of transitive verbs

4.1.3.2 Indirect Objects

Notionally, Indirect Objects refer to people or entities that carry the semantic role of Goal, Recipient, or Benefactive of an action or event (see section 4.2 below). The following sections discuss the grammatical properties of IOs.

4.1.3.2.1 Indirect Objects form a close bond with a lexical verb

Indirect Objects occur immediately after so-called *ditransitive verbs* (i.e. verbs that take an IO and DO), with which they have a close bond. Notice that IOs cannot generally occur without a following Direct Object. In the examples below the IOs have been italicized, the DOs underlined.

61 And then he tells *her* <u>the story of his life</u>.

62 They brought *me* <u>a bottle of Croft's Original</u>.

63 He left *us* <u>the first eyewitness account of the ancient Britons</u>.

64 I got *her* <u>a mini cake</u> and made *her* <u>a card</u>!

These examples alternate with a structure involving a prepositional phrase, as in (65)–(68):

65 And then he tells the story of his life *to her*.

66 They brought a bottle of Croft's Original *to me*.

67 He left the first eyewitness account of the ancient Britons *to us*.

68 I got a mini cake *for her* and made a card *for her*.

In these cases the PPs function as Complements which carry the same semantic roles as Indirect Objects, namely Goal, Recipient, and Benefactive. (See section 11.5 on the motivations for using the construction in (61)–(64), rather than the one in (65)–(68).)

In the following examples *me* and *Emily* function as Direct Object, but carry a role typically associated with an IO.

69 A: I live in Southgate. B: Oh that's right. You told *me*.

70 Sylvie came here today to teach *Emily*.

4.1.3.2.2 Indirect Objects are virtually always realized as noun phrases

Indirect Objects are much less frequent than Subjects or Direct Objects: there are only 1,771 in the ICE-GB corpus. Without exception they are realized as noun phrases.

4.1.3.2.3 A subset of pronouns heading NPs in the Indirect Object position take accusative case

When an NP functioning as Indirect Object is headed by a pronoun that can have a case contrast (e.g. first and third person personal pronouns, *who*), the pronoun carries accusative case (sections 2.2.2.2 and 3.2.2).

4.1.3.2.4 Indirect Objects of active clauses can become the Subjects of passive clauses

Indirect Objects share with Direct Objects the property that they can become the Subjects of passive clauses, as the passive versions of (61)–(63) show:

71 And then *she* is told the story of his life (by him).

72 *I* was brought a bottle of Croft's Original (by them).

73 *We* were left the first eyewitness account of the ancient Britons (by him).

However, the passive versions of both parts of (64), involving the verbs GET and MAKE, are unacceptable to many.

74 ?She was got a mini cake and she was made a card.

Table 4.5 summarizes the properties of typical Indirect Objects, whereas Table 4.6 lists a selection of ditransitive verbs.

Typical Indirect Objects...
• refer to people or entities that are Goals, Recipients, or Benefactives of an action or event (this is a notional property);
• occur immediately after the verb, with which they have a close bond;
• must be accompanied by a following DO;
• are realized as noun phrases;
• carry accusative case (if headed by a pronoun that can have a case contrast);
• can become the Subjects of passive clauses.

Table 4.5: The properties of typical Indirect Objects

A selection of ditransitive verbs		
DENY	LEND	SERVE
ENVY	OFFER	SELL
FIND	ORDER	SEND
FORGIVE	OWE	SHOW
GIVE	PAY	SPARE
GRANT	PROMISE	TEACH
HAND	RESERVE	TELL
LEAVE	SAVE	THROW

Table 4.6: A selection of ditransitive verbs

4.1.3.3 Predicative Complements

Predicative Complement is a function label used for constituents that specify a property that is ascribed to the referent of another constituent, or for constituents that identify the referent of another expression. We distinguish *Subject-related Predicative Complements* from *Object-related Predicative Complements*. Their properties will be discussed in the next two sections. In section 4.1.3.3.3 I will discuss how PCs differ from Direct and Indirect Objects.

4.1.3.3.1 Subject-related Predicative Complements

In the following examples the italicized Subject-related Predicative Complements are obligatory, and indicate a property that is ascribed to the underlined Subjects.

75 <u>The first London</u> was just [$_{NP}$ *a colonial outpost of the Roman empire*].

76 <u>The sky</u> was [$_{AdjP}$ *clear*] after the rainfall.

Semantically, Subject-related PCs can express *depictive* and *resultative* meanings. The former is illustrated in (75) where the bracketed NP expresses a property attributable to the Subject. Resultative meaning is illustrated in (77), where the PC expresses the result of a process of change.

77 <u>He</u> became [$_{AdjP}$ *convinced he could reach the North Pole unaided*].

Other verbs that take resultative PCs are GO (*crazy*), GROW (*old*), PROVE (*fatal*), TURN (*red*).

Mention should be made of the *specifying* use of BE, as in (78). Here the verb specifies or identifies the referent of the Subject.

78 His son was *Roderick*.

When a Subject-related PC is realized as a noun phrase headed by a pronoun that can have a case alternation the pronoun characteristically occurs in the accusative case, except in very formal styles.

79 Do you think it's *them*?

80 Hi, it's *me*.

There are 31,414 Subject-related Predicative Complements in the ICE-GB corpus. Of these 42 per cent are AdjPs, whereas 35 per cent are NPs (of which almost 5 per cent are headed by pronouns). Of the remaining Subject-related PCs around 11 per cent are realized as prepositional phrases, 8 per cent as clauses, and a very small percentage as adverb phrases. Examples of these will be discussed in section 5.4.1.3.

Verbs that license a Subject-related Predicative Complement are called *linking verbs* (section 3.6.1), further examples of which are listed in Table 4.7.

A selection of linking verbs	
APPEAR	PROVE
BE	REMAIN
BECOME	SEEM
FEEL	SMELL
GET	SOUND
GROW	TASTE
LOOK	

Table 4.7: A selection of linking verbs

4.1.3.3.2 Object-related Predicative Complements

Object-related Predicative Complements (italicized in the examples below) indicate a property that is ascribed to Direct Objects (underlined), which must therefore be present. Verbs that license a Direct Object and an Object-related Predicative Complement are called *complex transitive* verbs. Object-related Predicative Complements are relatively infrequent in the ICE-GB corpus. They are typically realized as noun phrases or adjective phrases. Here are two examples.

81 He'd worked for the company who had now made <u>him</u> [NP *a distributor*].

82 She found <u>him</u> [AdjP *really frustrating*], because he didn't seem bothered.

Prepositional phrases and clauses are also possible as Object-related PCs. These will be exemplified briefly in sections 5.4.1.4 and 8.3.5.

As with the Subject-related PCs, Object-related PCs can differ semantically: in (82) the PC expresses a depictive meaning, whereas in (83) it expresses a resultative meaning:

83 Police believe that although the suspects washed <u>the knife</u> [AdjP *clean of any blood*], they were unable to remove the DNA.

Table 4.8 lists some English complex transitive verbs.

A selection of complex transitive verbs	
BELIEVE	LABEL
BRAND	LEAVE
CONSIDER	PRESUME
DECLARE	PRONOUNCE
DEEM	PROVE
FIND	RATE
JUDGE	RENDER
KEEP	THINK

Table 4.8: A selection of complex transitive verbs

4.1.3.3.3 Predicative Complements vs Direct and Indirect Objects

How do Predicative Complements differ from DOs and IOs? They all occur after verbs with which they have a close bond (which is why they are called Complements), but PCs cannot be referring expressions. This means that in an example like (81) the noun phrase that functions as Object-related Predicative Complement (*a distributor*) does not point to an individual in the world, but ascribes a property (in this case the occupancy of a particular kind of job) to the referent of the DO. In other cases, as we have seen, PCs identify the referent of a Subject. Predicative Complements cannot become the Subject of a passive clause.

Table 4.9 summarizes the properties of Predicative Complements.

Typical Predicative Complements...
• specify a property ascribed to the referent of a Subject or Direct Object, or identify the referent of a Subject;
• are realized as noun phrases, adjective phrases, prepositional phrases, clauses, or (in the case of Subject-related PCs) adverb phrases;
• occur after linking verbs (in the case of Subject-related PCs);
• are obligatory (in the case of Subject-related PCs);
• follow a DO (in the case of Object-related PCs);
• cannot become the Subjects of passive clauses.

Table 4.9: The distributional properties of typical Predicative Complements

4.1.3.4 Prepositional Phrase as Complement

There are many verbs in English that license a Prepositional Phrase as Complement (PPC), with or without an accompanying Direct Object. Here are some typical examples.

84 Senior opposition figures have been arrested, and the government has <u>blamed</u> [NP *troublemakers*][PP *for the violence*].

85 You can <u>refer</u> [PP *to your notes*] whenever you need to.

86 Since reaching prominence he has <u>branched</u> [PP *out*], writing a newspaper column and presenting documentaries about boats and planes – and hosting a chat show.

87 It is best to <u>leave</u> [PP *out*] [NP *perennial weed roots*].

In the sections below the properties of PPCs will be discussed.

4.1.3.4.1 The verbs and prepositions can be transitive or intransitive

In (84) and (85) above the PP is headed by a transitive preposition (section 3.7.1), whereas in (86) and (87) the PPs are headed by intransitive prepositions (section 3.7.2).

The verbs in (84) and (87) are transitive, whereas those in (85) and (86) are intransitive. The DO in the last example can also be positioned after the PP, as in (88).

88 It is best to leave [_NP_ *perennial weed roots*] [_PP_ *out*].

4.1.3.4.2 The Head of the PP is licensed by the verb

The verb licenses not only the PP as Complement, but also the Head of the PP. Thus in (84) the verb BLAME licenses a PP headed by *for* (or *on* in the alternative structure *blamed the violence on troublemakers*), and in (85) REFER licenses a PP headed by *to*.

4.1.3.4.3 PPCs cannot become the Subjects of passive clauses

Unlike Indirect Objects, Direct Objects, and Complements of prepositions, PPCs cannot become the Subjects of passive clauses. For example, (89) is not a possible passive counterpart of (85).

89 *To your notes can be referred by you whenever you need to.

The distributional properties of PPCs are summarized in Table 4.10, whereas Table 4.11 lists a selection of verbs licensing PPCs.

Typical PPCs...
• involve a transitive or intransive verb, as well as a transitive or intransitive PP licensed by that verb;
• involve a PP whose Head is licensed by a verb;
• cannot become the Subjects of passive clauses.

Table 4.10: The distributional properties of PPCs

A selection of verbs licensing PPCs	
ENVY NP *for* NP	BACK *down*
INVEST NP *in* NP	CATCH *on*
ACCOUNT *for* NP	EAT NP *up*
DECIDE *on* NP	WRITE NP *down*

Table 4.11: A selection of verbs licensing PPCs

The full range of structures involving Prepositional Phrases as Complements will be discussed in section 5.4.1.5.

4.1.3.5 Complement Clauses

We assign the function label *Complement Clause* to clauses that are licensed by a verb, but cannot be assigned one of the other Complement functions Direct Object, Indirect Object, Predicative Complement, or PP as Complement. To illustrate, consider the bracketed finite and non-finite clauses in (90) and (91) which contain the matrix verb PERSUADE. In these examples the underlined phrases are assigned the function of Direct Object, whereas the bracketed clauses function as Complement Clause.

90 John persuaded <u>the local children</u> [clause *that the toy ought to be adapted so that instead of a human rider the toys featured a gorilla*].

91 So in the late sixties I persuaded <u>a tolerant secondary school head in Sudbury Suffolk</u> [clause *to let me loose on a class of fifteen- and sixteen-year-olds for one lesson a week*].

A full overview of structures that involve Complement Clauses will be presented in Chapters 7 and 8.

4.1.3.6 Adjuncts

Whereas Complements are licensed by a Head, and are often obligatory (in the sense that leaving them out may result in an ungrammatical structure), Adjuncts are not licensed. Because they are optional they have a much looser bond with their associated Head than Complements do. In the sections that follow I will discuss the grammatical properties of Adjuncts, focusing on those that occur inside verb phrases and at clause level. Adjuncts that occur inside other phrase types will be discussed in Chapter 5.

4.1.3.6.1 Adjuncts supply circumstantial information

Adjuncts supply circumstantial information about the 'when', 'where', 'how', or 'why' of a situation, and can express a very wide range of meanings. These include 'aspectuality', 'concession', 'degree', 'direction', 'duration', 'evaluation', 'extent', 'frequency', 'instrument', 'intensity', 'location', 'manner', 'modality', 'purpose', 'reason', 'result', 'source', 'time', and so on. (See also section 3.8.1.)

It is important to be aware of the fact that if a phrase specifies a reason, location, time, etc. this is a necessary, but not a sufficient reason for assigning the function label Adjunct to it. For example, the PP *there* in (92) specifies a location, but we nevertheless analyse it as a Complement, rather than as an Adjunct. The reason is that the PP is licensed by the verb LIVE, and is in fact obligatory. If we leave it out the example will have an entirely different meaning.

92 The girl I'm seeing at the moment lives [PP *there*].

See section 5.4.1.5 for discussion.

4.1.3.6.2 Adjuncts are typically realized as prepositional phrases and adverb phrases

The vast majority of Adjuncts inside verb phrases are realized either as prepositional phrases or as adverb phrases; the remainder are realized as noun phrases or clauses.

93 The sailing barges [VP had tremendous economic importance [PP *in the past*]].

94 I [VP go to church [PP *on Sundays*]].

95 We [VP need our countryside more [PP *because we are an urban society*]].

96 The engine [VP beat [AdvP *frantically*]].

97 Sometimes I think she [VP [AdvP *deliberately*] sets out to anger Marcus].

98 'Blind Date' [$_{VP}$ pulls in 12.5 million viewers [$_{NP}$ *each week*]].

99 Many [$_{VP}$ died [$_{NP}$ *that way*] [$_{PP}$ *for their faith*]].

100 I [$_{VP}$ let them have ten minutes [$_{clause}$ *to get there*]].

I will return to clausal Adjuncts in Chapters 7 and 8.

4.1.3.6.3 Adjuncts can be more or less integrated in clause structure

Adjuncts can be integrated to a greater or lesser extent within their containing clauses. The Adjuncts in (93)–(100) above directly modify the verb phrases in which they occur, and are called *VP-Adjuncts*. By contrast, the Adjuncts in (101)–(103) below are much less tightly linked to their host clauses. They are called *Clause Adjuncts*. They are intonationally set apart when uttered.

101 The prospects of getting a full-time or tenured post would be very difficult. [$_{AdvP}$ *However*], it would be possible to obtain hours at different colleges making up part-time work.

102 Now that we have adopted a system of my paying all expenses and then claiming, the problem should be solved. [$_{AdvP}$ *Nevertheless*], I hope these will be paid promptly.

103 [$_{AdvP}$ *Probably*], you won't want to go down and look at that today.

Syntactically VP-Adjuncts can be in the focus position of a cleft construction (section 11.8), whereas Clause Adjuncts cannot. Compare (104) and (105), where the focus positions have been italicized.

104 It was *in the past* that the sailing barges had tremendous economic importance. (= one of the cleft variants of (93))

105 *It was *however* that it would be possible to obtain hours at different colleges making up part-time work. (= an ungrammatical cleft variant of (101))

The adverb phrases in (101) and (102) have a linking function, whereas the AdvP in (103) conveys modal meaning. See also sections 3.8 and 10.3.11.4.

I will return to VP-Adjuncts in section 5.4.2.

4.1.3.6.4 Adjuncts are mobile

Adjuncts are typically mobile, and can often occupy different positions within clauses or phrases. For example, (95) has the alternative order in (106), and the AdvP *deliberately* in (97) can also be placed at the end of the VP, as in (107).

106 *Because we are an urban society*, we need our countryside more.

107 Sometimes I think she sets out to anger Marcus *deliberately*.

4.1.3.6.5 Adjuncts are stackable

As (108) shows, Adjuncts are *stackable*, which means that more than one Adjunct can appear in any one clause or phrase.

108 [NP *Yesterday*] the sun was just as it is [PP *in India*].

In Table 4.12 the distributional properties of Adjuncts are summarized.

Typical Adjuncts...
• are not licensed by a Head;
• add circumstantial information about the 'when', 'where', 'how', or 'why' of a situation;
• are realized by prepositional phrases and adverb phrases;
• can be more or less integrated in clause structure;
• are mobile;
• are 'stackable'.

Table 4.12: The distributional properties of typical Adjuncts

4.2   Semantic roles

In this section I will discuss *semantic roles*. Before doing so we first need to introduce the term *predicate* (with a lower case 'p'). This notion is a concept from the domain of meaning, and should be distinguished from the syntactic notion *Predicate*. Recall that the latter is a function label (hence the capital letter 'P') which we assign to a string of words other than the Subject in a clause. By contrast, predicates play a role in specifying the core meaning of a clause. In a sense, the predicate specifies 'what goes on'. In the following examples the words in italics are semantic predicates which require the underlined phrases as their *arguments* in order to make up a meaningful *proposition* (a specification of a situation, e.g. a state of affairs, an activity).

109 <u>Flintoff</u> *smirked* as he walked back to his mark.

110 <u>I</u> *opened* <u>my mouth</u>.

111 <u>Dave</u> *gave* <u>her</u> <u>one of the moist tissues from the plastic dispenser</u>.

Arguments carry semantic roles. Table 4.13 gives a list of such roles with examples. In each case the predicate is in italics, and the constituent carrying the role in question is underlined.

Semantic role	Description	Example
Agent	The animate instigator of a situation denoted by a predicate.	(a) <u>The police</u> *arrested* him.
Experiencer	The animate entity that experiences a situation denoted by a predicate.	(b) <u>I</u> *felt* very sad and very down.
Goal	The location, person, or other entity in the direction of which something is displaced.	(c) I've been *sending* them to <u>72 St Quintins Ave.</u>
Recipient/ Benefactive	The person or entity that receives something or benefits from a situation denoted by a predicate.	(d) I'll *give* <u>you</u> further directions. / (e) I'll *sew* your bag for <u>you</u>.
Instrument	The device or implement by means of which a situation denoted by a predicate is brought about.	(f) <u>The seaming</u> *holds* everything together well.
Patient	The animate or inanimate 'undergoer' of a situation denoted by a predicate.	(g) We *replaced* <u>everything</u>.
Theme	The entity that is displaced or affected by a situation denoted by a predicate.	(h) Walker tries to *kick* <u>the ball</u> into the stumps.
Proposition	The specification of a situation.	(i) I *think* <u>that's very important.</u>

(Continued)

Semantic role	Description	Example
Locative	The obligatory specification of the place where a situation denoted by a predicate takes place.	(j) Di *works* <u>in the library</u>.
Source	The location, person, or entity from which something is displaced.	(k) Heating *comes* from <u>the sun</u>.

Table 4.13: Semantic roles

Arguments can be linked to Subjects and Complements, but not to Adjuncts, because the latter supply optional information in clauses. Semantic roles are only assigned to arguments as *participants*. This means that any string of words that functions as an Adjunct in a clause or as a Predicative Complement is not assigned a semantic role. For example, if we expand (110) as in (112) we see that the AdvP *slowly* merely adds optional information, but is not one of the participants in the act of opening, which involves an Agent (*I*), and a Theme (*my mouth*).

112 <u>I</u> *opened* <u>my mouth</u> slowly.

4.3 Analysing clauses at the levels of form, function, and meaning

We have seen that clauses can be analysed at three distinct but related levels: grammatical form, grammatical function, and semantic role. Consider (113).

113 [NP <u>Our correspondent</u> (Agent)] *compiled* [NP <u>this report</u> (Theme)] [PP under <u>restrictions</u>].

In this clause the italicized predicate licenses the two underlined arguments which correspond to the grammatical Subject and Direct Object. Both arguments are realized as NPs, and are assigned the semantic roles of Agent and Theme, respectively. The PP *under restrictions* is an Adjunct. It is not licensed by the verb, and not an argument, and hence not assigned a semantic role.

4.4 Representing the structure of phrases and clauses

In this section I will discuss a way in which we can represent the structure of clauses graphically in so-called *tree diagrams*, and how we can recognize units of structure called *constituents*.

Tree diagrams (or *trees* for short) are graphical representations of syntactic structures that bear a resemblance to real trees, except that they are upside down. A simple Direct Object noun phrase like *the piano* in (114) can be represented as in (115).

114 She plays *the piano*.

115

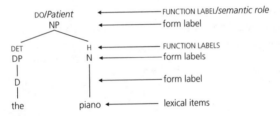

DO = Direct Object; NP = noun phrase; DET = Determiner;
DP = determinative phrase; D = determinative; H = Head; N = noun

This representation shows that the NP *the piano* consists of a determinative phrase (headed by a determinative) and a noun. The former functions as Determiner, whereas the latter functions as Head. In trees we will use SMALL CAPITALS to represent function labels and italic type to indicate semantic roles. The structure of *She plays the piano* can be represented by the tree in (116), which incorporates the tree in (115).

116

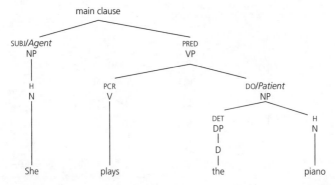

SUBJ = Subject; NP = noun phrase; H = Head; N = noun; PRED = Predicate; VP = verb phrase; PCR = Predicator; V = verb; DO = Direct Object; DET = Determiner; DP = determinative phrase; D = determinative

In this tree the highest level represents the main clause (section 3.9). The Subject NP is headed by a noun, to be precise by a personal pronoun, and the Predicate is realized by a verb phrase. The verb PLAY functions as Predicator which takes the noun phrase *the piano* as its Direct Object. Within that NP the word *the* is a determinative phrase headed by a determinative functioning as Determiner, while the noun *piano* functions as the Head of the NP. Each unit in the tree is called a *node*. We will say that nodes can *dominate* other nodes. For example, VP dominates V, NP, DP, D, and N.

If we add the Adjunct *beautifully* to (114) we obtain (117), and its associated tree structure representation in (118). Notice that the Adjunct carries no semantic role, because it is not licensed by the verb, hence there is no semantic role label on the Adjunct node.

117 She plays the piano beautifully.

118

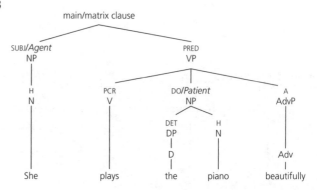

Within the trees in (116) and (118) we can clearly see that words group themselves together into constituents, which we informally defined at the beginning of this chapter as strings that syntactically behave as units. We can define constituents abstractly as follows: Y is a constituent of X if and only if Y is dominated by X. As an example, in (116) the nodes V and NP are constituents of VP (indicated by the fact that they are both dominated by the VP-node). The reason for this grouping is the close bond between the verb and its Complement, discussed in section 4.1.3.1.1. As we have seen, Adjuncts are not licensed by their associated Heads, and hence have a much less close bond with them. Nevertheless, an Adjunct like *beautifully* is still positioned inside the VP, as the tree in (118) shows, and this is because *beautifully* modifies the meaning of the verb: it specifies how the playing of the piano was carried out. However, notice that the Adjunct cannot break the much closer bond between the verb and the DO: it cannot be positioned between them, cf. *She plays beautifully the piano.*

Part III: Phrase and clause patterns

Chapter 5

Complex phrases and coordination

In this chapter we will take a closer look at the structure of English phrases. More specifically, we will examine the structure of the *complex phrase*, where that term is understood to denote a phrase that contains an array of elements in addition to its Head. I will begin with a discussion of phrase-level functions in section 5.1. We will see that the skeletal structure of the various phrase types is very similar. In sections 5.2–5.6 I will turn to a detailed treatment of the structure of each of the phrase types NP, AdjP, VP, PP, and AdvP. In section 5.7 I discuss coordination.

5.1   Phrase level functions

We distinguish the following functions within phrases: Head, Complement, and Adjunct. In noun phrases we additionally recognize the functions Determiner and Predeterminer. Adjuncts can be divided into several different kinds, as we will see in section 5.1.3 below. Table 5.1 provides a summary list.

Grammatical functions at phrase level
• Head (H)
• Complement (Comp)
• Adjunct (A)
▪ Pre-Head Adjunct
▪ Post-Head Adjunct
▪ External Adjunct (only in NPs)
• Determiner (Det) and Predeterminer (Predet) (only in NPs)

Table 5.1: Grammatical functions at phrase level

5.1.1   Head (H)

In Chapter 3 we defined the Head of a phrase as its most prominent element. Heads are obligatory, and for any one phrase they can be described as the element which the phrase as a whole is a 'kind of', and on which the other elements of the phrase are dependent. Thus the string *a quite ferocious cat* is a noun phrase headed by *cat* because the string as a whole denotes a kind of cat. The determinative phrase *a* and the adjective phrase *quite ferocious* are dependents of the Head. All phrases must be *endocentric*, which means that they must be *properly headed*. That is to say that noun phrases must be headed by a noun, adjective phrases must be headed by an adjective, verb phrases must be headed by a verb, and so on.

5.1.2   Complements in phrases

Within phrases Heads can license Complements of various types. As an example, consider the adjective *fond* in (1) below.

1 He wasn't particularly [~AdjP~ [~Adj~ fond] [~PP~ of Bax]].

The Head of this AdjP is the adjective *fond* which licenses the PP *of Bax* as its Complement. We cannot leave the PP out:

2 *He wasn't particularly fond.

The various phrasal Heads each license a different array of Complements, as we will see in the sections that follow.

5.1.3   Adjuncts in phrases

Adjuncts inside phrases specify circumstantial information at the level of the phrase. Here's an example of a noun phrase with an Adjunct.

3 [~NP~ a [~AdjP~ fairly wet] summer]

In this NP the Head is *summer*, which takes the adjective phrase *fairly wet* as an Adjunct. Another way of putting this is to say that the AdjP *modifies* the noun Head. (Indeed, the functional label used for phrasal Adjuncts in many grammars is *Modifier*.) Within the AdjP the

Head *wet* itself takes an Adjunct, namely *fairly*. Each of the phrase types we will be looking at has a different range of Adjuncts. We will distinguish between *pre-Head Adjuncts* and *post-Head Adjuncts*. For noun phrases we additionally recognize *External Adjuncts*.

5.1.4 Determiner (Det) and Predeterminer (Predet): only in noun phrases

The functional notions of *Determiner* and *Predeterminer* are used only for noun phrases. Determiners serve to 'specify' NPs. This means that the phrases that realize the Determiner function add fairly general and often abstract specificational meanings to NPs, for example 'definiteness', 'proximity', 'number', 'gender', 'possession', or a combination of these. For example, in a simple NP like (4), *the* is a determinative which functions as the Head of a determinative phrase which in turn functions as a Determiner within the larger NP.

4 [$_{NP}$ [$_{DP}$ *the*] shoe]]

The DP marks the NP as 'definite', a notion which we previously defined as 'uniquely identifiable' to the addressee in the most common cases.

The Predeterminer function can be realized by phrases with a quantifying meaning that are placed before NPs. They modify the NP as a whole. Here is an example of a DP functioning as Predeterminer.

5 No magic trick deals with [$_{NP}$ [$_{DP}$ *all*] [$_{NP}$ the problems]].

In any one NP only one constituent can be assigned the function of Determiner or Predeterminer.

5.1.5 The structure of phrases

We can represent the skeletal structure of NPs as in (6), and the structures of AdjPs, VPs, PPs, and AdvPs as in (7). As explained in section 4.4, in each case the function labels and form labels are given on separate lines. The symbol '¤' is used where the form label can be of different kinds (that is, where the function can be realized by different kinds of forms). Elements in brackets are optional. For example, phrases can consist of only a Head, as in *Dogs are lazy*, where *dogs* is an NP consisting solely of the Head noun, and *lazy* is an AdjP consisting of the Head *lazy*.

6

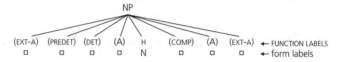

NP = noun phrase; (EXT-A) = External Adjunct; (PRE)DET = (Pre)Determiner; A = Adjunct; H = Head; N = noun; COMP = Complement; ◻ = variable form class

7

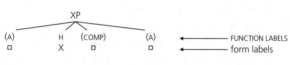

XP = AdjP, VP, PP, or AdvP; A = Adjunct; H = Head; X = Adj, V, P, or Adv

As these tree diagrams show, Adjuncts can occur before or after the Head, and they are stackable, as we saw in section 4.1.3.6.5. Complements virtually always occur after the Head. Within verb phrases more than one Complement may occur, as we will see in section 5.4.

Complements generally have a tighter relationship than Adjuncts with their associated Heads in phrases. Because of this they tend to be placed immediately to the right of the Head. If a phrase contains one or more post-Head Adjuncts, they occur to the right of any Complement(s) that may be present. As an example, consider the bracketed noun phrase below.

8 By 1978 Granger had contributed articles to *Time*, *The New Republic* and other magazines; and became a daily columnist, television critic and [**teacher** *of journalism* <u>at Columbia College</u> <u>in Chicago</u>].

In this NP the Head noun *teacher* takes a Complement in the shape of a PP (*of journalism*), as well as two PP Adjuncts (*at Columbia College* and *in Chicago*). As we will see in section 5.2.3.1, the phrase *of journalism* is regarded as a Complement because it can be related to a V + Complement (DO) sequence, in this case *teaches journalism*. Notice that because of the tight relationship between the Head noun and its Complement, the Adjuncts cannot be placed immediately after the Head, as the following examples show.

9 *He became [teacher at Columbia College of journalism in Chicago].
(N+Adjunct+Complement+Adjunct)

10 *He became [teacher in Chicago of journalism at Columbia College].
(N+Adjunct+Complement+Adjunct)

11 *He became [teacher at Columbia College in Chicago of journalism].
(N+Adjunct+Adjunct+Complement)

Exceptions to this general tendency occur when the Complement is 'heavy' (i.e. consists of many words), and is consequently extraposed (section 3.2.2.1.2) across the 'light' Adjunct, as in (12).

12 He became [**teacher** ___ <u>at Harvard</u> *of journalism, creative writing, linguistics, and political science*].

5.2 Complex noun phrases

5.2.1 Determiners in noun phrases

Within noun phrases the function of Determiner can be realized by determinative phrases, noun phrases, and prepositional phrases (Table 5.2). As noted in section 5.1.4, only one constituent in any one NP can function as Determiner.

Determiners in noun phrases
• determinative phrases;
• noun phrases;
• prepositional phrases.

Table 5.2: Determiners in noun phrases

5.2.1.1 Determinative phrases functioning as Determiner in noun phrases

An overview of determinatives was given in section 3.3. In each of the examples in Table 3.11 the determinative heads a DP which functions as a Determiner inside a noun phrase. This is also the case for the examples below, except that in these cases the determinative is itself modified.

13 By [NP [DP *almost all*] standard measures] Haiti, the poorest country of the region, stands at the opposite pole.

14 The prediction was that broking firms would expand their operations and that [NP [DP *very many*] new companies] would be created.

5.2.1.2 Noun phrases functioning as Determiner in noun phrases

Noun phrases can function as Determiner in English in the shape of genitive personal pronouns, as in (15), genitive interrogative pronouns, as in (16), genitive relative pronouns, as in (17), 'full' genitive noun phrases, as in (18), or 'ordinary' noun phrases, as in (19).

15 [NP [NP *My*] question] was about [NP [NP *your*] interview].

16 [NP [NP *Whose*] home] did you take her to _?

17 He found favour as a court physician among the various princedoms of Europe, but he also earned his bread as an itinerant doctor [NP [NP *whose*] reputation] always preceded him.

18 China's 100 million under-fives will have the chance to cuddle Postman Pat and his black and white cat and collect [NP [NP [NP *the man from Greendale*]'*s*] best exploits on DVD] after deals struck by his owner, Entertainment Rights.

19 With [NP [NP *this size*] zoom], image stabilisation is essential, and the SP-570UZ has two systems to reduce shake.

As we saw in section 3.2.2, we regard *my* in (15) and *whose* in (16) and (17) as pronouns, rather than as determinatives, by virtue of the fact that they carry genitive case. In (15) and (17) the larger bracketed NPs *my question* and *whose reputation* function as Subject. The NPs *your interview* in (15), *whose home* in (16), and *this size zoom* in (19) function as the Complements of the prepositions *about*, *to*, and *with*, respectively. Note that in (16) the NP *whose home* is associated with the gap indicated by '_'. In (18) -'*s* is attached to the NP *the man from Greendale* as a whole.

5.2.1.3 Prepositional phrases functioning as Determiner in noun phrases

In the following examples prepositional phrases function as Determiner within noun phrases.

20 [NP [PP *Over twenty*] Iranians] killed by avalanche. (headline)

21 Geneva-based United Nations humanitarian agencies and the International Red Cross said [NP [PP *up to a million*] people] were on the move, fleeing towns and cities for rural areas or trying to cross borders to Iran, Pakistan and Tajikistan.

The PPs cannot co-occur with other Determiners, cf. *over twenty the Iranians, *up to a million those people.*

5.2.2   Predeterminers in noun phrases

Determiners can be preceded by quantifying expressions, which can be realized by different types of phrases. These modify the noun phrase that follows as a whole, and function as *Predeterminer*. The Predeterminer function can be realized by determinative phrases, noun phrases, adverb phrases, and certain adjectival elements (Table 5.3).

Predeterminers in noun phrases
• determinative phrases;
• noun phrases;
• adverb phrases;
• adjectival elements.

Table 5.3: Predeterminers in noun phrases

5.2.2.1   Determinative phrases functioning as Predeterminer in noun phrases

Determinative phrases headed by *all* and *both* can function as Predeterminer, as in the examples below.

22 I buy books [NP [DP *all*] [NP the time]] for work.

23 [NP [DP *Both*] [NP the possible contractors I met this week]] spoke about putting in trunking ready for the ethernet cabling.

The determinative can itself be modified, as in (24).

24 The police admit that [NP [DP *almost all*] [NP the items seized]] had a legitimate purpose.

This example resembles (13), but differs from it by virtue of the presence of *the*, which functions as Determiner inside the NP.

5.2.2.2 Noun phrases functioning as Predeterminer in noun phrases

Examples of noun phrases functioning as Predeterminer are so-called *fractions*, such as *half, a quarter, one-sixth,* and a number of so-called *multipliers*, such as *two times, three times, double, triple.*

25 It's probably only [NP [NP *half*] [NP the population]] at best that are covered.

26 And yet Malawi has a lake [NP [NP *one-fifth*] [NP the size of the country]].

27 In all but the most exceptional circumstances, it will become "normal practice" again for loans to be limited to a maximum of [NP [NP *three times*] [NP the borrower's salary]].

28 The interface is extended, providing up to [NP [NP *double*] [NP the speed]].

Notice that in each case the Determiner slot within the inner NP is filled by *the*.

5.2.2.3 Adverb phrases functioning as Predeterminer in noun phrases

In the examples that follow, multiplier adverbs such as *once*, *twice*, and *thrice* function as Predeterminer.

29 That's [NP [AdvP *twice*] [NP the present population of Africa]].

30 They have found that emissions of carbon dioxide have been rising at [NP [AdvP *thrice*] [NP the rate]] in the 1990s.

5.2.2.4 Adjectival elements functioning as Predeterminer in noun phrases

A number of adjective-like elements can function as Predeterminer inside noun phrases. This set includes words like *such* and *exclamative <u>what</u>* (sections 1.6 and 6.4), as well as phrasal constituents.

31 You're [NP [AdjP *such*] [NP a snob]], honestly.

32 The second thing I want to say is [NP [AdjP *what*] [NP a remarkable week]] it's been.

33 It is interesting to remember, in this connection, [NP [AdjP *how impor-tant*] [NP *a part*]] wills and legacies play in Charles Dickens's fiction.

5.2.3 Complements in noun phrases

Nouns can take several types of Complements (listed in Table 5.4): prepositional phrases, clauses, and pre-Head reduced noun phrases (i.e. NPs without a Determiner).

Complements in noun phrases
• prepositional phrases;
• clauses;
• pre-Head reduced noun phrases (without a Determiner).

Table 5.4: Complements in noun phrases

5.2.3.1 Prepositional phrases functioning as Complement in noun phrases

Complements of nouns derived or converted from verbs (section 2.3.1) can occur in the shape of a PP, as in the examples below.

34 [NP Our review [PP *of the market*]] in Chapter 1 shows that spaceliners would be used initially for ferrying staff and cargo to and from government-funded space stations; and then for space tourism.

35 [NP The desire [PP *for money*]] has a corrupting influence.

36 [NP Achievement [PP *of the extra volume*]] was the subject of consider-able planning.

37 I refer to my telephone call the other day to check on [NP your receipt [PP *of my application for membership*]].

The head of the PP is usually the preposition *of*. In each of these cases the N + Complement sequence can be related to a V + Complement (DO) sequence.

38 We *reviewed the market*.

39 (They) *desire money*.

40 (They) *achieve extra volume*.

41 You *received my application for membership*.

In other cases a PP Complement is licensed by the noun without there being a link to a V + Complement sequence, as in the following set of examples.

42 The military is not ruling out [NP the possibility [PP *of contamination*]] as a result of the bombing.

43 It is [NP a form [PP *of dance*]].

44 And he's been looking at the possibilities of having [NP some meaning-ful dialogue [PP *between the parties*]].

The PPs are Complements here, rather than Adjuncts, because the noun licenses the preposition that heads the PP.

5.2.3.2   Clauses functioning as Complement in noun phrases

In the following examples clauses function as Complements of nouns inside noun phrases.

45 A spokeswoman for the London Ambulance Service refuted [NP the claim [clause *that lives were being put at risk*]].

46 I detect in the United States' latest position [NP a realisation [clause *that it is important to keep the United Nations Security Council consensus*]].

47 He strongly criticised [NP the Prime Minister's failure [clause Ø *to allow British entry into the Exchange Rate Mechanism*]].

48 But there's [NP no actual requirement [clause *for them to do it*]] under the terms of the office.

The symbol 'Ø' in (47) indicates that the Subject of the clause is implicit, that is, not overtly expressed; it is in this case understood to be the Prime Minister. I will return to this convention in Chapters 7 and 8. Again we can link the N + Complement sequence to a V + (NP) + Complement sequence, as (49)–(52) show.

49 Somebody *claimed* [*that lives were being put at risk*].

50 (They) *realised* [*that it is important to keep the United Nations Secu-rity Council consensus*].

51 The Prime Minister *failed* [Ø *to allow British entry into the Exchange Rate Mechanism*].

52 (Nobody) *requires them* [Ø *to do it under the terms of the office*].

There is a limited set of nouns whose Complements cannot be linked to verbal Complements. These also take finite or non-finite clausal Complements, for example *chance, fact, idea, occasion, proposition, question*. Examples follow.

53 [NP The fact [clause *that the accused was ignorant of the rules of English law*]] will not afford any defence.

54 You really must get used to [NP the idea [clause *that people will come up to you*]].

55 We need to knock on the head [NP the proposition [clause *that a short war will boost the international economy*]].

56 A declaration issued at the EU's Laeken summit in 2001 called for a Convention on the future of Europe to look into the simplification and reorganisation of the EU treaties, and raised [NP the question [*clause* *whether the end result should be a constitution*]].

57 This means that there is never [NP a chance [*clause* Ø *to have a complete weekend off*]].

58 He made the Queen's Speech debate on Wednesday [NP the occasion [clause Ø *to reassert mastery of a divided party*]].

59 That gives me [NP an opening [clause Ø *to pry further down the line*]].

The *that*-clauses and *to*-infinitive clauses specify the content of the claim, realization, failure, fact, idea, and so on.

Clauses that function as Complements of nouns are often called *appositive clauses*.

5.2.3.3 Noun phrases without a Determiner functioning as pre-Head Complement in noun phrases

To some extent nouns can also be complemented by noun phrases without a Determiner, as in (60)–(63), though note that, exceptionally, the Complements here *precede* the Head.

60 [$_{NP}$ an [$_{NP}$ *art*] student]

61 [$_{NP}$ the [$_{NP}$ *company*] representative]

62 [$_{NP}$ a [$_{NP}$ *banana bread*] eater]

63 [$_{NP}$ a [$_{NP}$ *ten percent*] saving]

Compare (60)–(63) with (64)–(67), where the NPs function as Direct Object, or as Complement of the preposition *of*.

64 s/he studies *art* — a student *of art*

65 s/he represents *the company* — a representative *of the company*

66 s/he eats *banana bread* — an eater of *banana bread*

67 s/he saved *ten percent* — a saving of *ten percent*

Structures like (60)–(63) are not always easy to distinguish from compounds (see section 2.3.2).

5.2.4 Adjuncts in noun phrases

Within noun phrases we distinguish between pre-Head Adjuncts, which occur before the Head, post-Head Adjuncts, which occur after the Head, and External Adjuncts, which modify NPs as a whole. Recall that Adjuncts are optional, and supply circumstantial information. An overview of Adjuncts in noun phrases is given in Table 5.5.

Adjuncts in noun phrases
• Pre-Head Adjuncts
▪ adjective phrases;
▪ determinative phrases;
▪ noun phrases (without a Determiner);
▪ prepositional phrases;
▪ verb phrases;
▪ adverb phrases;
▪ clauses and clause-like structures.

(Continued)

Adjuncts in noun phrases (*continued*)
• Post-Head Adjuncts
▪ noun phrases;
▪ adjective phrases;
▪ prepositional phrases;
▪ adverb phrases;
▪ determinative phrases;
▪ clauses.
• External Adjuncts
▪ adverb phrases;
▪ prepositional phrases;
▪ noun phrases.

Table 5.5: Adjuncts in noun phrases

5.2.4.1 Adjective phrases functioning as pre-Head Adjunct in noun phrases

Nominal Heads can be preceded by adjective phrases, as in (68).

68 [$_{NP}$ an [$_{AdjP}$ *interesting*] period]

Note that *interesting* is an adjective *phrase* in attributive position modifying the noun *period*, not just an adjective. We can show that *interesting* on its own occupies an AdjP-position by expanding (68) into (69).

69 [$_{NP}$ a [$_{AdjP}$ *very interesting*] period]

Because they are Adjuncts, adjective phrases can be stacked (see section 4.1.3.6.5):

70 [$_{NP}$ a [$_{AdjP}$ *lengthy*] [$_{AdjP}$ *enjoyable*] [$_{AdjP}$ *interesting*] period]

There are some restrictions on the order of adjective phrases within noun phrases. Consider (71), which sounds quite odd.

71 a *brown leather old practical* suitcase

The reason for this is that stacked adjectives tend to occur in a particular order, depending on the semantic domain they belong to. This order is shown in (72).

72 evaluation – property – age – colour – provenance – manufacture – type

Thus, evaluative adjectives tend to precede property adjectives, which in turn precede age adjectives, and so on. Here are a few examples:

this *excellent fresh* food

his *ugly thick red* socks

the *big old brown cotton* hat

a *practical old French leather* suitcase

The restrictions are semantic ordering *tendencies*, rather than hard-and-fast syntactic rules, given that slight changes in order do not always result in an unacceptable result (cf. *his thick ugly red socks*). This means that departures from the order in (72) are not so much ungrammatical as just odd-sounding.

5.2.4.2 Determinative phrases functioning as pre-Head Adjunct in noun phrases

In (73) and (74) below the determinatives *many* and *two* function as the Heads of determinative phrases which in turn function as pre-Head Adjuncts inside the bracketed NPs.

73 And if we're accepted in [NP [DP our] [DP *very many*] facets]], what's our problem?

74 [NP [DP These] [DP *two*] images] say it all.

The DPs *our* and *these* function as Determiner. Compare (73) with (14). Since the former already contains a Determiner (*our*) we analyse the DP *very many* as an Adjunct.

5.2.4.3 Noun phrases without a Determiner functioning as pre-Head Adjunct in noun phrases

Here are some examples of noun phrases without a Determiner functioning as pre-Head Adjunct. In (76) the NP takes genitive case.

75 Genesis also favoured the melotron's unique sound and they featured it heavily on many of [NP their classic [NP *early seventies*] albums].

76 She also revealed that [NP a [NP *men's*] magazine] had approached her for a photo session.

77 *Fly Me to the Moon* occasionally feels like it hasn't got as much energy or excitement as it could have, and [NP the real [NP *edge-of-your-seat*] action and drama] comes quite late in the film – but it's worth the wait.

Names can also function as pre-Head Adjunct, as in the example below from a famous novel.

78 If you really want to hear about it, the first thing you'll probably want to know is where I was born, and what my lousy childhood was like, and how my parents were occupied and all before they had me, and [NP all that [NP *David Copperfield*] kind of crap], but I don't feel like going into it, if you want to know the truth.

The Adjunct nature of the italicized pre-Head NPs becomes clear when we paraphrase the containing NPs. Thus *their classic early seventies albums* can be reworded as *their classic albums from the early seventies*. In (76) *a men's magazine* can be paraphrased as *a magazine for men*. Notice that the determinative *a* goes with *magazine*, not with *men's*, since the latter is plural.

Examples involving pre-Head noun phrases are not always easily distinguishable from compounds. We saw in section 2.3.2 that as a rule the stress in compounds is on the first component, while in phrases the second component tends to be stressed. In this connection consider the examples below.

79 Was it not the case that they responded to an advertisement that you placed in [NP *the trade press*]?

80 The hearing was told Ms Stewart threatened to start [NP *a grievance procedure*] if her lover was not allowed onto the same shift.

Here we could say that within the italicized NPs *trade* and *grievance* are NPs which function as pre-Head Adjunct. However, we can also regard *trade press* and *grievance procedure* as compounds, given that the stress is on *trade* and *grievance*, respectively.

5.2.4.4   Prepositional phrases functioning as pre-Head Adjunct in noun phrases

Prepositional phrases can premodify NP Heads, though this is quite rare. Some examples are shown in (81)–(83).

81 Forces chiefs back [NP [PP *under-fire*] minister].

82 [NP The [PP *under-threat*] Gatwick Express rail service] has been saved, the government announced today.

83 With the news that the EU has identified a risk of hearing loss to anyone listening to [NP [PP *in-ear*] music] over a volume of 89db, we must consider the way we consume music.

In all these examples the writers used a hyphen between the two components of the PP. This could indicate that these PPs are felt to be a bit like adjectives modifying nouns, cf. *the beleaguered minister, the endangered rail service*.

5.2.4.5 Verb phrases functioning as pre-Head Adjunct in noun phrases

In the following examples a verb phrase functions as pre-Head Adjunct.

84 In the Old Town, you can see mullet-haired skateboarders, scuttling nuns, transvestites and [NP the [VP *slowly growing*] numbers of foreigners] all putting this consensual approach into practice.

85 He was successful before, of course; he was well-known around media London as the master of [NP the [VP *quickly delivered*] opinion piece], first person or otherwise, to a tight deadline.

How do we know that the italicized strings are VPs, and not adjective phrases? First, notice that the words *growing* and *delivered* cannot be modified by typical adjectival Adjuncts like *very* (cf. **very growing*, **very delivered*). Secondly, in (84) and (85) *growing* and *delivered* are modified by *slowly* and *quickly*. These manner adverbs can only modify verbs.

Compare (84) and (85) with (86) and (87).

86 That's [NP a [AdjP *very interesting*] point] that Philip's made.

87 I'm used to working with [NP [AdjP *very able-bodied*] people].

In these cases the Head nouns are modified by *very interesting* and *very able-bodied*. The Heads of these phrases must be adjectives, because they are modified by *very*. (However, notice that *interesting* is converted from a verb; see section 2.3.3.)

5.2.4.6 Adverb phrases functioning as pre-Head Adjunct in noun phrases

It is rare for adverb phrases to modify nominal Heads, but examples like the following are possible:

88 A chanceless innings of patience and class from 20-year-old Gordon Muchall secured a tense finish and [NP [AdvP *almost*] victory] for Durham after a turgid low-scoring affair.

As with pre-Head PPs, we often find a hyphen between the adverb and the noun (*almost-victory*), which may indicate that the adverb–noun sequence is regarded as a compound noun of some sort.

5.2.4.7 Clauses and clause-like structures functioning as pre-Head Adjunct in noun phrases

In the following examples clauses and clause-like structures function as pre-Head Adjunct.

89 The international mobile telecoms provider is offering unlimited free international texts until 2 January to customers on [NP their [clause *pay-as-you-go*] sim card].

90 Gallons of ink have been spilled and [NP ['clause' *god knows how many*] pixels] have been burned to report the yearlong saga of the Foreign Intelligence Surveillance Act (Fisa), but it can be pretty well summarised in one paragraph.

Here again the words that make up the modifying clause are often, though not always, hyphenated, indicating that the words taken together are regarded as a unit, much like an adjective.

5.2.4.8 Noun phrases functioning as post-Head Adjunct in noun phrases

In the examples below the Head is postmodified by an NP.

91 Is my right honourable friend aware that on this side of the House we fully support the contents, as well as the style and tone of [NP his statement [NP *this afternoon*]]?

92 Easter found me supine and semi-naked on coral sand, doing a pretty good imitation of a crabstick, toying with a dewy Fanta, staring out at the sycophantic Caribbean and wondering, as ever, if I dared to wear [NP a shirt [NP *that colour*]].

93 This obviously helped [NP banks [NP *this side of the Atlantic*]].

In (91) and (93) *this afternoon* and *this side of the Atlantic* can also be construed as Adjuncts functioning at the VP level, rather than inside the noun phrase, in which case we can paraphrase the second part of (91) as 'that on this side of the House this afternoon we fully support the contents as well as the style and tone of his statement', and (93) can be reordered as *This side of the Atlantic, this obviously helped banks*. Intonation is often a clue as to the intended structure. There is no intonational break if the Adjunct is considered to be part of the NP, and passivization is possible: [NP *Banks this side of the Atlantic*] *were obviously helped by this.*

In the following example the italicized noun phrase is an *appositive* Adjunct of the noun *film*. The title refers to the same entity as the noun.

94 To read the wartime Williams is to be transported back to the suburban home front but a home front observed from the child's eye view just as John Boorman observed it in [NP his autobiographical film [NP *Hope and Glory*]].

5.2.4.9 Adjective phrases functioning as post-Head Adjunct in noun phrases

An adjective phrase can postmodify a Head noun, as in the examples below.

95 Some people have [NP ears [AdjP *full of wax*]].

96 I understood that it had not been possible to arrange [NP the separate debate [AdjP *recommended*]].

97 And their first ruler was very interested in [NP all things [AdjP *western*]].

98 Ordnance Survey takes its name from the Board of Ordnance which in the eighteenth century was an important element of the military being concerned with fortifications, artillery, engineering, and [NP all matters [AdjP *technical*]].

99 National troops retook the city in May, at the cost of [NP many thousands [AdjP-coordination *dead and imprisoned*]].

More often than not, the AdjPs can be regarded as reduced relative clauses (see sections 3.2.2.3 and 7.3.3). Thus, (95) is arguably a reduced version of (100), and (96) a reduced version of (101).

100 Some people have ears *which are full of wax.*

101 I understood that it had not been possible to arrange the separate debate *which was recommended.*

The italicized string of words in (99) is an adjective phrase coordination (see section 5.7.1 for discussion).

The following are set phrases.

102 [NP poet [AdjP *laureate*]]

103 [NP governor/secretary/attorney/surgeon [AdjP *general*]]

104 [NP astronomer [AdjP *royal*]]

5.2.4.10 Prepositional phrases functioning as post-Head Adjunct in noun phrases

PPs postmodifying nominal Heads are extremely common. They can add a very wide range of different types of circumstantial information, including 'location', 'time', 'source', as well as more abstract meanings. Some examples follow.

105 I think some people come initially to help [NP people [PP *in wheelchairs*]] dance.

106 We think we've got [NP the main point [PP *about that*]].

107 Anyway [NP other countries [PP *in Europe*]] such as Austria and Switzerland make far more money out of tourism than we do and they are republics.

108 I am awaiting [NP a leisure card [PP *from the library*]] but, meantime, enclose a copy of the relevant page of my passport as proof of my age.

109 I haven't had [NP a moment [PP *to myself*]].

5.2.4.11 Adverb phrases functioning as post-Head Adjunct in noun phrases

In the following examples adverb phrases function as post-Head Adjunct.

110 He'll find very large numbers of them have [NP very low incomes [AdvP *indeed*]].

111 We've not been playing badly, though, and [NP the results [AdvP *lately*]] have certainly been worse than the performances.

112 But of tax rises there was nothing, an echoing silence around the Commons chamber – yet it is an issue that [NP some day [AdvP *soon*]] he will have to address.

In these cases it is not always entirely clear exactly what the AdvPs modify. Thus, in (111) one could argue that *lately* functions as a VP-level Adjunct, though it would then be more likely to occur after *have* or after *certainly*. In (112) we could also say that *soon* is the Head, modified by the NP *some day* (see section 5.6.2.3 below).

5.2.4.12 Determinative phrases functioning as post-Head Adjunct in noun phrases

Some determinatives, for example *each*, *enough*, *less*, and *more*, can head determinative phrases which function as post-Head Adjunct, as in the following examples.

113 Nor will there be precise plans on the size of a future executive where the bigger states currently have [NP two seats [DP *each*]], with one apiece for the 10 smaller partners.

114 They have [NP reasons [DP *enough*]], without being handed more.

5.2.4.13 Clauses functioning as post-Head Adjunct in noun phrases

Relative clauses can function as post-Head Adjunct. As we saw in section 3.2.2.3, these are clauses that supply additional information about the referent of the Head of the noun phrase in which they occur, and are typically introduced by relative pronouns. Here are some further examples.

115 He's [NP the guy [clause *who is supposed to have left*]].

116 But it is [NP a form of dance [clause *which already exists*]].

Finite and non-finite relative clauses will be discussed in more detail in section 7.3.3.

5.2.4.14 External Adjuncts in noun phrases

A number of phrase types, specifically AdvPs, PPs, and NPs, can modify an entire NP, and function as External Adjunct. They can be attached either at the beginning or end of an NP. Examples are shown below.

117 The novels of Christina Stead span [NP [AdvP *almost*] [NP the entire century]].

118 At today's prices, [NP [NP those tracts] [AdvP *alone*]] are worth £130 million.

119 [NP [AdvP *Only*] [NP a handful of international relief agencies]] are currently working in the country.

120 I beg to differ from this survey and state that Heathrow is [NP [AdvP *perhaps* [NP the best airport in the world]], its facilities are second to none.

121 Today is [NP [AdvP *officially*] [NP the most depressing day of the year]] – but thankfully help is at hand.

122 By this time Castile was looking [NP [PP *by far*] [NP the most valuable ally]] again.

123 There he sits looking [NP [NP *every bit*] [NP a chief executive]] – grey suit, white shirt, red tie.

124 [NP [NP The Gauls] [NP *themselves*]] were part of the much larger family of Celtic-speaking peoples who in the last centuries BC occupied all the brown bits you see on this map.

External Adjuncts can be distinguished from Predeterminers (section 5.2.2) both syntactically and semantically. Positionally, when they occur before the Head of an NP they precede any Predeterminers (and Determiners) which are present, as the example below makes clear. The element functioning as Predeterminer is underlined.

125 It has been quite gratifying to read that [NP *even* [NP all [NP the ambitious, overworked managers that I see at the office (and fail to comprehend)]]] feel deep down that they're missing out on life.

Semantically External Adjuncts can express a wider range of meanings than Predeterminers, such as 'focus' (e.g. *alone, even, only*), 'degree' (*almost, entirely, much, nearly*), 'viewpoint' (*academically, financially, officially*), 'evaluation' (*fortunately, happily, regrettably*), 'modality' (*possibly, perhaps*), and so on. Predeterminers typically express quantifying meanings, as we have seen. External Adjuncts can often also appear as Adjuncts in clauses or other phrase types. Compare (13), (24), and (88), where the adverb *almost* functions as an Adjunct inside a phrase, with (117), where it functions as an External Adjunct modifying an entire NP. Compare also *perhaps* in (120) with the same adverb in (126), where it functions as a Clause Adjunct (section 4.1.3.6.3).

126 And we can *perhaps* leave aside whether they mean anything or not.

5.3 Complex adjective phrases

5.3.1 Complements in adjective phrases

Adjective Heads can be complemented by prepositional phrases, clauses, and noun phrases (Table 5.6).

Complements in adjective phrases
• prepositional phrases;
• clauses;
• noun phrases.

Table 5.6: Complements in adjective phrases

5.3.1.1 Prepositional phrases functioning as Complement in adjective phrases

In PP Complements of adjective phrases the preposition is always fixed. For example, *fond* always takes a PP Complement introduced by *of*.

127 I was getting [$_{AdjP}$ quite fond [$_{PP}$ *of him*]].

128 He is [$_{AdjP}$ mindful [$_{PP}$ *of the terror that must have been visited upon the victim that day*]].

129 The system is totally [$_{AdjP}$ dependent [$_{PP}$ *on employee goodwill*]] if it is to produce good information.

130 We're not [$_{AdjP}$ involved [$_{PP}$ *in that side of politics*]].

In a few cases leaving out the Complement leads to ungrammaticality, as in examples (127) and (128), though in others it may lead merely to a change in meaning, or a sense of information that is lacking. For example, with regard to (129), using *dependent* without a PP beginning with *(up)on* may lead an addressee to ask 'dependent on *who* or *what*?' about the system in question.

5.3.1.2   Clauses functioning as Complement in adjective phrases

Finite and non-finite clauses can function as Complement of adjectives. Non-finite clauses in this function can occur with or without a Subject of their own.

131 I'm [$_{AdjP}$ pleased [$_{clause}$ *that you had a cancellation this morning*]].

132 We're not [$_{AdjP}$ sure [$_{clause}$ *what these knives might have been like*]].

133 The Garda appear [$_{AdjP}$ eager [$_{clause}$ Ø *to help*]] though their resources are inadequate.

134 I'm [$_{AdjP}$ perfectly happy [$_{clause}$ *for you to clap and sing*]].

135 Were you [$_{AdjP}$ too busy [$_{clause}$ Ø *doing your projects*]]?

5.3.1.3   Noun phrases functioning as Complement in adjective phrases

Noun phrases can only function as Complement of a small set of adjectives, namely *due*, *like*, NEAR, *unlike*, and *worth*, as in the following examples. Notice that NEAR is in its comparative form in (137).

136 It's [$_{AdjP}$ worth [$_{NP}$ *a mention*]].

137 You can wait until [$_{AdjP}$ nearer [$_{NP}$ *the time*]] to go digital, or you can make the switch now.

5.3.2   Adjuncts in adjective phrases

The information supplied by Adjuncts inside AdjPs is always optional. They can be realized in a variety of ways, as Table 5.7 shows.

Adjuncts in adjective phrases
• Pre-Head Adjuncts
▪ adverb phrases;
▪ noun phrases;
▪ prepositional phrases;
▪ determinative phrases;
▪ 'verb phrases'.
• Post-Head Adjuncts
▪ prepositional phrases;
▪ adverb phrases;
▪ determinative phrases.

Table 5.7: Adjuncts in adjective phrases

The different types of Adjuncts in adjective phrases will be discussed in the sections that follow.

5.3.2.1 Adverb phrases functioning as pre-Head Adjunct in adjective phrases

Adjectives can be modified by adverb phrases headed by intensifier adverbs such as *extremely, fairly, quite, really, reasonably, slightly, too, totally, very*.

138 [$_{AdjP}$ [$_{AdvP}$ *fairly*] elaborate]

139 [$_{AdjP}$ [$_{AdvP}$ *quite*] small]

140 [$_{AdjP}$ [$_{AdvP}$ *really*] pleasant]

141 [$_{AdjP}$ [$_{AdvP}$ *totally*] idiotic]

142 [$_{AdjP}$ [$_{AdvP}$ *very*] narrow]

5.3.2.2 Noun phrases functioning as pre-Head Adjunct in adjective phrases

Less commonly, noun phrases modify the Head. The NPs typically indicate measures in time or space.

143 [$_{AdjP}$ [$_{NP}$ *six years*] older]

144 [$_{AdjP}$ [$_{NP}$ *nine miles*] long]

5.3.2.3 Prepositional phrases functioning as pre-Head Adjunct in adjective phrases

Also not very common are PPs functioning as pre-Head Adjunct.
Here are two examples.

145 [$_{AdjP}$ [$_{PP}$ *in no way*] radical]

146 [$_{AdjP}$ [$_{PP}$ *by no means*] clear]

5.3.2.4 Determinative phrases functioning as pre-Head Adjunct in adjective phrases

In the next battery of examples determinative phrases function as
pre-Head Adjunct inside AdjPs. In (149) the DPs function in this way
in paired AdjPs.

147 I don't think it's [$_{AdjP}$ [$_{DP}$ *that*] risky].

148 I've got a little garage and it's only [$_{AdjP}$ [$_{DP}$ *this*] small].

149 [$_{AdjP}$ [$_{DP}$ *The*] worse] it seemed, [$_{AdjP}$ [$_{DP}$ *the*] more cheerful] I felt.

5.3.2.5 'Verb phrases' functioning as pre-Head Adjunct in adjective phrases

Occasionally we find pre-Head Adjuncts that resemble verb phrases
inside AdjPs.

150 It's [$_{AdjP}$ [$_{VP'}$ *laugh-out-loud*] funny] which is pretty good for a book
on depression – comprehensive and very helpful.

5.3.2.6 Prepositional phrases functioning as post-Head Adjunct in adjective phrases

Post-Head Adjuncts that are realized as prepositional phrases are not
always easy to distinguish from PPs that function as Adjunct at a different level of clause structure. Thus *on Saturday mornings* in (153)
can be moved, as (154) shows.

151 It was [$_{AdjP}$ too early [$_{PP}$ *in the morning*]].

152 They are [$_{AdjP}$ rich [$_{PP}$ *beyond their wildest dreams*]].

153 It's a bit of a nuisance parking down there, but they are [$_{AdjP}$ open
[$_{PP}$ *on Saturday mornings*]].

154 It's a bit of a nuisance parking down there, but on Saturday mornings they are open.

5.3.2.7 Adverb phrases functioning as post-Head Adjunct in adjective phrases

Adverb phrases headed by the adverbs *indeed* and *still* can function as post-Head Adjunct inside AdjPs, as in (155) and (156).

155 It'll be [_AdjP_ very destructive [_AdvP_ *indeed*]] both for sick people and their businesses.

156 Her house was lovely and her family [_AdjP_ lovelier [_AdvP_ *still*]].

5.3.2.8 Determinative phrases functioning as post-Head Adjunct in adjective phrases

The determinative *enough* can function as post-Head Adjunct inside adjective phrases, as in the example below.

157 That's [_AdjP_ clear [_DP_ *enough*]].

5.4 Complex verb phrases

5.4.1 Complements in verb phrases

As we saw in section 3.6.2, the simplest verb phrases contain an intransitive verb with or without Adjuncts, or a transitive verb with a Complement and one or more Adjuncts. More complex verb phrases can contain more than one Complement, and can also contain one or more Adjuncts. The most typical Complements licensed by verbs inside verb phrases are shown in Table 5.8.

Complements in verb phrases
• noun phrases;
• adjective phrases;
• prepositional phrases;
• clauses (finite and non-finite).

Table 5.8: Complements in verb phrases

The Complements of verbs inside verb phrases will be discussed with reference to English *verb complementation* patterns. These specify which Complement(s) a Predicator licenses, if any. The patterns in question are shown in Table 5.9.

Basic complementation patterns
PCR (no complement): intransitive
PCR + DO: monotransitive
PCR + IO + DO: ditransitive
PCR + Subject-related PC: complex intransitive
PCR + DO + Object-related PC: complex transitive
PCR + (DO +) PPC: prepositional

PCR = Predicator, DO = Direct Object; IO = Indirect Object, PC = Predicative Complement, PPC = Prepositional Phrase as Complement

Table 5.9: Basic complementation patterns

Note that the patterns are formulated in terms of grammatical functions which can be realized in different ways. Examples will be given in the sections that follow. The intransitive pattern will not be discussed further here.

5.4.1.1 The pattern PCR + DO: monotransitive

5.4.1.1.1 Noun phrases, adjective phrases, and prepositional phrases functioning as Direct Object

As we saw in section 4.1.3.1.2, Direct Objects are overwhelmingly realized as noun phrases. Other types of phrases, including PPs and AdjPs, can only marginally function as Direct Object. Consider first (158), where the DO is a prepositional phrase.

158 They want [PP *between £8 billion and £9 billion*] from the Government.

In (159) the adjective phrase could be analysed as a Direct Object.

159 You mean [AdjP *close to Christmas*], I assume.

However, this example was uttered in response to someone saying 'In my own estimation the turning point of the economy certainly is not going to be till the back end of this year at the very earliest.' Because of this we could regard (159) as a shortened version of (160), in which the AdjP functions as Complement of a preposition.

160 You mean that the turning point of the economy is certainly not going to be till *close to Christmas*?

5.4.1.1.2 Clauses functioning as Direct Object

In the examples below the bracketed clauses function as Direct Object. The clause in (161) is finite, whereas (162) involves a non-finite clause.

161 We know [clause *that not all choices are wise*], but we're reluctant to let that fact serve as the basis for a moral conclusion.

162 I didn't expect [clause *Ø to get that sort of reaction*].

There exists a large number of patterns in which clauses can function as DO. These will be discussed in detail in Chapters 7 and 8.

5.4.1.2   The pattern PCR + IO + DO: ditransitive

As we saw in Chapter 4, Indirect Objects are almost always realized as noun phrases. Here are some additional examples. In both cases the Direct Object is also realized as a noun phrase.

163 You're in fact giving [NP *people in high-valued property*] [NP *a subsidy*].

164 She claimed that the new Prime Minister Jim Callaghan had offered [NP *his predecessor*] [NP *the job of Foreign Secretary in his government*].

Very rarely Indirect Objects are realized as prepositional phrases, as in the invented example that follows.

165 I gave *under the bed* a good clean.

5.4.1.3   The pattern PCR + Subject-related PC: complex intransitive

In this pattern a verb is complemented by a Predicative Complement that ascribes a property to a Subject, or identifies the referent of the Subject. The PC can be realized by an NP, AdjP, PP, AdvP, or clause.

5.4.1.3.1 Noun phrases functioning as Subject-related Predicative Complement

As we saw in section 4.1.3.3.1, Subject-related Predicative Complements are commonly realized as noun phrases. Here are some further examples. In each case the Subject to which the PC is related is underlined.

166 <u>It</u> seemed [_{NP} *a splendid way of getting my ideas straight*].

167 As with many children, <u>origami</u> became [_{NP} *an absorbing hobby of his*].

5.4.1.3.2 Adjective phrases functioning as Subject-related Predicative Complement

Subject-related Predicative Complements are also frequently realized as adjective phrases. As in the previous section, in the following examples the Subject to which the PC is related is underlined.

168 <u>Tanya</u> appeared [_{AdjP} *quite relieved*] as the telephone rang.

169 <u>He</u> became [_{AdjP} *convinced he could reach the North Pole unaided*].

5.4.1.3.3 Prepositional phrases functioning as Subject-related Predicative Complement

In the examples that follow the property expressed by the PP is ascribed to the underlined Subject.

170 <u>I</u> was [_{PP} *at a loss for words*].

171 <u>This</u> is [_{PP} *in apparent contrast to the findings of a larger survey by Hickson et al. (1986)*].

Notice that example (172) below is different from the examples above: here the property ascribed to the referent of the Subject is not expressed by the PP as a whole, but rather by the NP that complements the preposition *as*.

172 <u>That</u> counts [PP *as a draw in the ongoing battle between man and machine*].

5.4.1.3.4 Adverb phrases functioning as Subject-related Predicative Complement

Adverb phrases too can function as PC; they often provide a time specification:

173 <u>That</u> was [AdvP *later*].

174 I don't know for sure if <u>it</u> will be [AdvP *that soon*].

5.4.1.3.5 Clauses functioning as Subject-related Predicative Complement

In (175) and (176) the bracketed (finite and non-finite) clauses function as Predicative Complements related to the underlined Subjects.

175 <u>The problem with that</u> of course is [clause *that parties may not have a majority*].

176 Presumably <u>the first job</u> would be [clause *Ø to mark them up*].

Clausal Subject-related PCs will be exemplified further in Chapters 7 and 8.

5.4.1.4 **The pattern PCR + DO + Object-related PC: complex transitive**

In this pattern a verb is complemented by a Direct Object, as well as by a Predicative Complement that ascribes a property to the Direct Object. The PC can be realized by an NP, AdjP, PP, or clause.

5.4.1.4.1 Noun phrases functioning as Object-related Predicative Complement

As we saw in section 4.1.3.3.2, Object-related PCs are frequently realized as noun phrases, as in (177) and (178). The Direct Objects are underlined.

177 Some people call <u>this</u> [NP *a competitive system*].

178 [NP *What*] do <u>they</u> call it _?

(178) is a special case: here the Object-related PC is a clause-initial NP headed by an interrogative pronoun (section 3.2.2.5) which is associated with the gap following the Direct Object (indicated by '_').

This type of *interrogative clause* will be discussed further in section 6.2.1.

5.4.1.4.2 Adjective phrases functioning as Object-related Predicative Complement

Like noun phrases, adjective phrases also commonly function as Object-related PC.

179 I find <u>it</u> [_{AdjP} *fascinating*].

180 What's making <u>me</u> [_{AdjP} *sick*] this afternoon is the honourable gentleman for Wanstead and Woodford who was born in nineteen fifty-two.

5.4.1.4.3 Prepositional phrases functioning as Object-related Predicative Complement

Prepositional phrases functioning as Object-related PC are quite rare. Here's an example:

181 There must have been a time — maybe back in 1966 before live news coverage was common and Charles Whitman opened fire from a clock tower at the University of Texas in Austin and killed 16 people — when witnesses, officials and news announcers would find <u>themselves</u> [_{PP} *at a loss for words*].

Compare (181) with (170) where the same phrase functions as a Subject-related PC.

The examples in (182) and (183) below also contain PPs, but here it is the noun phrase Complements of the prepositions *as* and *for* that indicate the properties ascribed to the Direct Objects, not the PPs as a whole.

182 Until then Alice had felt paranoid and helpless, wounded by the thought that someone in authority saw <u>her</u> [_{PP} *as a threat*].

183 I first got <u>a millionaire</u> [_{PP} *for my neighbour*].

In (183) the most likely meaning is 'my first neighbour was a millionaire', rather than 'I first procured a millionaire for my neighbour'. As (184) and (185) show, it is possible for a preposition heading a PP functioning as Object-related PC to have an AdjP as Complement.

184 He left <u>them</u> [_{PP} *for dead*].

185 Anyway she's given us <u>an article</u> [PP *for free*] which is good.

Notice that in (185) the PP functions as Object-related PC in a ditransitive construction.

5.4.1.4.4 Clauses functioning as Object-related Predicative Complement

In the example below the two bracketed NPs and the bracketed clause function as Object-related PCs. They are associated with the underlined Direct Objects. Only *-ing* clauses can function as Object-related PC. This is rare.

186 Call <u>it</u> [NP *a rebirth*], call <u>it</u> [NP *a renewal*], call <u>it</u> [clause *Ø fooling fate*]. Whatever this thing is, it's helping the Kings win hockey games and they think it's about time.

5.4.1.5 The pattern PCR + (DO +) Prepositional Phrase as Complement: prepositional

English allows a large number of patterns involving one or more prepositional phrases functioning as Complement. The verbs occurring in these patterns can be transitive or intransitive. Table 5.10 offers an overview of constructions in which the PP Complements are not locative. They will be discussed in detail after the table.

Constructions involving non-locative PPs functioning as PPC
1. Intransitive verb + PPi
Example:
(a) Somehow his comeback as a 50s "commie basher" in the Cold War and Korea never <u>caught</u> [PP *on*].
Other combinations:
BACK *down,* BRANCH *out,* CLIMB *up,* CLOSE *in,* COME *apart/in,* CROP *up,* DIE *down,* DRAG *on,* GET *by,* GET *up,* GROW *up,* MOVE *on,* RUN *off,* SIT *up,* TOUCH *down,* WORK *out*
2. Transitive verb + NP + PPi <u>or</u> Transitive verb + PPi + NP
Example:
(b) I'll <u>turn</u> [NP *the light*] [PP *off*] there, so you can see better. / (c) I'll <u>turn</u> [PP *off*] [NP *the light*] there, so you can see better.
Other combinations:
BRING NP *over,* CLEAN NP *off,* EAT NP *up,* FILL NP *in,* GIVE NP *back,* HAND NP *over,* LEAVE NP *out,* PAY NP *back,* SEND NP *back,* TEAR NP *up,* TURN NP *on,* WIPE NP *off,* WRITE NP *down*

(Continued)

Constructions involving non-locative PPs functioning as PPC (*continued*)

3. Intransitive verb + PPt

Examples:

Type 1: (d) He <u>relied</u> [~PP~ *on the forensic evidence*].

Type 2: (e) He <u>served</u> [~PP~ *as defence minister*] from 2000-03.

Other combinations:

Type 1: ACCOUNT *for* NP, ASK *for* NP, ATTEND *to* NP, CONSIST *of* NP^-P^, COMPLAIN *about* NP, DAWN *on* NP^-P^, DEAL *with* NP, DECIDE *on* NP, DIFFER *from* NP^-P^, FALL *for* NP^-P^, FEEL *for* NP^-P^, FORGET *about* NP, HOPE *for* NP, INSIST *on* NP, LAUGH *at* NP, LOOK *at* NP, OBJECT *to* NP, PAY *for* NP, REFER *to* NP, RESORT *to* NP, SEND *for* NP, TALK *to* NP, VOTE *for* NP, WAIT *for* NP, WORK *for* NP, WORRY *about* NP

Type 2: COUNT *as* NP/AdjP, DOUBLE *as* NP, PASS *for* NP/AdjP, POSE *as* NP, RESIGN *as* NP, RETIRE *as* NP

4. Transitive verb + NP + PPt

Examples:

Type 1: (f) And so Bob drafted this questionnaire and <u>gave</u> [~NP~ *it*] [~PP~ *to Dick*].

Type 2: (g) The US president <u>paid</u> [~NP~ *tribute*] [~PP~ *to Islam's influence on religion, culture and civilisation*].

Type 3: (h) Personally I agree with H. G. Wells that it is a great mistake to <u>regard</u> [~NP~ *the head of state*] [~PP~ *as a sales promoter*].

Other combinations:

Type 1: LEND NP *to* NP, OFFER NP *to* NP, SEND NP *to* NP, TELL NP *to* NP

Type 2: BLAME NP *on* NP, DO *justice to* NP, ENVY NP *for* NP, GIVE *way to* NP, INVEST NP *in* NP, PERSUADE NP *of* NP, PROVIDE NP *with* NP, RAISE *an objection to* NP, REFER NP *to* NP, REMIND NP *of* NP, THANK NP *for* NP

Type 3: ACCEPT NP *as* NP/AdjP, ACKNOWLEDGE NP *as* NP/AdjP, BRAND NP *as* NP/AdjP, CONDEMN NP *as* NP/AdjP, DIAGNOSE NP *as* NP/AdjP, HAIL NP *as* NP/AdjP, IDENTIFY NP *as* NP/AdjP, INTERPRET NP *as* NP/AdjP, PORTRAY NP *as* NP/AdjP, RECOGNIZE NP *as* NP/AdjP, TAKE NP *for* NP/AdjP, TREAT NP *as* NP/AdjP, VIEW NP *as* NP/AdjP

5. Intransitive verb + PPi + PPt

Examples:

Type 1: (i) He also has to <u>put</u> [~PP~ *up*] [~PP~ *with a soppy elder brother Robert*].

Type 2: (j) Their son Harry was born in 2003, 10 years after he <u>took</u> [~PP~ *over*] [~PP~ *as host of the Late Show*].

Other combinations:

Type 1: BREAK *up with* NP^-P^, CHECK *up on* NP, COME *down with* NP^-P^, GET *away with* NP^-P^, GET *down to* NP^-P^, KEEP *away from* NP^-P^, LOOK *forward to* NP, LOOK *in on* NP, LOOK *out for* NP^-P^, LOOK *up to* NP, RUN *away with* NP^-P^, STAND *out from* NP^-P^, STAND *up for* NP, WALK *out on* NP

Type 2: COME *across/over as* NP/AdjP, END *up as* NP, FINISH *up as* NP

(*Continued*)

Constructions involving non-locative PPs functioning as PPC (*continued*)

6. Transitive verb + NP + PPi + PPt <u>or</u> Transitive verb + PPi + NP + PPt

Examples:

Type 1: (k) They found bored staff who <u>fobbed</u> [$_{NP}$ *customers*] [$_{PP}$ *off*] [$_{PP}$ *with leaflets*]. /
(l) They found bored staff who <u>fobbed</u> [$_{PP}$ *off*] [$_{NP}$ *customers*] [$_{PP}$ *with leaflets*].

Type 2: (m) Authorities say Curry-Demus killed Johnson and tried to <u>pass</u> [$_{NP}$ *Johnson's infant son*] [$_{PP}$ *off*] [$_{PP}$ *as her own*]. / (n) Authorities say Curry-Demus killed Johnson and tried to <u>pass</u> [$_{PP}$ *off*] [$_{NP}$ *Johnson's infant son*] [$_{PP}$ *as her own*].

Other combinations:

Type 1: BRING NP *in on* NP, FIX NP *up with* NP, GIVE NP *up to* NP, LET NP *in on* NP, PLAY NP *off against* NP, PUT NP *up for* NP, PUT NP *up to* NP, TAKE NP *up on* NP

Type 2: LAY NP *down as* NP, PASS NP *off as* NP/AdjP, PUT NP *down as* NP/AdjP, RULE NP *out as* NP/AdjP, SHOW NP *up as* NP/AdjP, WRITE NP *off as* NP/AdjP

7. Intransitive verb + PPt + PPt

Examples:

Type 1: (o) After walking for some time he came to a Georgian police checkpoint and <u>appealed</u> [$_{PP}$ *to them*] [$_{PP}$ *for help*].

Type 2: (p) From an early age I <u>conceived</u> [$_{PP}$ *of myself*] [$_{PP}$ *as a rationalist*] and though I made spasmodic efforts at belief, I never felt a divine presence.

Other combinations:

Type 1: AGREE *with* NP *about* NP, ARGUE *with* NP *about* NP, ARRANGE *with* NP *for* NP, BOAST *to* NP *about* NP, COMPLAIN *to* NP *about* NP, LOOK *to* NP *for* NP

Type 2: LOOK *(up)on* NP *as* NP/AdjP, REFER *to* NP *as* NP/AdjP, THINK *of* NP *as* NP/AdjP

8. Ditransitive verb + NP + PPi + NP

Example:

(q) Ask nicely, and I'll <u>write</u> [$_{NP}$ *you*] [$_{PP}$ *out*] [$_{NP}$ *a list*].

Other combinations:

PAY NP *back* NP, RUN NP *off* NP, SEND NP *over* NP

PPi = PP headed by an intransitive preposition; PPt = PP headed by a transitive preposition. In each case the NP is a DO, except in construction 8 where the first NP is an IO. The patterns marked '-P' resist passivization.

Table 5.10: An overview of constructions involving non-locative PPs functioning as PPC

In construction 1 an intransitive verb takes a PP headed by an intransitive preposition as its PPC.

In construction 2 the verb licenses either an NP and a PP or a PP and an NP as Complements. The PPs are headed by intransitive prepositions. The order is determined by a number of factors, including information structuring (see Chapter 11). When the NP is headed by a pronoun it must occur immediately after the verb, unless it is stressed. Thus we have (187), (188), and (189) as possible structures, but not (190).

187 I turned off the light.

188 I turned the light off.

189 I turned it off.

190 *I turned off it.

Construction 3 involves an intransitive verb followed by a PP functioning as PPC headed by a transitive preposition. We have two subtypes here. In Type 1 constructions the preposition takes an ordinary NP as Complement. In Type 2 constructions the Complement PP functions as Subject-related Predicative Complement, but it is the NP contained in this PP that ascribes a property to the Subject of the clause; the Complement of the preposition can also be an adjective phrase, as in *That counts as radical* and *She could have passed for dead*. Notice that in (191) we can insert a phrase between the verb and the PP, which shows that the PP is a constituent. Unlike in the case of construction 2, the order V–NP–PP in (192) is impossible.

191 He relied *completely* on the evidence.

192 *He relied the forensic evidence on.

Passivization involving the NP inside the PP is possible for many Type 1 items of construction 3, but not for all.

In construction 4 we have a transitive verb followed by an NP functioning as DO, and a PP functioning as PPC, headed by a transitive preposition. This pattern involves three subtypes. The Type 1 pattern alternates with the ditransitive pattern, discussed in section 4.1.3.2. The NP that complements the Head of the PP carries the semantic role of Recipient. Type 2 is less flexible, in that in many cases the NP following the verb is fixed (*tribute* in the example given in the table). In the Type 3 pattern the transitive PP (headed by *as* or *for*) functions as Object-related Predicative Complement, but it is the NP contained in the PP that ascribes a property to the DO. In some cases an AdjP functions as Complement of the preposition, as in *We portrayed her as foolish*.

In construction 5 an intransitive verb is complemented by two PPs. The first of these is headed by an intransitive preposition, whereas the second is headed by a transitive preposition. We have two subtypes here. Type 1 sometimes allows passivization involving the NP inside the second PP; Type 2 does not allow this. In the Type 2 pattern the transitive PP functions as Subject-related Predicative Complement, but it is the NP contained in the second PP that ascribes a property to the Subject of the clause. An AdjP can sometimes also function as Complement of the preposition, as in *He came across as intelligent*.

Construction 6 is like construction 5, except that it involves a transitive verb which is followed by a noun phrase functioning as DO, and two PPs. The first PP can also follow the verb, with the NP in second position. The PP in the Type 2 pattern functions as Predicative Complement, but again it is the NP contained in the PP that ascribes a property to the Object of the clause, rather than the PP as a whole. As above, in some cases an AdjP can also function as Complement of the preposition, as in *They wrote the manager off as useless*.

Construction 7 involves two PPs as Complements of an intransitive verb, each headed by a transitive preposition. In the Type 1 pattern both PPs take ordinary NPs as their Complements. In the Type 2 pattern the NP contained in the second PP ascribes a property to the NP contained in the first PP.

In construction 8 a ditransitive verb is followed by an NP functioning as IO, a PP headed by an intransitive preposition functioning as PPC, and an NP functioning as DO. This pattern is versatile to some degree in that it allows for an alternative ordering of the Complements if the IO is 'heavy' enough. Compare the following three possibilities, ranked in order of acceptability.

193 I'll write your brother out a list.

194 I'll write your brother a list out.

195 I'll write out your brother a list.

Notice that some of the patterns shown in the table have literal meanings (e.g. *get up*, *clean* (NP) *off*), while others have unpredictable meanings, and can be regarded as idiomatic. For example, the preposition *out* in the combination WORK *out* does not carry its literal sense.

The noun phrases inside the prepositional phrases can often be replaced by clauses. For example, in construction 3 (Type 1), instead of *He relied on the forensic evidence* we can also have *He relied on what he had seen.*

In sections 7.3.1.2.3 and 8.3.3.1 I will discuss further patterns that involve a PP functioning as Complement, namely 'MENTION ([$_{pp}$ *to* NP]) [$_{clause}$ *that*...]', as in *I mentioned to Harry that it was late*, and 'PREVENT NP [$_{pp}$*from* [$_{clause}$ *-ing* participle...]]', as in *She prevented the louts from destroying the sculpture.*

Next we consider the constructions in Table 5.11, which all involve PP Complements that express a location.

Constructions involving locative PPs functioning as PPC

1. Intransitive verb + locative PPi or PPt

Examples:

(a) The girl I'm seeing at the moment <u>lives</u> [$_{pp}$ *there*].

(b) I <u>work</u> [$_{pp}$ *in the Physiology Department*].

Other verbs:

BE, DWELL, REMAIN, RESIDE

2. Transitive verb + NP + locative PPi or PPt

Examples:

(c) I cleared off the desk and <u>put</u> [$_{NP}$ *everything*] [$_{pp}$ *inside*].

(d) He's <u>put</u> [$_{NP}$ *his certificate*] [$_{pp}$ *on his wall*].

Other combinations:

KEEP NP *out*, LEAVE NP *in*, PUT NP *up*

3. Intransitive verb or transitive verb + locative PPt + locative PPt

Examples:

(e) Seaman then <u>went</u> [$_{pp}$ *from end*] [$_{pp}$ *to end*].

(f) This <u>brought</u> [$_{NP}$ *him*] [$_{pp}$ *from Dublin*] [$_{pp}$ *to England*], where he received excellent reviews.

Other combinations:

SEND NP *from* NP *to* NP, TRANSPORT NP *from* NP *to* NP, TRAVEL *from* NP *to* NP

(Continued)

Constructions involving locative PPs functioning as PPC
4. Transitive verb + NP + locative PPi + locative PPt + locative PPt

Examples:

(g) Martin Brundle has actually <u>brought</u> [$_{NP}$ *that car*] [$_{PP}$ *up*] [$_{PP}$ *from last*] [$_{PP}$ *to third*].

Other combinations:

GUIDE NP *down/out/up from* NP *to* NP, SEND NP *down/out/up from* NP *to* NP

PPi = PP headed by an intransitive preposition; PPt = PP headed by a transitive preposition.

Table 5.11: An overview of constructions involving locative PPs functioning as PPC

In construction 1 an intransitive verb is followed by a locative PP headed by either an intransitive or transitive preposition. In the examples given here the PPC is obligatory. If it is left out their meaning changes.

Construction 2 is like construction 1, except that a DO now follows the verb. How does a PPC like *on his wall* in the example shown differ from an Object-related PC like *at a loss for words* in (181)? While both are realized as prepositional phrases, the former does not ascribe a property to the DO, while the latter does. Thus in (181) the property of 'being at a loss for words' is ascribed to the referent of *themselves*, while *on his wall* obligatorily specifies a location.

In construction 3 an intransitive or transitive verb is complemented by two locative PPs, both headed by transitive prepositions.

Construction 4 involves a transitive verb followed by a DO and three locative PPCs.

5.4.2 Adjuncts in verb phrases

Adjuncts inside verb phrases are not licensed by verbs, as we saw in section 4.1.3.6. They modify verb + Complement sequences, and can occur in various guises, expressing a wide variety of meanings. Table 5.12 shows the various types of VP-Adjuncts.

Adjuncts in verb phrases
• Pre-Head Adjuncts
▪ adverb phrases.
• Post-Head Adjuncts
▪ adverb phrases;
▪ noun phrases;
▪ prepositional phrases;
▪ clauses.

Table 5.12: Adjuncts in verb phrases

5.4.2.1 Adverb phrases functioning as pre-Head Adjunct in verb phrases

Pre-Head Adjuncts are often realized as adverb phrases which can express a range of meanings such as 'manner', 'frequency', and 'time' (see also section 3.8.1).

196 I [$_{VP}$ [$_{AdvP}$ *quickly*] looked away], knowing that he was trying to hide the shaking.

197 Dickens [$_{VP}$ [$_{AdvP}$ *usually*] does that].

198 And the people [$_{VP}$ [$_{AdvP}$ *still*] play cricket on it].

199 I [$_{VP}$ [$_{AdvP}$ *never*] saw it, though].

200 I [$_{VP}$ [$_{AdvP}$ *definitely*] like Americans].

5.4.2.2 Adverb phrases functioning as post-Head Adjunct in verb phrases

In the following three examples the post-Head Adjuncts are realized as adverb phrases. Like their pre-Head counterparts, they can express many different kinds of meanings.

201 You want a shoe with a rigid sole that decreases the amount of pronation so you [$_{VP}$ cycle [$_{AdvP}$ *efficiently*]].

202 I [$_{VP}$ wear this [$_{AdvP}$ *occasionally*]].

203 But I [$_{VP}$ did it [$_{AdvP}$ *really badly*]].

5.4.2.3   Noun phrases functioning as post-Head Adjunct in verb phrases

Noun phrases functioning as Adjunct typically express the semantic notions of time and manner.

204 Well, I [vp had chips [NP *yesterday*]], and they were delicious.

205 Someone [vp introduced it to me [NP *the other day*]].

206 I [vp had a really, really good supper [NP *last night*]].

207 Many [vp died [NP *that way*]].

5.4.2.4   Prepositional phrases functioning as post-Head Adjunct in verb phrases

Prepositional phrases functioning as post-Head Adjunct are extremely frequent, and can express a huge range of meanings.

208 Charlemagne [vp was successful [PP *in 799*]], but he [vp still had to secure control of the peninsula [PP *after this date*]].

209 Fran [vp is very happy [PP *at Cheltenham*]].

210 You [vp looked very fat [PP *in my waistcoat*]] pal.

211 Let's [vp stop it [PP *for the moment*]].

The Head of a PP functioning as an Adjunct inside a VP can be a conjunctive preposition (section 3.7.1) which takes a clausal Complement. This type of PP will be discussed in detail in section 5.5.1.5.

5.4.2.5   Clauses functioning as post-Head Adjunct in verb phrases

Subordinate clauses can function as Adjunct in verb phrases. Here are two examples. The first is finite, the second non-finite.

212 It [vp also has six manually controlled "steps" [clause *should you wish to assume control yourself*]].

213 I [vp rushed over to the library [clause Ø *to get a couple of the books that Robins had recommended*]].

Further examples will be discussed in Chapters 7 and 8.

5.5   Prepositional phrases

5.5.1   Complements in prepositional phrases

Prepositions (simple or complex) very commonly take NPs as Complements, but they can also take AdjPs, AdvPs, PPs, and clauses, though much less frequently. Table 5.13 provides a summary list.

Complements in prepositional phrases
• noun phrases;
• adjective phrases;
• adverb phrases;
• prepositional phrases;
• clauses.

Table 5.13: Complements in prepositional phrases

5.5.1.1   Noun phrases functioning as Complement in prepositional phrases

Noun phrase Complements of prepositions have already been discussed in section 3.7.1. Here are some additional examples:

214 The earliest examples [PP in [NP *England*]] are the bifora windows [PP in [NP *the transepts* [PP at [NP *Winchester*]]]].

215 She slid and tumbled [PP down [NP *the grassy outcrop*]] and tugged the star [PP out of [NP *the moon-slurried waters*]].

5.5.1.2   Adjective phrases functioning as Complement in prepositional phrases

In the examples below the prepositions take adjective phrases as their Complements. In (216) the PP functions as an Object-related Predicative Complement (section 4.1.3.3.2). The adjective inside the PP ascribes a property to the underlined Direct Object. In (217) the PP functions as an Adjunct within the verb phrase.

216 How can you describe <u>someone else</u> [PP as [AdjP *jealous*]]?

217 If you get a descaler which really fizzes [PP like [AdjP *crazy*]] when you put it in the kettle, that stuff will clean it.

See also example (160) where the adjective phrase functions as Complement of a preposition.

5.5.1.3 Adverb phrases functioning as Complement in prepositional phrases

Adverb phrases function as Complement in the PPs below.

218 [PP Until [AdvP *recently*]], all that was known was what had been written by Vincent's sister-in-law Jo in 1914.

219 I won't leave the slide on [PP for [AdvP *long*]].

220 The dominant class remains as dominant [PP as [AdvP *ever*]].

221 And there's been a lot of changes of leadership and no significant break [PP as [AdvP *yet*]].

5.5.1.4 Prepositional phrases functioning as Complement in prepositional phrases

It is quite common for prepositions to take prepositional phrases as Complements, as in (222)–(224).

222 Try to light the room [PP from [PP *behind the set*]].

223 Wait [PP until [PP *after tomorrow night*]].

224 [PP Since [PP *before dawn*]] today Britain's forces have been in action in the Gulf.

5.5.1.5 Clauses functioning as Complement in prepositional phrases

Conjunctive prepositions take (mostly finite) clauses as Complements. They associate subordinate clauses (sections 1.7 and 7.1) with matrix clauses. The meanings expressed by conjunctive prepositions are very varied, as the examples below show.

Time (*after, as, before, since, until, when, while, whilst*)

225 [PP After [clause *he left university*]] he started a career in journalism and worked for the *Newcastle Chronicle*.

226 I think it happened [PP before [clause *I was eight*]].

227 I've always kept very good ties with Jeremy [PP since [clause *we broke up*]].

Reason (*as, because, for, seeing* [*that*], *since*)

228 [PP As [clause *the top models now have Jaguar-style price tags*]], they must have Jaguar-style luxury too.

229 These birds are usually found on islands [PP because [clause *there are no predators*]].

230 They say that [PP since [clause *we own the building*]], they won't increase the amounts of money with inflation.

Concession (*although, despite, even though, though, whereas, while, whilst*)

231 [PP Although [clause *water was a kind of god to the Romans*]], the bridge itself had no religious meaning.

232 The narrator, [PP despite [clause Ø *identifying possible ways to freedom for women*]], is blind to the anomaly of women taking little part in political or social action.

233 [PP Whereas [clause *Germany was seen to personify victory at all costs*]], Britain's war effort was pictured in archaic, chivalric images made readily available by the Victorians' medieval revival and its popularisation in the didactic literature of social heroism.

Condition (*if, even if, only if, unless*)

234 They think that [PP if [clause *you pay*]] it must by definition be better.

235 [PP Unless [clause *something's done about her*]] she'll end up like her mother.

Contrast (*whereas, while, whilst*)

236 Jets take in oxygen from the air, [PP whereas [*clause* *rockets have to carry their own*]].

237 [PP Whilst [clause *my fiancée seems to have been quite lucky*]] others are not so.

Purpose (*in order* [*that*], *so*, *so as*)

238 [PP In order [clause *that they can carry out this role*]], some generally agreed notions about what is and is not acceptable behaviour towards children must be arrived at and written down.

239 More nationalities had been recognized, assisted in inverse proportion to their numerical importance and historic seniority, [PP so as [clause Ø *to divide the population into smaller categories and speed up their integration*]].

Result (*so* [*that*])

240 Today suitcases arrived [PP so [clause *that she could start to pack*]].

As will be clear from these examples, some prepositions can express more than one meaning. For example, *since* can express 'time' and 'reason', and *while* can express 'time' and 'concession'.

Do not confuse the conditional preposition *if* with *interrogative if*, exemplified in (241), which we analysed as a subordinating conjunction (see section 3.9).

241 She asked [clause *if* she might see a hand-mirror].

A number of prepositions belong both to the class of regular prepositions (section 3.7.1) and to the class of conjunctive prepositions, for example *after*, *before*, and *since*. Compare the use of *after* in (242) and (243).

242 Rotas introduced [PP after [NP *the dispute*]] are also falling apart. [P + NP]

243 And that's a trend that's likely to continue well [PP after [clause *the economy begins to upturn*]]. [P + subordinate clause]

Analysing words like *although, because, since, when, where*, and *while* as prepositions is a major departure from traditional grammar, where they are regarded as subordinating conjunctions. We will see in section 7.1 that subordinating conjunctions connect matrix clauses and subordinate clauses in a different way from conjunctive prepositions.

Non-finite clauses are less common as Complements of prepositions than finite clauses. They can occur with or without a Subject of their own. If they have a noun phrase headed by a pronoun as Subject the pronoun can be in the accusative case (as in (244)) or in the genitive case (as in (245)).

244 You can't just put it on [$_{PP}$ [$_P$ without] [$_{clause}$ *them knowing*]].

245 She had voiced no exception [$_{PP}$ [$_P$ to] [$_{clause}$ *his being there*]], but if she had he would have stopped this activity too.

246 I'm looking forward [$_{PP}$ [$_P$ to] [$_{clause}$ Ø *seeing it*]].

Table 5.14 lists some common conjunctive prepositions.

English conjunctive prepositions			
after$^{±NP}$	despite^{+NP}	once	whenever
(al)though	for (all)$^{±NP}$	since$^{±NP}$	where^{-NP}
as^{+NP}	from^{+NP}	than^{+NP}	whereas
at^{+NP}	if (conditional)	through$^{±NP}$	while^{-NP}
because	into^{+NP}	till^{+NP}	whilst^{-NP}
before$^{±NP}$	lest	unless	with^{+NP}
beside(s)$^{±NP}$	like^{+NP}	until^{+NP}	without$^{±NP}$
between$^{±NP}$	of $^{+NP}$	upon^{+NP}	
by$^{±NP}$	on$^{±NP}$	when^{-NP}	

All the prepositions listed in the table can occur with a clause as Complement (some only with non-finite clauses). Annotations indicate additional possibilities. Prepositions marked '$^{±NP}$' can occur either with an NP Complement or without one (i.e. intransitively), while those marked '$^{+NP}$' have only the first of these possibilities and those marked '$^{-NP}$' only the second. Note that some prepositions can also take a PP as Complement, e.g. *because* in *He didn't play because of his injury*.

Table 5.14: Conjunctive prepositions

Complex prepositions that take clauses as Complements (predominantly *-ing* participle clauses) are called conjunctive complex prepositions, as we saw in section 3.7.3. A sample are listed in Table 5.15. With the exception of *as if, as long as, in case, in order* [*that*], and *so* [*that*], all items can also license an NP as Complement.

Conjunctive complex prepositions			
ahead of	by dint of	in case of	in view of
as for	by virtue of	in lieu of	on account of
aside from	due to	in order [that]$^{-NP}$	owing to
as if^{-NP}	far from	in relation to	prior to
as long as^{-NP}	for (the) sake of	in/with respect to	so [that]$^{-NP}$
as soon as	for/from want of	in return for	subsequent to
as to	in accordance with	in spite of	with a view to
as well as	in addition to	instead of	
at (the) risk of	in between	in terms of	
because of	in case^{-NP}	in (the) light of	

Those marked '–NP' cannot occur with an NP.

Table 5.15: Conjunctive complex prepositions

5.5.2 Adjuncts in prepositional phrases

As in the other phrase types, in PPs we distinguish between pre-Head Adjuncts and post-Head Adjuncts. The former can be realized as AdvPs, PPs, and NPs, the latter only as PPs (Table 5.16).

Adjuncts in prepositional phrases
• Pre-Head Adjuncts
▪ adverb phrases;
▪ prepositional phrases;
▪ noun phrases.
• Post-Head Adjuncts
▪ prepositional phrases.

Table 5.16: Adjuncts in prepositional phrases

5.5.2.1 Adverb phrases functioning as pre-Head Adjunct in prepositional phrases

Among the pre-Head Adjuncts are adverb phrases headed by adverbs that have an intensifying meaning (e.g. *clean*, *quite*, *right*, *straight*, and *very*), as in (247)–(254). Notice that some of the PPs shown here, and in subsequent sections, are headed by an intransitive preposition.

247 It was from that bridge that Edmund Foster "escaped this world" when a new train left the rails and went [PP [AdvP *clean*] through the railing].

248 Luton captain Kevin Nicholls created the opening with skilful footwork just outside the Wednesday penalty area and a pass that left the home defence flat-footed and put Howard [PP [AdvP *clean*] through].

249 She's [PP [AdvP *quite*] into carpentry].

250 It's also a valuable stretch of agricultural land [PP [AdvP *right*] on the edge of Prince Charles's estate].

251 He's hardly likely to suddenly come [PP [AdvP *right*] down] again.

252 The best thing to do is to turn [PP [AdvP *straight*] to the index].

253 I'm going to go [PP [AdvP *straight*] back] to London.

254 You were [PP [AdvP *very*] on time].

5.5.2.2 Prepositional phrases functioning as pre-Head Adjunct in prepositional phrases

Examples like (255)–(256) contain prepositional phrases which function as pre-Head Adjunct and are headed by intransitive prepositions that have a directional meaning (e.g. *down*, *out*, *over*).

255 The whole area [PP [PP *down*] by the beach] and [PP [PP *down*] by the sea] is actually flattened.

256 He'd been to a lecture the previous night [PP [PP *up*] in London].

5.5.2.3 Noun phrases functioning as pre-Head Adjunct in prepositional phrases

In (257)–(261) the PPs take an intransitive preposition as Head, and are modified by pre-Head Adjuncts realized as noun phrases.

257 And if you wear it [PP [NP *that way*] up] it means you're going out with them.

258 Check in [PP [NP *about an hour*] before].

259 Well they're [PP [NP *a goal*] down] at the moment.

260 But the referee says it was knocked on and he gives the scrum to England [$_{PP}$ [$_{NP}$ *fifteen metres*] in].

261 And so I was asking the question about what would happen [$_{PP}$ [$_{NP}$ *twenty-five years*] on].

Note that in (258) the word *about* is an adverb which functions as Predeterminer.

5.5.2.4   Prepositional phrases functioning as post-Head Adjunct in prepositional phrases

Post-Head Adjuncts within PPs can be realized by other PPs, as in (262) and (263).

262 Hodge is now [$_{PP}$ in [$_{PP}$ *with a chance of victory*]].

263 They go [$_{PP}$ out [$_{PP}$ *in the cold*]] with no clothes on.

Here the Heads of the higher-level PPs are the intransitive prepositions *in* and *out*, which take the PPs *with a chance of victory* and *in the cold* as Adjuncts. There is some doubt as to whether these PPs are separate VP-level Adjuncts, though notice that they cannot be moved elsewhere (cf. *With a chance of victory Hodge is now in;?*In the cold they go out*), which suggests that they are linked with the prepositions *in* and *out*, respectively.

5.6   Adverb phrases

5.6.1   Complements in adverb phrases

Adverbs are not as versatile as the other word classes in their Complement- and Adjunct-taking properties. Complements of adverbs can be prepositional phrases or clauses (Table 5.17).

Complements in adverb phrases
• prepositional phrases;
• clauses.

Table 5.17: Complements in adverb phrases

5.6.1.1 Prepositional phrases functioning as Complement in adverb phrases

Complements of adverbs are mostly prepositional phrases, often with *for* or *to* as Head.

264 But [_{AdvP} unfortunately [_{PP} *for its creator*]], the new design has already been compared to wallpaper, shop bar-codes and deckchair fabric.

265 [_{AdvP} Happily [_{PP} *for the Tottenham supporters*]], Vinnie Samways is fit and well.

266 Surely it would be better for the government to control cannabis' consumption and make profit from it, [_{AdvP} comparably [_{PP} *to other dangerous substances such as alcohol, cigarettes and petrol etc. that other readers have listed above*]].

267 This faculty may of course exist [_{AdvP} independently [_{PP} *of Reason*]].

5.6.1.2 Clauses functioning as Complement in adverb phrases

In (268) and (269) clauses function as Complement of the adverbs.

268 Did they hand Jeanette to you [_{AdvP} immediately [_{clause} *she was born*]]?

269 The Sun admits that it set out to find Hoare [_{AdvP} directly [_{clause} *he was released from prison*]] and often came close to discovering him during a rigorous six-month search across Britain – from Bristol, through Wales and on to the north-east.

5.6.2 Adjuncts in adverb phrases

Pre-Head Adjuncts can be realized as AdvPs, DPs, and NPs, whereas post-Head Adjuncts can be realized as PPs, AdvPs, and DPs (Table 5.18).

5.6.2.1 Adverb phrases functioning as pre-Head Adjunct in adverb phrases

Adverbs can be premodified by other adverbs (or adverb phrases, to be precise), as in the examples below.

Adjuncts in adverb phrases
• Pre-Head Adjuncts
▪ adverb phrases;
▪ determinative phrases;
▪ noun phrases.
• Post-Head Adjuncts
▪ prepositional phrases;
▪ adverb phrases;
▪ determinative phrases.

Table 5.18: Adjuncts in adverb phrases

270 With base-jumping, stuff happens [AdvP [AdvP *really*] fast] and small problems can lead to big accidents.

271 I [AdvP [AdvP *very*] often] supply one of these reports and will be happy to do so for him.

272 There is a particular range of values for the greenhouse effect where the Earth can exist [AdvP [AdvP *quite*] happily] either with or without an icecap over the Arctic Ocean.

5.6.2.2 Determinative phrases functioning as pre-Head Adjunct in adverb phrases

Examples of determinative phrases functioning as pre-Head Adjunct are shown below.

273 [AdvP [DP *The*] longer] this dish cooks [AdvP [DP *the*] better] it tastes, and an hour is ideal.

274 First, I never need to see things [AdvP [DP *that*] clearly] again.

5.6.2.3 Noun phrases functioning as pre-Head Adjunct in adverb phrases

Noun phrases functioning as pre-Head Adjunct inside AdvPs often express the extent to which the meaning of the adverb applies.

275 It's now come full circle [AdvP [NP *seventeen years*] later].

276 I could have done it [AdvP [NP *a lot*] better].

5.6.2.4 Prepositional phrases functioning as post-Head Adjunct in adverb phrases

Post-Head Adjuncts in adverb phrases can be realized by PPs, as in the following example, where the PP further specifies the meaning of the adverb *later*.

277 Ministers refused to cave into teachers' demands for an improved annual salary – and further strikes were averted [AdvP later [PP *in the year*]].

5.6.2.5 Adverb phrases functioning as post-Head Adjunct in adverb phrases

Adverbs like *indeed* and *still* can head AdvPs which function as post-Head Adjunct inside AdvPs.

278 We've taken it [AdvP very, very seriously [AdvP *indeed*]], the issue of racism.

279 She was not piteous, enjoyed life and spent a good deal of time talking to servants, first in Sheffield, later in London and [AdvP later [AdvP *still*]] in her father's country house on the outskirts of Esher.

5.6.2.6 Determinative phrases functioning as post-Head Adjunct in adverb phrases

The determinative *enough* can head a DP which functions as post-Head Adjunct in an AdvP.

280 I don't know Ian [AdvP well [DP *enough*]].

281 [AdvP Funnily [DP *enough*]], many patients who show such learning consequently deny ever having done the task before!

5.7 Coordination

5.7.1 Coordinated structures

Coordination was discussed briefly in section 3.9. Coordinated structures involve two or more phrases or clauses that are linked by coordinating conjunctions such as *and*, *or*, and *but*. The following examples show coordinated noun phrases, adjective phrases, prepositional phrases, verb phrases, adverb phrases, and clauses.

282 We have [NP-coordination [NP *tutorials*], [NP *lectures*] and [NP *practicals*]].

283 I'm [AdjP-coordination [AdjP *very surprised at their commitment*] and [AdjP *pleased*]].

284 They spread through the blood system and the lymphatic system particularly [PP–coordination [PP *to the brain*] and [PP *to the liver*]].

285 The light [VP-coordination [VP *flared*] and [VP *diminished*]], casting a flickering light across the streets.

286 The Government has also [AdvP-coordination [AdvP *quietly*] but [AdvP *steadfastly*]] maintained its opposition to commercial whaling.

287 I hope [clause-coordination [clause *Simey is well*] and [clause *his exams were OK*]].

We will refer to coordinated NPs as *NP-coordinations*, to coordinated AdjPs as *AdjP-coordinations*, and so on. The constituents that are coordinated are called *coordinates*, and are at the same syntactic level. What this means is that the coordinated phrases have equal syntactic status, and together perform a particular grammatical function. Thus in the case of (283) the two conjoined adjective phrases together function as Subject-related Predicative Complement.

Note that different types of phrases can also be coordinated. In (288) we have an AdjP/PP-coordination.

288 As for all shots, you need to be [AdjP/PP-coordination [AdjP *alert*] and [PP *on your toes*]].

5.7.2 Syndetic, asyndetic, and polysyndetic coordination

We distinguish between *syndetic coordination* and *asyndetic coordination*. The former involves the use of a coordinating conjunction, whereas in the latter coordinating conjunctions are omitted, as in the following examples.

289 They were often *musicians, philosophers, physicists*.

290 He's going all round *Italy, Austria, Switzerland*.

Omitting the conjunctions creates the feel of an open-ended list of items.

When we have multiple coordinators we speak of *polysyndetic coordination*:

291 So for somebody involved in the visual arts it's a very liberating process to suddenly be going public in a way, working with ideas of *movement and shape and form*.

By using more than one coordinating conjunction the individual coordinates are emphasized, and in this way their individual importance is signalled.

5.7.3 Correlative coordination

Correlative coordination involves the use of the strings *both... and, either... or,* or *neither... nor.*

Examples are given below.

292 I believe <u>both</u> Parliament <u>and</u> Sterling have served our country and the rest of the world very well.

293 As the prosecuting counsel, Brian Brown is hampered first by a lack of eyewitnesses most of them being <u>either</u> dead <u>or</u> too ill to testify.

294 <u>Neither</u> you <u>nor</u> your partner have to be a parent of the child or children provided they live with you as members of your family.

The use of the correlative pattern again highlights the different coordinates individually, as well as the relationship between them.

Chapter 6
Clause types and negation

In English we can define a number of different *clause types* based on their syntactic characteristics. We distinguish between *declarative*, *interrogative*, *imperative*, and *exclamative* clauses. With the exception of imperatives, the system of clause types applies to main and subordinate clauses. In this chapter we will focus on main clauses. The final section of this chapter will discuss negation, both clausal and subclausal.

6.1 Declarative clauses

Declarative clauses display the regular constituent order of Subject – Predicator – (Complement(s)) – (Adjunct(s)). The latter two functions are optional, as indicated by the brackets. As an example, consider (1), where *I* functions as Subject, *interviewed* functions as Predicator, *Andrew* is the Direct Object, and *on Friday* is an Adjunct.

1 I interviewed Andrew on Friday.

Declarative clauses are characteristically used to make *statements* which the speaker believes to be true. As we saw in Chapter 2, English used to have inflectional forms to realize mood. However, in contemporary English it does not make sense to regard mood as an inflectional notion, and we say instead that mood is grammatically implemented through the use of the clause types, and/or through the use of modal auxiliary verbs. We will see in section 6.5 that declarative clauses are not exclusively used for making statements.

As noted above, we will also use the label 'declarative' for subordinate clauses (see section 1.3 and Chapters 7 and 8). The bracketed string in (2) is a *declarative subordinate clause* which functions as the

Direct Object of the verb SAY. It is introduced by the subordinating conjunction *that*.

2 I said [*that I interviewed Andrew on Friday*].

Table 6.1 summarizes the properties of declarative clauses.

Declarative clauses...
• have a regular constituent order Subject + Predicator + (Complement(s)) + (Adjunct(s)); • are typically used to make statements which the speaker believes to be true.

Bracketed clause elements are optional.

Table 6.1: The properties of declarative clauses

6.2 Interrogative clauses

Interrogative clauses are characteristically used to ask *questions*. We distinguish between *open interrogatives* and *closed interrogatives*.

6.2.1 Open interrogative clauses

Open interrogative clauses are typically used to ask questions which can solicit an unrestricted set of answers. Examples are given below.

3 [NP *Who*] said that?

4 [NP *What*] do we want to achieve _ from the expenditure?

5 [NP *Which*] did you enjoy _ the most?

6 [NP *Whom*] did you telephone _ after the discovery?

7 [PP *When*] is your birthday _?

8 [PP *Where*] did she see me _?

9 [AdvP *Why*] do you want that _?

10 [AdvP *How*] did you manage to make the mistake _?

The first thing to note is that, except in (3), the constituent order in these examples is markedly different from that of declarative

clauses: in each case the clause has an initial _wh_-_phrase_ headed by a
_wh_-_word_ (section 3.2.2.3). Example (3) is exceptional because the _wh_-
phrase is in Subject position. These interrogative clauses are called
'open' because in principle they can solicit a limitless array of answers,
as we have seen. Thus, in answer to (8) we can say 'at Joe's house', 'in
the restaurant around the corner', 'in Amsterdam', and so on.

A second observation is that interrogative clauses with a non-
Subject initial _wh_-phrase display Subject–auxiliary inversion, first
discussed in section 3.6.3.1. Any of the different types of auxiliary
verb, as well as the lexical verbs BE and HAVE, can invert with a Subject.
As we will see in section 7.3.1.2.2, inversion does not occur in subordinate clauses.

The third observation we can make is that in each case, again with
the exception of (3), the _wh_-phrase is associated with a 'gap' later in
the clause, indicated by '_'. As we saw in section 3.2.2.3, we can conceptualize the association between the _wh_-phrase and the gap as
involving _movement_ from the gap position to a clause-initial position. In (4), (5), and (6) we associate _what, which_, and _whom_ with the
Direct Object positions of the verbs ACHIEVE, ENJOY, and TELEPHONE,
respectively. In (3) _who_ functions as Subject, and is not associated
with a gap. In (7) we associate _when_ with a Predicative Complement
position (cf. _Your birthday is when?_), while in (8)–(10) the gaps are
Adjunct positions.

Fourthly, in (3)–(6) the _wh_-phrases are noun phrases headed by
interrogative pronouns. In (3) and (6) respectively they carry nominative and accusative case. Accusative case is not obligatory in (6):
both _who_ and _whom_ are possible. The difference is that accusative
case is more formal, and more common in written than in spoken
language. Recall that _when_ and _where_ in (7) and (8) are analysed as
prepositions heading PPs (see sections 3.7 and 5.5.1.5), whereas _why_
and _how_ in (9) and (10) are adverbs heading adverb phrases.

Finally, it is important to point out that it is also possible for open
interrogatives to involve _wh_-phrases which contain more than just a
single _wh_-word, as in (11)–(15).

11 [NP _What sort of information_] do we want to collect _?

12 [NP _Which car_] did you take _?

13 [NP _Whose project_] is it _?

14 [PP *In which book*] is a villain turned to mincemeat by the snow-fan of a train _?

15 [PP *To what degree*] will you go _ to succeed?

In (11) and (12) *what* and *which* are analysed as interrogative determinatives functioning as Determiners (section 3.3.4), whereas in (13) *whose* is an interrogative pronoun in the genitive case (sections 3.2.2.5 and 5.2.1.2), also functioning as Determiner. The *wh*-phrases in the last two examples are prepositional phrases. Within these PPs the *wh*-words are interrogative determinatives.

Table 6.2 summarizes the properties of open interrogative clauses.

Open interrogative clauses...

- are typically used to ask questions which can have an open-ended list of answers;
- contain a *wh*-phrase headed by a *wh*-word which is normally in clause-initial position, and is associated with a position later in the clause (except when the *wh*-phrase is a Subject);
- display Subject–auxiliary inversion when the *wh*-phrase precedes the Subject in main clauses.

Table 6.2: The properties of open interrogative clauses

6.2.2 Closed interrogative clauses

Here are some examples of closed interrogatives.

16 Is your back better enough for you to do all that samba dancing?

17 Did you get her telephone number?

18 Will you have another cup of tea, grandpa?

19 Can they appoint me as their agent?

Syntactically, these interrogative clauses are characterized by Subject–auxiliary inversion. They are referred to as 'closed' because they can only solicit the answers 'yes' or 'no'. While it is of course perfectly possible to reply to (18) by saying 'I'm fine' or 'maybe later', or to (19) by saying 'I hope so', these are considered to be *responses*, not answers. In general, the structure of an interrogative clause determines the answers that can be given, but this is not the case for responses.

We can distinguish a special type of closed interrogative clause, called an *alternative interrogative*, exemplified in (20):

20 Is it a tragedy or a comedy?

In this case the possible answers are limited to 'a tragedy' and 'a comedy'.

It is important to be aware of the fact that the term 'question' is not used in its everyday sense in this chapter, but in a specialized way: a question is the typical use that is made of an interrogative structure in order to solicit an answer. Although interrogatives are typically used to ask questions, this is not always the case, as I will make clear in section 6.5.

Table 6.3 summarizes the properties of closed interrogative clauses.

Closed interrogative clauses...
• are typically used to ask questions which solicit the answers 'yes' or 'no';
• display Subject–auxiliary inversion.

Table 6.3: The properties of closed interrogative clauses

6.3 Imperative clauses

Imperative clauses contain a verb in the plain form, and usually lack a Subject, though see (27) and (28) below. They are typically used to issue *directives*, which can be orders, instructions, and the like exhorting an addressee to do something. Unlike the other clause types, they can only occur in main clauses. DO can optionally be added for emphasis, as in (25), but it is required in negative imperatives, cf. (26).

21 Tell him we are waiting for the order.

22 Have a guess.

23 Hang on.

24 Think.

25 (Do) be careful!

26 Don't be shy.

27 You be careful going back.

28 Somebody please tell me I'm right otherwise my little remaining faith in the UK's voters will evaporate completely.

Imperatives can be (perceived to be) rude, depending on the relationship between the speaker and the addressee.

Not all verbs allow imperatives equally easily. As a rule of thumb, verbs that do not allow the referents of their Subjects to control the event expressed by the verbs (e.g. verbs expressing cognitive states: KNOW, UNDERSTAND, etc.) are generally not used in imperative clauses, simply because it is pragmatically odd to tell someone to know or understand something. Exceptions are possible, as the following example shows.

29 *Realise* that this program is directed at you. *Realise* that group hysteria is the feed of the New World Order, and *realise* that you are in the War of your life.

A special type of imperative is the <u>*let*</u> *imperative*, exemplified in (30) and (31). In these cases the speaker is included in the directive. Thus we can interpret (30) as 'Let's you and I have a look at the list'. The negated versions of *let* imperatives are formed with the negated dummy auxiliary verb DO.

30 Let's have a look at the list.

31 Don't let's tell the police.

Table 6.4 summarizes the properties of imperative clauses.

Imperative clauses...
• are typically used to issue directives;
• usually lack a Subject;
• occur only as main clauses;
• take a verb in the plain form;
• mostly occur with dynamic verbs.

Table 6.4: The properties of imperative clauses

6.4   Exclamative clauses
· ·

Exclamative clauses are typically used to make exclamative statements. They are characterized either by a word order that involves an exclamative *wh*-word *what* at the beginning of a clause-initial noun phrase, or by *how* used in front of an adjective or adverb in a clause-initial AdjP or AdvP. *How* can also occur on its own. There is normally no Subject–auxiliary inversion, and in writing an exclamation mark is often used. Here are some examples. In each case the bracketed phrases are associated with the positions indicated by '_'.

32 [NP What a worrying man] he is _!

33 [NP What rubbish] she talked _.

34 [NP What shameful decisions] they took _!

35 It showed [clause [NP what a bargain] CEC was getting _] and [clause [AdvP how hard] people actually worked _]!

36 Linda gets off on this big business about snob appeal: [clause [AdjP how clever] all her acquaintances are _], and [clause [AdjP how wonderful] they are _ in one way or another].

37 [AdjP How true] that is _!

38 [AdvP How] he laughed _.

In (32) the Subject of the clause is *he*, while the phrase *what a worrying man* functions as a (preposed) Subject-related Predicative Complement. Notice that *what* precedes the determinative *a*. In (33) and (34) Direct Objects are fronted, whereas a DO and Adjunct, respectively, are preposed in (35). Note that the exclamative clauses in (35) and (36) are coordinated (see section 5.7). In (36) and (37) AdjPs containing *how* and functioning as Subject-related Predicative Complement are preposed. Finally, in (38) *how* occurs on its own, and functions as a (preposed) Adjunct.

Table 6.5 summarizes the properties of exclamative clauses.

Exclamative clauses...
• are typically used to utter exclamatory statements; • involve exclamative *what* or *how* in preposed phrases; • do not normally display Subject–auxiliary inversion.

Table 6.5: The properties of exclamative clauses

6.5   The clause types and their uses

In the sections above we looked at the syntax of each of the clause types, as well as their typical uses in main clauses. The discussion is summarized in Table 6.6.

Clause type	Syntax	Typical use
declarative	• normally Subject + Predicator + (Complement(s)) + (Adjunct(s)) order.	to make a statement, believed to be true by the speaker.
open interrogative	• interrogative *wh*-phrase (usually clause-initial); • Subject–auxiliary inversion when the *wh*-phrase precedes the Subject in main clauses.	to ask questions with a potentially open set of answers.
closed interrogative	• Subject–auxiliary inversion.	to ask questions with 'yes' or 'no' as answers.
imperative	• usually no Subject; • verb in the plain form; • only in main clauses; • mostly with dynamic verbs.	to issue a directive.
exclamative	• preposed phrase with exclamative *what* or *how*; • normally no Subject–auxiliary inversion.	to make an exclamative statement.

Table 6.6: Overview of the clause types: syntax and use

The syntax of a particular clause can be determined with reference to the criteria discussed in this chapter. However, the *use* that is made of that same clause, and how it is understood, is dependent on the context in which it is uttered. In cases where a clause in a particular context is used in an expected, typical way (as shown in Table 6.6) we speak of a *direct speech act*. For example, if a speaker utters (39) they are using a declarative structure which is likely to be an informative statement which they believe to be true, perhaps in response to someone asking *What did he write?*

39 He wrote *Death in Venice*.

Similarly, if a speaker utters (40) they are likely to be asking a question.

40 Did you go to that meeting?

You may have wondered why I used the word 'likely' twice in the text above. The reason is that the various clause types can also be used as *indirect speech acts*. This happens when a clause is used in an untypical way. As an example, consider again (39), which is syntactically declarative. If it is uttered with a rising intonation at the end, that is, with a voice rising in pitch, the speech act is no longer 'making a statement', but 'asking a question'. Another example which can be used as an indirect speech act is (41).

41 Can you answer the question I posed earlier?

This utterance is a closed interrogative by virtue of its syntax, and could be used to ask if someone is able or in a position to answer a particular question. This would be a direct speech act. However, in many situations, for example in a confrontational radio interview, (41) could be used to (politely) direct someone to *do* something, that is, answer a question. If the word *please* is added to (41) the directive force of the utterance becomes apparent, because we do not normally use this word when we ask a question.

Consider next (42).

42 Did you realise that the redesign of the roof meant that the blue wall would be carrying a substantially greater part of the roof than before?

Syntactically this clause is again a closed interrogative, and it can be used to solicit either 'yes' or 'no' as an answer. However, when a speaker who utters (42) does not expect an answer, they are in effect making a statement equivalent to the declarative structure in (43). In such a situation (42) is called a *rhetorical question*.

43 The redesign of the roof means that the blue wall will be carrying a substantially greater part of the roof than before.

The possibilities for using indirect speech acts are endless, and allow for variation in language use. Here are some further examples. In each case the utterances can have a literal meaning, but can also be used indirectly, depending on the context of utterance. Some possible interpretations are given in brackets. As we will see, the list of speech acts is not limited to those shown in the right-hand column of Table 6.6.

Declaratives used as…

directive

44 I'm telling you to go.

45 I am working. (In a situation in which someone does not want to be disturbed: 'Go away.')

46 I am a secretary. (In a situation in which someone is being asked to do something that is not part of their job: 'I don't want to empty the office bins.')

47 It's late now. (In a situation in which someone wants to leave: 'Let's go.')

48 He is serious. (In a situation in which someone believes someone else not to have been joking: 'Stop laughing.')

question

49 Jaycee was a male? (With a rising intonation: 'Was he really a male?')

50 Perhaps this represents cash advanced? (With a rising intonation: 'Does this represent cash advanced?')

apology

51 I'm sorry it's gone on so long.

52 I beg your pardon.

Interrogatives used as…

statement

> **53** What do *you* know about how I feel? (with stress on *you*:'You know nothing about this.')

> **54** How can you possibly know that? ('You do not know that.')

offer

> **55** Dad, will you have some more juice?

invitation

> **56** Would you like to take a seat while I tell him you're here?

directive/request

> **57** Joe, would you like to nominate Katherine? (i.e. 'Please nominate Katherine.')

> **58** Can you point me in the right direction? (i.e. 'Point me in the right direction.')

> **59** Will you please send it to me now? (i.e. 'Send it to me now.')

Imperatives used as…

expression of wish/hope

> **60** Have a lovely day, my dear. ('I hope you have a lovely day.')

apology

> **61** Please forgive me for inadvertently sending my subscription to the wrong address.

> **62** Please excuse me being lazy by word processing this letter!

statement

> **63** Please find enclosed cheque no. 123456. (i.e. 'Cheque no. 123456 is enclosed.')

6.6   Negation

Negation in English can operate at the clausal and subclausal levels. In the former case an entire clause is negated, whereas in the latter case a constituent of a clause is negated.

6.6.1   Clausal negation

Clauses can be negated by using negative words such as *never, not, nobody*, or *nothing*, or by using the ending *-n't* on verbs. Examples are shown below.

64 I will *not* offer you rash promises about how quickly this can be done.

65 That place *never* closes.

66 I did*n't* give it to her.

67 *Nobody* knows about it.

We can determine whether a clause is positive or negative by adding an interrogative tag to it: negative clauses are usually followed by a positive interrogative tag (as in (68) and (69)), whereas positive clauses are usually followed by a negative interrogative tag (as in (70) and (71); section 4.1.1.8).

68 Well they wo*n't* learn anything if they mess about, *will they*?

69 Oh god, she just does*n't* listen, *does she*?

70 And he will be happy sticking to blue wallpaper, *won't he*?

71 The Levites had a role in the other temples, *didn't they*?

This is not a hard-and-fast rule: positive clauses occasionally have positive tags, and negative clauses occasionally have negative tags.

Clauses containing words such as *barely, few, hardly*, or *scarcely* are also negative. This can be demonstrated by adding an interrogative tag. Thus, (72) is a negative clause, because we can add *can you*?

72 You can *hardly* ask for it back.

6.6.2 Subclausal negation

With subclausal negation only a constituent is negated. It is typically brought about by using affixes (section 2.1): a prefix such as *dis-*, *in-*, *un-*, *non-*, or a suffix such as *-less*.

73 Britain and Germany will no doubt continue to <u>*dis*agree</u> on particular policy issues.

74 Well, I think it's a bit <u>*un*reasonable</u>.

75 Well we're going to have *end<u>less</u>* discussions over what kind of film to get out, aren't we?

The fact that (75) has a negative interrogative tag shows that the clause as a whole is positive.

Chapter 7

Finite subordinate clauses

In this chapter I will discuss the notion of *subordination*, specifically with regard to finite clauses that function as Complements or Adjuncts in verb phrases. Finite clauses that function as Complements or Adjuncts in other types of phrases were discussed in Chapter 5. Chapter 8 will deal with non-finite subordinate clauses.

7.1 Subordination defined

Subordination is a grammatical phenomenon which involves an arrangement of two or more units (words, phrases, or clauses) that are in an unequal relationship. We will say that when a unit is subordinate to another it is *dependent* on it. For example, in (1) the clause introduced by the subordinating conjunction *that* (section 3.9) is dependent on the verb FEEL because it is licensed by it (section 4.1.3): it functions as its Direct Object. We refer to it as a *subordinate clause*.

1 I feel [clause *that this area has too much development*].

In (1) we distinguish two clauses: a *matrix clause*, which is coextensive with the structure as a whole, indicated by the solid arrow in (2), and a *subordinate clause*, indicated by the dashed arrow.

2 [main/matrix clause I feel [clause 2 *that this area has too much development*]].

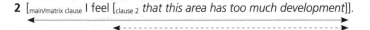

As we saw in section 3.9, matrix clauses are defined as clauses that contain subordinate clauses within them. Clauses that are themselves not subordinate to another clause are called *main clauses*. In (2) the matrix clause is also a main clause. (In what follows I will use the label 'main clause' only if it is significant to draw attention to the fact that the clause in question is not subordinate to another.)

Notice that the subordinate clause in (2) has a Subject of its own (*this area*), a Predicator (*has*), and a Direct Object (*too much development*). Further layers of subordination are possible, as in (3), which contains two subordinate clauses.

3 [main/matrix clause They are describing [clause 2 *that they think* [clause 3 *that the person is jealous*]]].

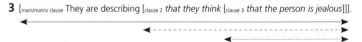

Here clause 2 is licensed by the verb DESCRIBE, whereas clause 3 is licensed by the verb THINK. More specifically, clause 2 functions as the Direct Object of DESCRIBE, whereas clause 3 is the DO of THINK. Notice that clause 2 is a matrix clause for clause 3.

Recall from section 2.2.1.5 that a clause that is tensed is also finite. Given that in (1) the verb *has* is a present tense form, it is part of a finite clause. Similarly, clauses 2 and 3 in (3) are finite because the verbs *think* and *is* carry tense.

7.2   Markers of subordination

Subordination can be marked syntactically. There are a number of ways in which this can be done in English.

First, as we saw in section 7.1, subordinate clauses can be introduced by *subordinating conjunctions* (also called simply *subordinators*; see section 3.9) which function as *markers of subordination*. English has three subordinators for finite clauses, namely *that*, *whether*, and *if*, and one subordinator for non-finite clauses, namely *for*. (Recall from sections 3.7.1 and 5.5.1.5 that we do not include items such as *since*, *before*, *although*, *because* in the class of subordinators.)

It is also possible to signal subordination through constituent order. For example, in the bracketed clause in (4) the preposed *wh*-phrase *why* is combined with the 'regular' order of a Subject followed by a verb. This is typical of subordinate interrogative clauses (see section 7.3.1.2.2).

4 The author seems to have realised [clause *why he had to leave* _].

Recall from section 6.2.1 that main interrogative clauses have Subject–auxiliary inversion (cf. *Why <u>did</u> <u>he</u> have to leave?*).

Consider also the example in (5):

5 [clause *Had I spent my time in some other hostelry*], I should now be returning to Oxford.

Here again the constituent order in the bracketed clause marks it as subordinate. The order we would expect in a main clause does not involve Subject–auxiliary inversion (cf. *I had spent my time in some other hostelry*). I will return to this type of subordinate clause in section 7.3.1.5.

7.3 The classification of finite subordinate clauses

In English we distinguish three types of finite subordinate clauses (Table 7.1): content clauses, comparative clauses, and relative clauses.

Finite subordinate clauses
content clauses
comparative clauses
relative clauses

Table 7.1: Finite subordinate clauses

Each type of subordinate clause will be discussed separately.

7.3.1 Content clauses

Content clauses are defined as finite subordinate clauses that syntactically resemble main clauses, but lack the features attributable to comparative clauses and relative clauses. They can be syntactically characterized in terms of the clause types we discussed in Chapter 6. We distinguish between the three types of content clauses shown in Table 7.2.

Content clauses
declarative content clauses
interrogative content clauses
exclamative content clauses

Table 7.2: Content clauses

(Because imperatives can only occur in main clauses, there is no such thing as an imperative content clause.)

Content clauses can perform a variety of functions, some of which were already discussed in sections 5.2.3.2, 5.3.1.2, and 5.5.1.5, namely Complement of a noun, Complement of an adjective, and Complement of a preposition. In the sections that follow I will discuss content clauses functioning as Subject, Direct Object, Complement Clause, Subject-related Predicative Complement, and Adjunct. I will use model verbs to exemplify complementation patterns, and I will list a sample of verbs occurring in these patterns. It is important to be aware of the fact that if a verb appears in one of the tables in this chapter, this does not mean that it does not occur in any other pattern(s). For example, the verb BELIEVE can take a Direct Object (*We believed the story*, *We believed that the story was true*), or a Direct Object and a Complement Clause (*We believed the story to be true*). The latter pattern will be discussed in Chapter 8.

7.3.1.1   Content clauses functioning as Subject

In the examples below the italicized clauses function as Subject.

6 [clause *That the appetite comes with eating*] may be an adage as old as the hills.

7 [clause *Whether technology can be considered as the 'motor of society'*] is a chicken and egg debate.

8 [clause *What he needs _*] is mental flexibility.

9 [clause *What a disaster the conference had been*] became clear two weeks later.

The clause in (6) is declarative, whereas the clauses in (7) and (8) are interrogative. Closed interrogative content clauses are introduced by *whether*, whereas open interrogative content clauses are introduced by a *wh*-phrase which is headed by a *wh*-word, and is associated with a gap marked by '_' (unless the *wh*-phrase is a Subject; see sections 3.2.2.3 and 6.2.1 on *wh*-words and gaps). The Subject clause in (9) is exclamative.

The subordinators *whether* and *if* are often interchangeable, as we will see in section 7.3.1.2.2, but not in interrogative content clauses functioning as Subject. Here only *whether* is possible. Although the bracketed clause in (8) resembles a free relative clause (to be discussed in section 7.3.3.5), it is an interrogative clause because we can paraphrase it as follows: 'The answer to the question *what does he need?* is mental flexibility.'

If the Subject clause is felt to be lengthy, it may be extraposed to the end of the clause (section 3.2.2.1.2). The extraposition process for (6), (7), and (9) is shown in (10)–(12). (The Subject clause in (8) cannot be extraposed.) There are two stages. In the first stage the content clause is displaced to the end of the matrix clause, after which *anticipatory it* (section 3.2.2.1.2) is slotted into the matrix clause Subject position.

10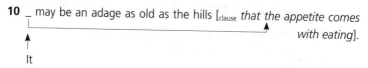

11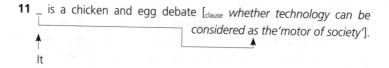

12

I present extraposition in this way only for expository purposes. There is no suggestion that the two stages are processes which take place in the mind.

Extraposition will be discussed further in section 11.3.2.2.

7.3.1.2 Content clauses functioning as Direct Object

7.3.1.2.1 The pattern 'DECIDE [$_{clause}$ *that* …]'

As in (1) above, in the examples below declarative content clauses function as Direct Object.

13 We decided [$_{clause}$ *that we would work together*].

14 I thought [$_{clause}$ *Ø$_{sub}$ he was here*].

Notice that in (14) the subordinator *that* has been omitted (indicated by '*Ø$_{sub}$*'). (This is not possible for the other subordinators. For example, we cannot omit *whether* from *I wondered whether they're any good* in pattern 7.3.1.2.2 below.)

We regard the content clauses in the examples above as Direct Objects because they can become the Subjects of passive clauses, although they are then usually extraposed. As an example, consider the two passive versions of (13) in (15) and (16). While the former is clumsy, if not unacceptable, the latter, which involves extraposition, is fine.

15 [$_{clause}$ *That we would work together*] was decided.

16 _ was decided [$_{clause}$ *that we would work together*].

    It

Declarative content clauses functioning as Direct Object seem to be less closely related to the verb that licenses them than noun phrases functioning as DO. This is because such clauses do not need to follow the verb immediately: adverbs may intervene, as (17) shows.

17 I think *really* [$_{clause}$ it's very difficult to produce any form of art unless you are driven].

Noun phrases functioning as DO are generally positioned immediately after the verb (see section 4.1.3.1.1), though even here there are exceptions, especially in spoken English.

Other verbs that can take a declarative clause functioning as Direct Object are listed in Table 7.3.

'DECIDE [clause *that* ...]' The *that*-clause functions as Direct Object.		
ACCEPT	CONFIDE	PRETEND
ACKNOWLEDGE	CONFIRM	REALIZE
ADD	CONSIDER	REMARK
ADMIT	DECIDE	REPLY
AGREE	DECLARE	SAY
ANNOUNCE	DEMAND	SENSE
ARGUE	DEMONSTRATE	SHOW
ARRANGE	DISCLOSE	STATE
ASSERT	EXPECT	SUGGEST
ASSUME	FIND	SWEAR
BELIEVE	GUARANTEE	THINK
BET	HINT	UNDERSTAND
CHECK	INSIST	WARN
CLAIM	KNOW	WRITE
COMPLAIN	MENTION	
CONFESS	PREFER	

Table 7.3: Verbs occurring in the pattern 'DECIDE [clause *that* ...]'

7.3.1.2.2 The pattern 'WONDER [clause *whether/if/wh*-phrase ...]'

This pattern involves subordinate interrogative and exclamative clauses functioning as Direct Object. As we have seen, closed interrogative clauses are introduced by *whether* or *if*, whereas open interrogative clauses are introduced by a *wh*-phrase which is headed by a *wh*-word, and is associated with a gap marked by '_' (unless the *wh*-phrase is a Subject). Subordinate interrogative clauses differ from main interrogative clauses in lacking Subject–auxiliary inversion. The italicized clauses in (18) and (19) are closed interrogatives, whereas those in (20)–(23) are open interrogatives.

18 Can you recall [clause *whether there was a trial within a trial in Payne's case*]?

19 I don't know [clause *if they're any good*].

20 I wonder [clause *who supplies them at the moment*].

21 It is then sent to the taxonomist dealing with that family, who will discover [clause *what genus it belongs to* _] and [clause *what species it is* _].

22 I don't know [clause *what you did* _ *with it*].

23 Although regret is displayed it is not self pitying, for the author seems to have realised [clause *why he had to leave Oxford* _].

In examples where we have the sequence *whether … or not*, the subordinator cannot normally be exchanged for *if*. However, occasional exceptions do occur, as in the following example.

24 He didn't know [clause *if Sally had heard him or not*].

In (25) and (26) the bracketed constituents are exclamative clauses, introduced by an adjectival *wh*-word (section 5.2.2.4).

25 You know [clause *what a good friend I am* _], Jafar, don't you?

26 I want to underscore [clause *how extremely essential your efforts are* _].

Some further verbs that can license interrogative or exclamative clauses functioning as Direct Object are listed in Table 7.4.

'WONDER [clause *if/whether/wh*-phrase …]' The *wh*-clause functions as Direct Object.		
ASCERTAIN	DISCOVER	MIND
ASK	DOUBT	NOTICE
CARE	ENQUIRE	OBSERVE
CHECK	ESTABLISH	PREDICT
CONFIRM	ESTIMATE	REALIZE
CONSIDER	FORGET	REMEMBER
DECIDE	GUESS	SAY
DISCLOSE	KNOW	WONDER

Table 7.4: Verbs occurring in the pattern 'WONDER [clause *if/whether/ wh*-phrase …]'

7.3.1.2.3 The pattern 'MENTION ([pp *to* NP]) [clause *that* ….]'

In this pattern the verb licenses two Complements: an optional prepositional phrase, and a declarative content clause functioning as Direct Object. An example is shown in (27).

27 He mentioned [PP *to you*] [clause *that he was writing it*].

The head of the PP can also be *from*, *of*, or *with*, as in (28)–(30).

28 Many commentators have concluded [PP *from this*] [clause *that voters care most about fairness — the sense that there should be a level playing field with opportunities for all*].

29 He had repeatedly demanded [PP *of the Europeans*] [clause *that they "step up to the plate" and at least match the $335m the US has made available*].

30 Now £64,000 is not a million, but Tarrant pleaded [PP *with us*] [clause *that "in these very tough times it's a massive amount of money"*].

Some verbs that can occur in this pattern are listed in Table 7.5.

'MENTION ([PP *to* NP]) [clause *that* …]' The PP is a Complement of the verb. The *that*-clause functions as Direct Object.		
ACKNOWLEDGE	DISCLOSE	PROPOSE
ADMIT	DISCOVER[F]	PROTEST
AGREE[W]	ELICIT[F]	PROVE
ANNOUNCE	EXPLAIN	RECOMMEND
ARRANGE[W]	HINT	REMARK
ASK[O]	INFER[F]	REPLY
ASSERT	INSIST	REPORT
BEG[O]	LEARN[F]	REVEAL
BOAST	MENTION	SAY
COMPLAIN	NOTICE[F]	SEE[F]
CONCLUDE[F]	OBJECT	SIGNAL
CONFESS	OBSERVE[F]	STATE
CONFIRM[W]	PLEAD[W]	SUGGEST
DECLARE	POINT [*out*]	TESTIFY
DEMAND[O]	PROMISE	

Verbs marked '[F]', '[O]', or '[W]' license a PP headed by *from*, *of*, or *with*, respectively.

Table 7.5: Verbs occurring in the pattern 'MENTION ([PP *to* NP]) [clause *that* …]'

7.3.1.2.4 The pattern 'TELL NP [$_{\text{clause}}$ *that* ...]'

A handful of verbs that occur with Indirect Objects license declarative clauses functioning as Direct Object, as in the example below, where the italicized NP functions as Indirect Object.

31 She told [$_{\text{NP}}$ *me*] [$_{\text{clause}}$ *that she was starting this class with Adam*].

The IO can become the Subject of a passive clause, as in (32).

32 I was told that she was starting this class with Adam.

The verbs that occur in this pattern are listed in Table 7.6. They can also occur in the pattern V + IO + DO, where the IO and DO are noun phrases (e.g. *I told her a lie*).

'TELL NP [$_{\text{clause}}$ *that* ...]'	
The NP functions as Indirect Object, and can become the Subject of a passive clause. The *that*-clause functions as Direct Object.	
PROMISE$^{\pm NP}$	TEACH$^{\pm NP}$
SHOW$^{\pm NP}$	TELL

Verbs marked '$^{\pm NP}$' can occur with or without an NP. When they occur without an NP the clause functions as Direct Object.

Table 7.6: Verbs occurring in the pattern 'TELL NP [$_{\text{clause}}$ *that* ...]'

7.3.1.2.5 The pattern 'ASK NP [$_{\text{clause}}$ *whether/if/wh*-phrase ...]'

In this pattern the verb is followed by an NP functioning as Indirect Object, and a closed interrogative ((33) and (34)), open interrogative ((35)), or exclamative ((36)) content clause functioning as Direct Object.

33 May I ask [$_{\text{NP}}$ *her*] [$_{\text{clause}}$ *whether she thinks that the eleven are not now both isolated and intransigent in relation to agricultural policy and the GATT round*].

34 He didn't tell [$_{\text{NP}}$ *us*] [$_{\text{clause}}$ *if he wanted top slicing of the licence fee to help fund public service programming on Channel Four*].

35 I don't think he's ever asked [$_{\text{NP}}$ *me*] [$_{\text{clause}}$ *what I was doing _*].

36 We've got to have mechanisms in place so that when we go back for more money, we'll be able to tell [NP *Congress*] [clause *what a great job we did _ spending the money they've already given us*].

As with the pattern discussed in the previous section, verbs that occur in this pattern can also occur in the pattern V + IO + DO, where the IO and DO are noun phrases (e.g. *I asked them a question*). The IO can become the Subject of a passive clause. For example, the passive version of (35) is (37).

37 I don't think I've ever been asked what I was doing.

Verbs that can occur in this pattern are shown in Table 7.7.

'ASK NP [clause *whether/if/wh*-phrase …]'
The NP functions as Indirect Object, which can become the Subject of a passive clause. The *wh*-clause functions as Direct Object.

ASK⁺ᴺᴾ	TEACH
SHOW⁺ᴺᴾ	TELL

The verbs ASK and SHOW can occur with or without an NP. When they occur without an NP the clause functions as Direct Object.

Table 7.7: Verbs occurring in the pattern 'ASK NP [clause *whether/if/wh*-phrase …]'

7.3.1.2.6 The pattern 'CONSIDER _ NP/AdjP [clause *that/wh*-phrase …]'

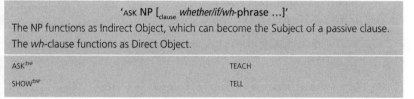

In this unusual complex transitive pattern the content clause functions as a Direct Object. In the example that follows the declarative content clause is extraposed. Anticipatory *it* (section 3.2.2.1.2) is inserted into its original position.

38 Some scientists consider_ possible [clause *that microbes could have survived for aeons below the Martian permafrost layer, where water changes from ice into liquid*].

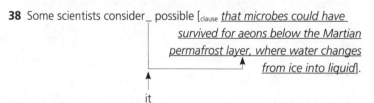

In (39) the content clause is interrogative. This time it has not been extraposed.

39 We consider [clause *how the problem is dealt with _*] [NP *a major concern*].

The noun phrase or adjective phrase in this pattern functions as Object-related Predicative Complement.

7.3.1.3 Content clauses functioning as Complement Clause

7.3.1.3.1 The pattern 'PERSUADE NP [clause *that …*]'

In this pattern the NP functions as Direct Object, whereas the *that*-clause functions as Complement Clause. As we saw in Chapter 4, we use the function label Complement Clause for any clause that is licensed by a verb, but cannot be assigned one of the other Complement functions Direct Object, Indirect Object, or Predicative Complement. Here is an example.

40 We persuaded [NP *them*] [clause *that we could do it*], and in the end they gave in.

The DO can become the Subject of a passive clause, as in (41):

41 They were persuaded that we could do it by us, and in the end they gave in.

Although there is some indeterminacy here, we will not regard the NP as an Indirect Object. The reason is that PERSUADE cannot occur in the typical V + IO + DO pattern, where the IO and DO are realized as noun phrases (cf. **I persuaded him a course of action*).

Some further verbs that can occur in this pattern are listed in Table 7.8.

'PERSUADE NP [clause *that …*]'		
The NP is the DO of the verb; it can become the Subject of a passivized matrix clause. The *that*-clause functions as Complement Clause.		
ADVISE$^{\pm NP}$	FOREWARN$^{\pm NP}$	SATISFY
ASSURE	INFORM	WAGER$^{\pm NP}$
BET$^{\pm NP}$	NOTIFY	WARN$^{\pm NP}$
CAUTION$^{\pm NP}$	REASSURE	
CONVINCE	REMIND	

Verbs marked '$^{\pm NP}$' can occur with or without an NP. When they occur without an NP the clause functions as Direct Object.

Table 7.8: Verbs occurring in the pattern 'PERSUADE NP [clause *that …*]'

7.3.1.3.2 The pattern 'REMIND NP [clause whether/if/wh-phrase …]'

As in the previous section, in this pattern the NP functions as Direct Object, whereas the interrogative clause functions as Complement Clause. Closed interrogative clauses are introduced by *whether* or *if* (cf. (42)), whereas open interrogative content clauses are introduced by a *wh*-phrase which is associated with a gap marked by '_' (cf. (43)), unless the *wh*-phrase is a Subject (see sections 3.2.2.3 and 6.2.1 on gaps).

42 Why have three shelves of histories of imperial India, when you could just type the key words into Google, and remind [NP *yourself*] [clause *whether it was Dyer or O'Dwyer who ordered the shooting at Amritsar*]?

43 It's a completely different job but it's good that I can advise [NP *them*] [clause *what it's like _*] when they get back to Birmingham.

A preposition can be placed before the clause, as in (44).

44 The scenes there reminded [NP *me*] [PP *of* [clause *what I saw _*]] when I went to Sri Lanka after the tsunami.

However, in this case the verb occurs in the pattern 'transitive verb + NP + PP' (see section 5.4.1.5), and the clause is a free relative clause (see section 7.3.3.5 below).

The DO can become the Subject of a passive clause, as the contrast between (43) and (45) shows.

45 It's a completely different job but it's good *that they can be advised what it's like* when they get back to Birmingham.

The verbs in this pattern are not ditransitive (cf. section 7.3.1.2.5), because they cannot occur with an IO and DO realized as noun phrases, cf. *He reminded me the problem.* (Although this is acceptable with a PP, cf. *He reminded me of the problem*, the PP does not function as DO here, but as a PP Complement. See section 5.4.1.5.)

Verbs that can occur in this pattern are listed in Table 7.9.

> **'REMIND NP [**clause *whether/if/wh*-phrase ...]'**
> The NP is the DO of the verb; the interrogative clause functions as Complement Clause.
> The DO can become the Subject of a passive clause.

ADVISE	INSTRUCT	WARN
INFORM	REMIND	

Table 7.9: Verbs occurring in the pattern 'REMIND NP [clause *whether/if/wh*-phrase ...]'

7.3.1.3.3 The pattern '*It* SEEM (PP) [clause (*that/as if*) ...]'

In this pattern the matrix clause contains the linking verb SEEM (section 3.6.1) which licenses two Complements: an optional PP and a clause functioning as Complement Clause. The latter is introduced by *that* or *as if*, which can be left out. The Subject of the matrix clause is the dummy pronoun *it* (section 3.2.2.1.2).

46 It seems [clause *that there must be quite a lot of late parrots in Cloud Cuckoo Land if the right honourable gentleman can come out with that stuff*].

47 Sometimes it appears [clause *as if social workers cannot win in the eyes of the public, no matter what they do*].

48 It appears [PP *to me*] [clause *that we can fund many useless projects*] but when it comes down to life or death, in this particular instance we fall short.

49 It was [clause *as if I had been hypnotised by the fear*]. I could only feel fear and I could only visualise a block.

Other verbs that can occur in this pattern are listed in Table 7.10.

> **'*It* SEEM (PP) [**clause (*that/as if*) ...]'**
> The matrix clause Subject is the dummy pronoun *it*. The subordinate clause functions as
> Complement Clause.

APPEAR	CHANCE[-PP]	HAPPEN[-PP]
BE	COME ABOUT[-PP]	TURN OUT[-PP]

Verbs marked '-PP' cannot take a PP complement.

Table 7.10: Verbs occurring in the pattern '*It* SEEM (PP) [clause (*that/as if*) ...]'

7.3.1.4 Content clauses functioning as Subject-related Predicative Complement: the pattern 'BE [_{clause} *that/wh*-phrase …]'

Recall from sections 3.6.1 and 4.1.3.3 that strings that complement linking verbs function as Subject-related Predicative Complement. Of the linking verbs only BE can license a content clause with that function.

50 The second myth is [_{clause} *that embryo experimentation is necessary*].

51 What I wonder is [_{clause} *whether we could take it further*].

52 But the only surprising thing is [_{clause} *how few coronaries senior ministers suffer _*].

The clauses in (50), (51), and (52) are declarative, interrogative, and exclamative, respectively. The difference between this pattern and the one in the previous section is that the clause identifies the referent of the Subject, and hence has a predicative function (see section 4.1.3.3.1).

7.3.1.5 Content clauses functioning as Adjunct

Content clauses functioning as Adjunct almost always display Subject–auxiliary inversion. Despite this, we regard them as declaratives. This is because the subordinate clauses can in all cases be paraphrased by using conditional *if*-clauses, which have a declarative word order. In the absence of *if*, Subject–auxiliary inversion marks the clauses as subordinate.

53 [_{clause} *Had I spent my time in some other hostelry*], I should now be returning to Oxford. (= (5))

54 That might not have mattered [_{clause} *had we continued to regard Europe as somebody else's problem*].

55 You can keep in touch with old friends (and enemies), and revisit old haunts [_{clause} *should you wish to*].

The example in (55) sounds slightly formal.

7.3.2 **Comparative clauses**

Before discussing comparative clauses we need to distinguish different cross-cutting types of comparisons. First, consider *scalar* and *non-scalar comparisons.* The former involve predicates on a scale, such as *hot* and *cold, old* and *young,* which can be preceded by words like *very.* The latter concern predicates that are normally not located on a scale, such as *(the) same* and *different* (though these can also occur as scalar predicates when modified by *more* or *much*). Next we distinguish comparisons of *equality* and *inequality.* The former are concerned with expressing parity between the terms that are compared in a particular respect, whereas the latter express non-parity. Finally, comparisons of inequality can be subdivided into *comparisons of superiority* and *comparisons of inferiority.*

We can apply these different types of comparisons to *comparative clauses.* Examples (italicized) are shown in Table 7.11.

	equality		inequality
scalar	(a) You can be as personal [$_{PP}$ as [$_{clause}$ *you like*]].	superiority	(b) Well your memory is better [$_{PP}$ than [$_{clause}$ *mine is*]].
		inferiority	(c) Leaf mould is less acid [$_{PP}$ than [$_{clause}$ *peat*]].
non-scalar	(d) The stretch of tablecloth in front of my companion looked the same [$_{PP}$ as [$_{clause}$ *mine did*]].	(e) The total flow from the well was different [$_{PP}$ than [$_{clause}$ *it was before the leak was found*]].	

Table 7.11: The scalar/non-scalar and equality/inequality contrasts

In (a) and (d) the comparisons of equality involve a comparative clause that functions as a Complement of the preposition *as,* whereas the comparisons of inequality in (b), (c), and (e) are Complements of *than.* In (b) the matrix clause expresses the fact that a particular property ('being good') applies to a higher degree to the addressee's memory than to the speaker's. We refer to this as a *comparison of superiority,* which is a subtype of comparison of inequality. Example (56) below also involves a comparison of superiority, despite appearances. The adjective *shorter* here means 'short to a greater degree than something else'. Note that the conflict referred to may in fact have been very long.

56 The conflict has proved shorter [PP than [clause *so many people predicted*]].

In (c) in Table 7.11 we have a *comparison of inferiority*, another sub-type of comparison of inequality. This involves the word *less*. The meaning here is that leaf mould is acid to a lesser degree than peat.

A very notable feature of comparative clauses is that they involve *reduction*, which is sometimes obligatory. It is possible for only one constituent to remain in the comparative clause, as in (c) in Table 7.11 and in (57) and (58) below, where only NPs remain.

57 My still life studio is as big [PP as [clause *this room*]] actually.

58 My dad is bigger [PP than [clause *your dad*]].

In the examples we have looked at so far the matrix clause conforms to the pattern Subject + Predicator + Subject-related Predicative Complement, where the Predicative Complement is an adjective phrase. Other patterns are also possible. Thus in (59) the comparative clause is part of an adverb phrase in the matrix clause, and in (60) it is part of an NP.

59 Standard Oil got its money back [AdvP a damn sight quicker [PP than [clause *most tax rebates come through*]]].

60 It's got [NP more contours [PP than [clause *mine has*]]] actually.

7.3.3 Relative clauses

The third class of finite subordinate clauses are called *relative clauses*. These are clauses that provide additional information about the Head noun to which they are linked, called the *antecedent*.

7.3.3.1 *Wh* relative clauses

In the examples below the bracketed relative clauses are introduced by the underlined relative pronouns *who(m)* and *which* (section 3.2.2.3).

61 And she told me that my **father**, [clause [NP <u>*who*</u>] *had died many years before*], was standing by my side.

62 The only **colleague**, [clause [NP _whom_] I knew _ already], was the social and physical geographer Doctor Dudley Stamp.

63 This is a dance **group** [clause [NP _which_] does not exclude people].

The relative pronouns function as the Head of *simple relative phrases* which consist of only one word. Because relative pronouns are nouns, the simple relative phrases are noun phrases. We refer to the *wh*-word in each of these examples as the *relativized element*. This is the element inside a relative phrase that takes the noun in bold as its antecedent.

Relative phrases can perform a variety of functions in relative clauses. Thus in (61) and (63) they function as Subject, while in (62) the relative phrase functions as the Direct Object of the verb KNOW and is associated with the gap indicated by '_' (see sections 3.2.2.3 and 6.2.1 on gaps). Notice that the pronoun takes accusative case (section 2.2.2.2). Using *who* in such constructions is equally acceptable.

The examples below involve *complex relative phrases*, that is, relative phrases that contain more than one word. They are typically NPs, AdjPs, or PPs within which the relativized elements are contained. As before, in the following examples the nouns in bold are the antecedents of the underlined relativized elements.

64 I've got a **friend** [clause [NP _whose_ parents] are Catholic].

65 You will go through a series of basic **manoeuvres** [clause [NP the routine of _which_] will become the foundation of your road riding technique].

66 Over the course of two decades, 1965-85, he undertook major construction **projects** in Saudi Arabia, [clause [AdjP most important among _which_] were the oil refinery and port installations at Rabigh on the Red Sea and King Fahd's palace and adjacent missile base at Riyadh].

67 The Family Practitioner **Committee** [clause [PP to _whom_] your form will be sent _] may check your claim.

68 Those few **minutes** of her life, [clause [PP of _which_] she was then conscious _], are lost to her memory.

In (64) the word *whose* is a relative pronoun in the genitive form which functions as a Determiner in the complex relative noun phrase *whose parents*. In (65)–(68) the relativized element is the Complement of a preposition. Where there are gaps they are associated with the relative phrase as a whole. Thus the gap after *sent* in (67) is associated with *to whom*, and the gap after *conscious* in (68) is associated with *of which*.

Recall that words like *when, where, while,* and so on are treated as prepositions in this grammar (see section 5.5.1). This means that in the following examples the underlined relativized elements are intransitive prepositions heading PPs. They function as Adjunct in the relative clauses, and are associated with the positions indicated by '_'.

69 In the **period** [clause [PP *when*] *he was writing in the fifties* _], he was reaching the climax of his career.

70 Nothing is put away and nothing really has a fixed **place** [clause [PP *where*] *it is kept*_].

The word *why* in (71) is the Head of an adverb phrase, associated with the gap indicated by '_'.

71 The **reason** [clause [AdvP *why*] *a revived Halloween is approved* _] is because it is a massive new advertising opportunity, in particular in the children's market.

Finally, in *sentential relative clauses*, the relativized element does not have a noun as its antecedent, but an entire clause. Here is an example.

72 I feel at home in Virginia, [clause *which is odd*].

7.3.3.2 Non-*wh* relative clauses

Relative clauses can also be introduced by the word *that*, as in (73) and (74) below.

73 The **power** [clause *that enables this union*] Coleridge categorized as the imagination.

74 The **nature** of the work [clause *that we do*] is no different from any other creative arts group.

In this grammar we analyse *that* as a subordinating conjunction. We do not regard it as a relative pronoun because pronouns can function as the Complements of prepositions (cf. *to whom/to which*), whereas the conjunction *that* cannot (cf. **the person to that...*).

Even though there is no overt relativized element in (73) and (74), it makes sense to say that there are *implicit* relativized elements present in these cases, indicated by '$\emptyset_{rel.}$' in (75) and (76), which have the nouns in bold type as their antecedents.

75 The **power** [$_{clause}$ *that $\emptyset_{rel.}$ enables this union*] Coleridge categorized as the imagination.

76 The nature of the **work** [$_{clause}$ *that we do $\emptyset_{rel.}$*] is no different from any other creative arts group.

In (75) the implicit relativized element functions as Subject, whereas in (76) it is a Direct Object, positioned after the verb DO. When the implicit relativized element is associated with a non-Subject gap, as in (76), *that* can be omitted.

7.3.3.3   Restrictive and non-restrictive relative clauses

Consider the examples below.

77 Successive surges of **violence**, [$_{clause}$ *which swept through jails on a single night in 1986*], have focused attention on living conditions.

78 The **cycle** [$_{clause}$ [$_{NP}$ *which*] *you ordered _*] is now complete and ready for collection.

In (77) and (78) the relative clauses are introduced by the relative pronoun *which*. There is a difference between (77) and (78) with regard to the information that the relative clauses impart. The former involves a *non-restrictive relative clause*. Such clauses are often (though not always consistently) set apart by commas. When the clause is uttered, a lower pitch is used for the relative clause. The example in (78) contains a *restrictive relative clause* which is not set off by commas, and is not uttered at a lower pitch. The difference is subtle, but important. The non-restrictive relative clause in (77) merely furnishes additional information about the violence in question, whereas the restrictive relative clause in (78) provides identifying information about the cycle: it is the one that was ordered by the addressee. The subordinating conjunction *that* is generally used in restrictive relative clauses, whereas *who/which* can be used in both restrictive and non-restrictive relative clauses, though this is by no means a hard-and-fast rule. Notice that the relative clause in (78) could also have been introduced by *that*.

The restrictive/non-restrictive distinction also applies to relative clauses introduced by *who*. An example of a restrictive relative clause with *who* is shown in (79), whereas (61) and (62) above contain non-restrictive relative clauses with *who*.

79 He's the guy [clause *who is supposed to have left*].

7.3.3.4 Non-finite relative clauses

Relative clauses can also be non-finite. I discuss some examples here, rather than in Chapter 8 on non-finite subordinate clauses, so as to be able to discuss all relative clause types in one place.

80 If required the user may have only two **squares** [clause *from which Ø to select _*].

81 The point the Tories seem to be making is that anything is better than going to the sort of university that most graduates go to, and if you can't go to Oxford and Cambridge the best **thing** [clause *Ø to do _*] is not to go anywhere.

The bracketed relative clauses in (80) and (81) are relative *to*-infinitive clauses, both with an implicit Subject (indicated by 'Ø'), though in (81) we can add a Subject preceded by the subordinating conjunction *for*, as shown in (82).

82 … the best **thing** [clause *for you to do*]…

Notice that (80) contains a *wh*-phrase headed by *which* functioning as the Complement of the preposition *from*, but (81) does not contain a *wh*-phrase.

Non-finite relative clauses can often be regarded as incomplete finite clauses, as in the examples below. Here the strings *who was*, *who are*, *which is*, and *which was*, respectively, can be said to have been omitted from the italicized relative clauses.

83 [NP The young **lady** [clause *sitting next to you*]] was wearing the T-shirt.

84 The one real problem is the number of [NP homeless **people** [clause *begging on the streets*]].

85 The Mansion House itself is [NP a fine neoclassical **building** [clause *sustained by a portico of six Corinthian columns*]].

86 Many head teachers believe [NP the national **curriculum**, [clause *introduced by the government two years ago to improve standards*]], has become too prescriptive.

In other cases, such as (87) below, an account of the structure of the non-finite relative clause in terms of clipping is less attractive, because verbs like RESEMBLE generally do not occur in the progressive construction.

87 Wealthy females would find the prospect of having an affair with [NP a **man** [clause *resembling a Swiss bank manager*]] irresistibly erotic.

Here the non-finite relative clause is an alternative version for *who resembles a Swiss bank manager*, not for *who is resembling a Swiss bank manager*.

7.3.3.5 Free relative clauses

We need to distinguish a special type of relative clause, namely *free relative clauses*, briefly discussed in section 3.2.2.4. These clauses are said to be 'free' because what characterizes them syntactically is the fact that there appears to be no overt Head for the relative clause to be anchored to. Within free relative clauses, bracketed in the examples below, the *wh*-phrase is headed by a *free relative pronoun* (section 3.2.2.4). As before, the *wh*-phrase is associated with a gap indicated by '_', unless it functions as Subject.

88 The point is you can do [*what* you like _].

89 [*What* Boccioni said _] was this: life is not a stationary thing.

90 This reinforces the earlier statement, that man is blind to [*what* he cannot see _].

91 You choose [*which* you prefer _].

92 You can also choose [*who* you wish _] to deal with your affairs after you have gone.

93 We bribe [*whoever* needs to be bribed] to get on that plane.

94 It makes for an enjoyable night just to try [*whichever* of the bars seems liveliest] and, on fine evenings, the partying goes on well into the early hours.

95 You forget the reason that you wanted to write [*whatever* you were writing _] to begin with.

As these examples show, free relative clauses can perform a variety of functions in the matrix clause, such as Subject, Direct Object, and Prepositional Complement.

Free relative clauses can perform the same grammatical functions as noun phrases, but they look like clauses by virtue of the fact that they always contain a tensed verb. In the examples above it is possible to explicitly mention the Head noun. Thus, we interpret (88) as in (96).

96 The point is you can do <u>that</u> *which* you like.

There is a sense in which the free relative pronoun *what* in (88) is the result of a fusion of *that* and *which* (*that which* > *what*). In (97) there are two instances of a Head and relative pronoun which have *not* fused into a free relative pronoun. The alternative version of (97) in (98) contains fused relative clauses.

97 But if you want a short answer to why the humanities matter, it's this: we repeat [~NP~ *that which* is worth repeating], and [~NP~ *that which* is in danger of being forgotten].

98 But if you want a short answer to why the humanities matter, it's this: we repeat [~clause~ *what is worth repeating*], and [~clause~ *what is in danger of being forgotten*].

As we saw in section 3.3.5, free relative clauses can also involve *free relative determinatives*, as the following example shows.

99 The cheapest option of all, however, is a set of four knife magnets that can be attached to the wall in [*whatever* arrangement you wish _].

Free relative clauses structurally resemble interrogative content clauses, but can often be distinguished from them by looking at the verb of the matrix clause. Compare (100) and (101).

100　I wondered [interrogative clause *what he said _*].

101　I rejected [free relative clause *what he said _*].

Because WONDER does not normally take an NP as Complement, and because free relative clauses resemble noun phrases in their distribution, the bracketed string in (100) must be an interrogative clause. Conversely, because REJECT cannot take a regular clause as Complement, but does take an NP as Complement (e.g. *he rejected the proposal*), the bracketed string in (101) must be a free relative clause. We can demonstrate that the subordinate clause in (100) is interrogative by paraphrasing it as in (102).

102　I wondered what is the answer to the question 'what did he say?'.

In the examples below the bracketed strings are also free relative clauses, and *when, whenever, where*, and *wherever* are *free relative conjunctive prepositions* (see sections 3.7.1 and 5.5.1.5 on conjunctive prepositions).

103　However, you can move your money [*when* you like], with no penalties or restrictions.

104　Louis XIV, it has been said, used to start a war [*whenever* he felt bored], and we seem to need a bit of risk to reduce ennui.

105　I put the straw in the glass and I put it [*where* he could sip it].

106　It's not a done deal that he can go [*wherever* he likes] given his record.

The motivation for this analysis is that the bracketed strings can be paraphrased, though not always equally easily, by a Head noun + relative clause structure. Thus (103) can be paraphrased as in (107).

107　You can move your money at a **time** [clause *when you like*].

However, these free relative clauses differ from the others we looked at because they do not occupy typical NP positions.

Free relative clauses also occur as components of pseudocleft constructions, which will be discussed in section 11.8.2.

Chapter 8

Non-finite and verbless subordinate clauses

This chapter will deal with non-finite subordinate clauses functioning as Complements or Adjuncts in verb phrases. Non-finite clauses that function as Complements or Adjuncts in other phrases were discussed in Chapter 5.

Recall from section 2.2.1.5 that we distinguish four types of non-finite clauses, as listed in Table 8.1. These clauses can perform various functions within the matrix clauses they are part of. They will be discussed in turn in sections 8.1–8.4.

Non-finite clauses
to-infinitive clause
bare infinitive clause
-ing participle clause
past participle clause

Table 8.1: Non-finite clauses

In section 8.5 I will discuss degrees of clause integration. Section 8.6 looks at the structure of clauses with one or more auxiliary verbs, and the final section in this chapter briefly discusses clauses that do not contain a verb.

8.1   *To*-infinitive clauses
. . . .

To-infinitive clauses can function as Subject, Direct Object, Complement Clause, Subject-related Predicative Complement, and Adjunct.

8.1.1 *To*-infinitive clauses functioning as Subject

In (1) and (2) below *to*-infinitive clauses function as the Subject of the matrix clause. Neither clause has an overt Subject of its own, though in both cases there is an implicit Subject, indicated by 'Ø', which is interpreted as 'people in general'. The *to*-infinitive clause in (2) is an infinitival interrogative clause introduced by a *wh*-phrase which is associated with the gap indicated by '_' (see sections 3.2.2.3 and 6.2.1 on gaps).

1 [clause Ø *To make moral judgements*] is to be judgemental.

2 [clause *What Ø to eat _ at Christmas*] is a difficult question.

In (3) and (4) the *to*-infinitive clauses also function as Subject of the matrix clause. This time they have a Subject of their own (underlined), and are introduced by the subordinator *for*. As example (5) shows, the Subject can be realized as a noun phrase headed by a pronoun in the accusative case.

3 [clause *For <u>those in the third age</u> to want a job*] is to go back on the system.

4 [clause *For <u>the roles</u> to be reversed*] would be a tragedy for many Conservative MPs and voters.

5 [clause *For <u>them</u> to know that Helen Duncan is not classed as a witch*] would be the icing on the cake.

Notice that the *to*-infinitive clause in (4) is passive.

8.1.2 *To*-infinitive clauses functioning as Direct Object

In the following sections I will use model verbs to discuss patterns in which *to*-infinitive clauses with or without a Subject of their own function as Direct Object.

8.1.2.1 The pattern 'WANT [clause (*for*) NP *to*-infinitive…]'

The verb WANT in the following example licenses a *to*-infinitive clause functioning as Direct Object with its own Subject (underlined).

6 I just want [clause *you to alter the scenario very slightly*].

We regard the NP *you* as the Subject of the subordinate clause, rather than as the Direct Object of the matrix clause, because it cannot become the Subject of a passive matrix clause, as (7) shows.

7 *You were wanted to alter the scenario very slightly by me.

Some matrix verbs allow the postverbal NP to take genitive case, as in (8) and (9), though this is rare. Genitive NPs cannot function as Direct Object, so this is further evidence for analysing the postverbal NPs in this pattern as Subjects.

8 I hate [clause *his always humiliating them*].

9 I love [clause *the President's continually defending the rights of students*].

The fact that the postverbal NP after WANT can take accusative case if it is headed by a pronoun that can have a case contrast, as in (10), is not a sufficient reason for assigning Direct Object status to it.

10 I just want *him to alter the scenario very slightly.*

Notice that the postverbal NP in (6) is not a semantic argument of the verb WANT (see section 4.2), but a Subject argument of ALTER. Thus in (6) it is not the case that 'I want you', but what I want is 'that you alter the scenario'. Consider also (11), which is the result of passivizing the bracketed clause in (6).

11 I just want [the scenario to be altered very slightly by you].

What is noteworthy about this example is that it means exactly the same as (6), despite the fact that the NP following the verb is different in the two examples. This again shows that the postverbal NP in (6) is not a semantic argument of WANT. As a final piece of evidence that the NP after WANT is not one of its arguments, consider (12) and (13).

12 Ideally we would want *there to be good contact between the child and both parents.*

13 It's been hot when you want *it to be cold, and cold when you want it to be hot.*

Because existential *there* and dummy *it* are meaningless (section 4.1.1.5) they cannot be regarded as semantic arguments of WANT. Put differently, WANT does not assign a semantic role to *there* and *it*.

In the pattern under discussion the syntactic analysis matches the semantic analysis. We will see below that this is not always the case for the patterns discussed.

A limited set of verbs occurring in this pattern take the subordinator *for* (see sections 3.9 and 7.2) before the postverbal NP, as in the examples below.

14 He rarely ventured beyond his small circle of friends, and his girlfriend complained about his reclusiveness – he always preferred [clause *for them to sit home*].

15 If you know that you are likely to be alone when you get off a bus at a remote destination, try to arrange [clause *for someone to meet you*].

16 On the one hand I admire his speed and agility, take pride in his stature as a genuine world-class player, rejoice in his 100 per cent Britishness, yearn [clause *for him to win Wimbledon*], and rather fancy his wife. On the other hand, he reminds me of a spoilt, rather sullen child.

Verbs that pattern like WANT are shown in Table 8.2.

'WANT [clause (*for*) NP to-infinitive...]'

The *to*-infinitive clause is the DO of the verb, and the NP is the Subject of the subordinate clause. The latter cannot become the Subject of a passivized matrix clause.

ACHE[+F]	LIKE
ARRANGE[+F]	LONG[+F]
CAN'T AFFORD[+F]	NEED
CAN'T BEAR[+F]	OPT[+F]
CAN'T STAND[+F]	PINE[+F]
CLAMOUR[+F]	PREFER[+F]
DESIRE	WANT[+F]
HATE[+F]	WISH[+F]
INTEND[+F]	YEARN[+F]

Verbs marked '[+F]' can occur with the subordinator *for*, sometimes obligatorily.

Table 8.2: Verbs occurring in the pattern 'WANT [clause (*for*) NP *to*-infinitive...]'

As before, it is important to be aware of the fact that if a verb appears in one of the tables in this chapter, this does not mean that it does not occur in any other pattern(s). For example, the verb INTEND can also license a Direct Object followed by a Complement Clause (e.g. *They intended John to write a book for her*); see section 8.1.3.3 below. WANT can also occur in the pattern described in the next section.

8.1.2.2 The pattern 'HESITATE [$_{clause}$ Ø *to*-infinitive…]': Subject control

In the examples below the *to*-infinitive clauses function as Direct Object, and do not have their own overt Subjects.

17 I$_i$ hesitate [$_{clause}$ Ø$_i$ *to mention this*].

18 I$_i$'d like [$_{clause}$ Ø$_i$ *to answer that in a slightly different way*].

We will say that in both cases the matrix clause Subject *controls* the implicit Subject of the subordinate clause (indicated by 'Ø'), in the sense that the referent of the matrix Subject determines the interpretation of the referent of the implicit Subject of the subordinate clause. The subscript indices ('$_i$') indicate coreference.

Verbs that behave like HESITATE are listed in Table 8.3.

'HESITATE [$_{clause}$ Ø *to*-infinitive…]'		
The *to*-infinitive clause is the Direct Object of the verb, and Ø is the implicit Subject of the *to*-infinitive clause. This Subject is interpreted as being coreferential with the Subject of the matrix clause.		
ASK	LIKE	REFUSE
BEG	LOVE	RESOLVE
DECLINE	MEAN	THREATEN
CAN'T BEAR	NEED	TRY
DEMAND	PLAN	UNDERTAKE
FORGET	PROCEED	VOW
HASTEN	PROMISE	WANT
HATE	PROPOSE	WISH

Table 8.3: Verbs occurring in the pattern 'HESITATE [$_{clause}$ Ø *to*-infinitive…]'

8.1.2.3   The pattern 'wonder [_clause_ *whether/wh*-phrase Ø *to*-infinitive...]': Subject control

In (19) the *to*-infinitive clause is a closed infinitival interrogative clause (cf. section 7.3.1.2.2 on finite subordinate interrogative clauses) introduced by *whether* (*if* is not possible here).

19 [_NP_ The more nervy pro-Europeans]_i_ have wondered [_clause_ *whether Ø_i_ to run for cover*].

Such clauses can also be of the open type, as in (20), introduced by a *wh*-phrase associated with the position indicated by '_'.

20 But now that we are taking the pirates on, does anyone_i_ know [_clause_ *what Ø_i_ to do _*] when we catch them?

In these examples the subordinate clauses function as Direct Object. As in the previous section these are cases of Subject control: we interpret the Subject of the subordinate clause (indicated by 'Ø') to be coreferential with the Subject of the matrix clause.

Verbs that pattern like wonder are shown in Table 8.4.

'wonder [_clause_ *whether/wh*-phrase Ø *to*-infinitive...]'		
The *to*-infinitive clause is the Direct Object of the verb and Ø is the implicit Subject of the *to*-infinitive clause. This Subject is interpreted as being coreferential with the Subject of the matrix clause.		
ASK	DISCUSS	NOTE
CHECK	ENQUIRE	NOTICE
CHOOSE	ESTABLISH	OBSERVE
CONSIDER	EXPLAIN	PONDER
DECIDE	FORGET	REMEMBER
DEMONSTRATE	JUDGE	SAY
DISCOVER	KNOW	SHOW

Table 8.4: Verbs occurring in the pattern 'wonder [_clause_ *whether/wh*-phrase Ø *to*-infinitive...]'

8.1.2.4   The pattern 'tell NP_i_ [_clause_ Ø_i_ *to*-infinitive...]': Indirect Object control

To-infinitive clauses can also function as Direct Object when they are preceded by an Indirect Object. Consider (21) below.

21 They told [$_{NP}$ *them*]$_i$ [$_{clause}$ *Ø$_i$ to gather round water holes*].

In this example the NP is an argument of the matrix clause and functions as its Indirect Object. Notice that the NP is headed by a pronoun in the accusative case. The *to*-infinitive clause does not have a Subject of its own, but we interpret the implicit Subject of the subordinate clause to be coreferential with the Indirect Object. This is a case of Indirect Object control.

The IO can become the Subject of a passive clause, as in (22).

22 They were told to gather round water holes.

PROMISE also occurs in this pattern, but with this verb the Subject of the subordinate clause is coreferential with the Subject of the matrix clause. With PROMISE we thus exceptionally have a case of Subject control.

23 [$_{NP}$ President Kibaki]$_i$ promised [$_{NP}$ *us*] [$_{clause}$ *Ø$_i$ to fight corruption*].

Here President Kibaki was the person who made a promise, such that he would fight corruption. (23) does not have a passive counterpart.

Verbs that occur in this pattern can also occur in the pattern V + IO + DO, where the IO and DO are noun phrases (e.g. *I told him a lie*).

Other verbs that can occur in this pattern are listed in Table 8.5.

'TELL NP$_i$ [$_{clause}$ *Ø$_i$ to*-infinitive...]'
The NP is the IO of the verb; the *to*-infinitive clause functions as DO. The IO can become the Subject of a passive matrix clause. The implicit Subject of the *to*-infinitive clause (Ø) is understood as being coreferential with the IO (except for PROMISE).

ASK	TEACH
PROMISE	TELL

The verb ASK can occur with or without an NP. When it occurs without an NP the clause functions as Direct Object, e.g. *I asked to leave*.

Table 8.5: Verbs occurring in the pattern 'TELL NP$_i$ [$_{clause}$ *Ø$_i$ to*-infinitive...]'

8.1.2.5 The pattern 'TELL NP$_i$ [$_{clause}$ *wh*-phrase Ø$_i$ *to*-infinitive...]': Indirect Object control

Some verbs can be followed by an Indirect Object in the shape of an NP and a Direct Object in the shape of an open interrogative clause, as in (24).

24 The Chinese, unsurprisingly, told [NP *her*]i [clause *what Øi to do _ with her suggestions*].

In this example the subordinate clause does not have a Subject of its own, but, as in section 8.1.2.4, we interpret the implicit Subject of the subordinate clause (indicated by 'Ø') to be coreferential with the Indirect Object. This is thus another case of Indirect Object control. The IO can become the Subject of a passive clause, as (25) shows.

25 Unsurprisingly, she was told what to do with her suggestions by the Chinese.

Verbs that occur in this pattern can also occur in the pattern V + IO + DO, where the IO and DO are noun phrases (e.g. *I told her a joke*).

In (26) we also have an Indirect Object in the shape of an NP (*me*) and a Direct Object in the shape of an interrogative clause. Notice, however, that this time the interrogative clause is of the closed type, and its implicit Subject is not controlled by the IO, but by the NP *anyone*, which functions as the Complement of the preposition *to*. *If* cannot be substituted for *whether* here. Only the verb ASK can license a closed non-finite interrogative clause after an IO in this unusual pattern.

26 "I'd say to [NP *anyone*]i who asked [NP *me*] [clause *whether Øi to join a street retreat*], 'Try it, wake up'," says Pierre Racine, 54, a psychologist and another retreater.

Verbs occurring in the pattern discussed in this section are shown in Table 8.6.

'TELL NPi [clause *wh*-phrase Øi *to*-infinitive…]'
The NP is the IO of the verb; the *to*-infinitive clause functions as DO. The IO can become the Subject of a passive matrix clause. The implicit Subject of the *to*-infinitive clause (Ø) is understood as being coreferential with the IO.

ASK	TEACH
SHOW	TELL

Some verbs can occur with or without an NP. When they do so the clause functions as Direct Object.

Table 8.6: Verbs occurring in the pattern 'TELL NPi [clause *wh*-phrase Øi *to*-infinitive…]'

8.1.3 *To*-infinitive clauses functioning as Complement Clause

The following patterns all involve clauses that function as Complement Clause. As we saw in Chapters 4 and 7, we assign this label to any clause that is licensed by a verb, but cannot be assigned one of the other Complement functions Direct Object, Indirect Object, or Predicative Complement.

8.1.3.1 The pattern 'PERSUADE NP$_i$ [$_{clause}$ Ø$_i$ *to*-infinitive…]': Direct Object control

Consider the structure in (27).

27 The Americans persuaded [$_{NP}$ *the UN*]$_i$ [$_{clause}$ *Ø$_i$ to impose the deadline*].

In this example the postverbal NP functions as a Direct Object, and the *to*-infinitive clause functions as a Complement Clause. Here the Direct Object controls the Subject of the subordinate clause. In other words, the referent of the implicit Subject of the *to*-infinitive clause is determined by the referent of the DO. The NP is an argument of the matrix clause verb. It functions as DO because it can become the Subject of a passive clause, as in (28).

28 The UN was persuaded to impose the deadline by the Americans.

If the postverbal NP is headed by a pronoun that can have a case contrast, it must take accusative case, as (29) shows.

29 The Americans persuaded *them* to impose the deadline for withdrawal.

In (27) the NP is a semantic argument of the matrix verb in this pattern because the UN was directly affected by the Americans' persuasion. Notice that we cannot have existential *there* or dummy *it* immediately following PERSUADE:

30 *Sarah persuaded *there* to be a meeting next week.

31 *Leon persuaded *it* to rain on Wednesday.

Compare (30)/(31) with (12)/(13). Furthermore, contrast (27) with (32).

32 *The Americans persuaded the deadline to be imposed by the UN.

In this case the string *the UN to impose the deadline* in (27) has been passivized, resulting in a structure that is unacceptable because one cannot persuade deadlines. This again shows that the postverbal NP in this pattern is an argument of the verb. Compare (27)/(32) with (6)/(11).

The verbs occurring in this pattern are not ditransitive (cf. section 8.1.2.4), because they cannot occur with an IO and DO realized as noun phrases, cf. *The thief persuaded the judge his innocence.* (Although this is acceptable with a PP, cf. *The thief persuaded the judge of his innocence*, the PP does not function as DO here, but as a PP Complement. See section 5.4.1.5.)

Verbs that pattern like PERSUADE are shown in Table 8.7.

'PERSUADE NP$_i$ [$_{clause}$ Ø$_i$ *to*-infinitive...]'

The NP is the DO of the verb and one of its semantic arguments; the *to*-infinitive clause functions as Complement Clause. The DO can become the Subject of a passive matrix clause. The implicit Subject of the *to*-infinitive clause (Ø) is understood as being coreferential with the DO.

ADVISE	INCITE
BEG	INSPIRE
BESEECH	INSTRUCT
CHALLENGE	INVITE
COMMAND	ORDER
COMPEL	PROMPT
DIRECT	REMIND
ENCOURAGE	REQUEST
ENTICE	TEMPT
ENTREAT	URGE
FORCE	WARN
IMPLORE	

Table 8.7: Verbs occurring in the pattern 'PERSUADE NP$_i$ [$_{clause}$ Ø$_i$ *to*-infinitive...]'

8.1.3.2 The pattern 'ADVISE NP$_i$ [$_{clause}$ *whether*/*wh*-phrase Ø$_i$ *to*-infinitive...]': Direct Object control

In the examples below the NPs function as Direct Object (they are arguments of the matrix clause verb), and the interrogative *to*-infinitive clauses (of the closed and open types) function as Complement Clause.

33 Please advise [NP *us*]i [clause *whether Ø*i *to turn the computer off or Ø*i *leave it on standby*].

34 No one has instructed [NP *me*]i [clause *what Ø*i *to prepare* _], but I have to produce a solid deck with a balance between bat and ball.

The subordinate clauses do not have a Subject of their own, but, as in section 8.1.3.1, we interpret the implicit Subjects of the *to*-infinitive clauses (indicated by 'Ø') to be coreferential with the Direct Objects. These are thus further cases of Direct Object control.

The verbs in this pattern are not ditransitive (cf. section 8.1.2.5) because they cannot occur with an IO and DO realized as noun phrases, cf. *He advised me a course of action*. (Although this is acceptable with a PP, cf. *He advised me of a course of action*, the PP does not function as DO here, but as a PP Complement. See section 5.4.1.5.)

Verbs occurring in this pattern are shown in Table 8.8.

'ADVISE NPi [clause *whether/wh*-phrase Øi *to*-infinitive...]'
The NP is the DO of the verb and one of its semantic arguments; the *to*-infinitive clause functions as Complement Clause. The DO can become the Subject of a passive matrix clause. The implicit Subject of the *to*-infinitive clause (Ø) is understood as being coreferential with the DO.

ADVISE	INSTRUCT	WARN
INFORM	REMIND	

Table 8.8: Verbs occurring in the pattern 'ADVISE NPi [clause *whether/wh*-phrase Øi *to*-infinitive...]'

8.1.3.3 The pattern 'INTEND NPi [clause Øi *to*-infinitive...]': raising to Object

Consider (35).

35 He intended [NP *them*]i [clause *Ø*i *to sell only 50 per cent of Test matches to satellite television*].

In this example the postverbal NP *them* is the Direct Object of the matrix clause verb INTEND, whereas the *to*-infinitive clause functions as Complement Clause. The implicit Subject of the *to*-infinitive clause (indicated by 'Ø') is understood as being coreferential with the DO.

The DO status of the postverbal NP becomes clear when we consider that it can become the Subject of a passive matrix clause:

36 They were intended to sell only 50 per cent of Test matches to satellite television.

What's more, notice that the postverbal NP in (35) is headed by a pronoun that takes accusative case.

In this pattern, although the postverbal NP is grammatically the DO of the matrix verb, semantically it is not one of its arguments. In other words, INTEND does not assign one of the semantic roles shown in Table 4.13 of section 4.2 (e.g. Agent, Patient, Experiencer) to its Direct Object. After all, 'he' did not intend 'them'; 'he' intended a situation to come about, namely 'their selling 50 per cent of Test matches'. Instead, the DO is assigned a semantic role by the lexical verb SELL inside the *to*-infinitive clause. We can demonstrate that the postverbal NP in (35) is not a semantic argument of the verb by taking a close look at (37) which involves a passive clause (*to be sold to satellite television by them*).

37 He intended only 50 per cent of Test matches to be sold to satellite television by them.

Here the Direct Object of INTEND is the NP *only 50 per cent of Test matches*. Importantly, notice that (37) means the same as (35). This means that the NP following INTEND cannot be one of its semantic arguments.

The grammaticality of the following example also shows that the postverbal NP position cannot be filled by an argument of INTEND.

38 I certainly intend *there* to be an increase in ranger and warden services to ensure that responsibilities are exercised by those who have the new right.

As noted before, *there* (along with dummy *it*) is meaningless, and cannot therefore be a semantic argument of the verb that precedes it.

The pattern 'INTEND NP [$_{clause}$ Ø *to*-infinitive]' differs in the above respects from the pattern 'PERSUADE NP [$_{clause}$ Ø *to*-infinitive]', discussed in section 8.1.3.1, in which the postverbal NP is a DO as well as a semantic argument of the matrix verb.

The verb INTEND is called a *raising-to-Object verb* because we can conceptualize the Subject of the subordinate clause as having been 'raised' to the Direct Object position of the matrix clause, as shown by the arrow in (39).

39 He intended [NP *them*]i [clause *Øi to sell only 50 per cent of Test matches to satellite television*].

The DO of a raising-to-Object verb is called a *raised Object*, which we define as an Object that does not receive a semantic role from the verb that licenses it (INTEND in (39)), but from a lexical verb inside a subordinate clause; in this particular case the verb SELL inside the *to*-infinitive clause. In this grammar we will use the arrow annotation as a way of visualizing the dual nature of the postverbal NP as the grammatical Direct Object of the matrix clause, and as the semantic Subject of the subordinate clause. There is no suggestion that the Subject of the subordinate clause has actually been displaced.

Other verbs that pattern like INTEND are shown in Table 8.9.

'INTEND NPi [clause Øi *to*-infinitive...]'

The NP is the raised Object of the verb, and it is not one of its semantic arguments; the *to*-infinitive clause functions as Complement Clause. The DO can become the Subject of a passive matrix clause. The implicit Subject of the *to*-infinitive clause (Ø) is understood as being coreferential with the DO.

ALLEGE	GUESS
ASSUME	JUDGE
BELIEVE	KNOW
CONCLUDE	MEAN
CONSIDER	PRESUME
DECLARE	PRONOUNCE
EXPECT	SUSPECT
FIND	UNDERSTAND

Table 8.9: Verbs occurring in the pattern 'INTEND NPi [clause Øi *to*-infinitive...]'

8.1.3.4 The pattern 'NP$_i$ SEEM [$_{clause}$ $\emptyset_i$ to-infinitive…]': raising to Subject

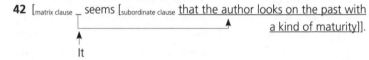

In the example below the subordinate clause functions as Complement Clause, and does not have an overt Subject.

40 [$_{NP}$ The author]$_i$ seems [$\emptyset_i$ *to look on the past with a kind of maturity*].

The matrix clause predicate in this example is the verb SEEM. Its Subject *the author* does not have a semantic role to play with respect to it, but only with respect to the verb in the subordinate clause, in this case LOOK. Put differently, SEEM does not assign a semantic role to its Subject. This becomes clear when we paraphrase (40) using a finite subordinate clause, as in (41), analysed as in (42).

41 It seems that the author looks on the past with a kind of maturity.

42 [$_{matrix\ clause}$ _ seems [$_{subordinate\ clause}$ <u>that the author looks on the past with a kind of maturity</u>]].

It

Here the Subject of the matrix clause (*that the author looks on the past with a kind of maturity*) has been extraposed, and is replaced by anticipatory *it* (section 3.2.2.1.2). This pronoun is meaningless, and hence by definition cannot carry a semantic role. The same point can be made by showing that another kind of semantically empty element can function as the Subject of *seem*, namely *there*, as (43) shows.

43 *There* seems to be a good repertoire about Lewis.

Now, notice that in (40) and (41) the NP *the author* is an Agent with respect to the verb LOOK. Bearing this in mind we can represent the structure of (40) as in (44), where the Subject of the matrix clause is associated with the Subject position in the subordinate clause (indicated by '$\emptyset$').

44 [$_{NP}$ <u>The author</u>]$_i$ seems [$_{clause}$ $\emptyset_i$ *to look on the past with a kind of maturity*].

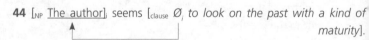

The verb SEEM is a *raising-to-Subject verb* because we can conceptualize the Subject of LOOK as having been 'raised' out of the subordinate clause to the matrix clause Subject position, as indicated by the arrow.

The Subject in this example is called a *raised Subject*, which we define as a Subject that does not receive a semantic role from the verb that follows it, but from a lexical verb inside a subordinate clause; in this particular example the verb LOOK inside the *to*-infinitive clause. As with raising-to-Object verbs we again use the arrow annotation, this time to visualize the dual nature of the clause-initial NP as the grammatical Subject of the matrix clause, and as the semantic Subject of the subordinate clause. Again, there is no suggestion that the Subject of the subordinate clause has actually been displaced.

Other verbs that pattern like SEEM are shown in Table 8.10.

'NP$_i$ SEEM [$_{clause}$ $\emptyset_i$ *to*-infinitive…]'

The matrix clause Subject is not one of the semantic arguments of the verb. The NP Subject has been 'raised' out of the *to*-infinitive clause from the position marked by the symbol '$\emptyset$'. The *to*-infinitive clause functions as Complement Clause.

APPEAR	LOOK
BEGIN	OUGHT
CEASE	PROVE
COMMENCE	START
CONTINUE	TEND
HAPPEN	TURN OUT

Table 8.10: Verbs occurring in the pattern 'NP$_i$ SEEM [$_{clause}$ $\emptyset_i$ *to*-infinitive…]'

8.1.4 *To*-infinitive clauses functioning as Subject-related Predicative Complement: the patterns 'BE [$_{clause}$ $\emptyset$ *to*-infinitive…]' and 'BE [$_{clause}$ *for* NP *to*-infinitive…]'

In (45) and (46) the *to*-infinitive clauses function as Subject-related Predicative Complement after the linking verb BE. In these examples the *to*-infinitive clauses do not have their own Subjects. The referents of the implicit Subject cannot always be retrieved from within the matrix clause. When they cannot they can usually be interpreted from the wider context.

45 Presumably the first job would be [$_{clause}$ $\emptyset$ *to mark them up*].

46 The immediate response of some senior American officers was [$_{clause}$ $\emptyset$ *to start planning a retaliatory strike against the Soviet Union*].

When the *to*-infinitive clause does have its own Subject, it must be preceded by *for*.

47 The idea was [clause *for me to see the material*].

48 The other option was [clause *for them to vote for the debate to be continued*].

8.1.5   *To*-infinitive clauses functioning as Adjunct

To-infinitive clauses functioning as Adjunct often express a purposive meaning. In (49) the bracketed clause has its own Subject (underlined), introduced by the subordinator *for*, whereas the clauses in (50)–(52) are Subjectless.

49 [clause *For <u>such a system</u> to be successful*], accurate mapping of a generic head model onto an actual head is required.

50 You will also get a voucher [clause Ø *to help you pay for your glasses or contact lenses*].

51 [clause Ø *To be fair*], I think people will take this into consideration.

52 I can't remember, [clause Ø *to be honest*].

The clausal Adjuncts typically appear in initial or final position.

8.2   Bare infinitive clauses
. . . .

Bare infinitive clauses can function as Direct Object, Complement Clause, and Subject-related Predicative Complement.

8.2.1   Bare infinitive clauses functioning as Direct Object: the pattern 'HAVE [clause NP bare infinitive...]'

In (53) the subordinate clause, which has a Subject of its own, functions as Direct Object. The NP in this pattern is not a semantic argument of the matrix verb. What (53) expresses is that something was brought about, namely 'that the Queen opened the refurbishment'.

53 "She entertained people like Melvyn Bragg, Cherie and Tony Blair and had [$_{clause}$ *the Queen open the refurbishment*]," said the source.

We do not analyse the postverbal NP as the DO because it cannot become the Subject of a passive clause:

54 *The Queen was had open the refurbishment.

However, a few verbs occurring in this pattern do allow matrix clause passivization, but *to* is then inserted. Compare (55) and (56).

55 Alcohol makes you feel invincible when you are most vulnerable.

56 You are made *to* feel invincible when you are most vulnerable by alcohol.

If the postverbal NP is headed by a pronoun that can take a case contrast, it must take accusative case, as (57) shows.

57 We let *him* keep the gun.

Verbs that occur in this pattern mostly carry the meanings of 'causation' and 'perception'. They are shown in Table 8.11.

'$_{HAVE}$ [$_{clause}$ NP bare infinitive…]'	
The clause is the Direct Object of the verb. The postverbal NP cannot become the Subject of a passive matrix clause; exceptions are marked '+P'.	
FEEL	MAKE[+P]
HAVE	NOTICE[+P]
HEAR[+P]	OBSERVE[+P]
HELP[+P]	SEE[+P]
LET	WATCH

Table 8.11: Verbs occurring in the pattern '$_{HAVE}$ [$_{clause}$ NP bare infinitive…]'

8.2.2 Bare infinitive clauses functioning as Complement Clause: the pattern 'NP$_i$ modal verb/dummy DO [$_{clause}$ Ø$_i$ bare infinitive…]': raising to Subject

In the examples below, the modal verbs license bare infinitive clauses functioning as Complement Clause. The bare infinitive clauses do not have an overt Subject: these have been raised to the Subject position of the matrix clause. We understand the implicit Subjects of the subordinate clauses as being coreferential with the matrix clause Subjects.

58 She$_i$ can [$_{clause}$ $\emptyset_i$ *come with Anna and Peter*].

59 They$_i$ will [$_{clause}$ $\emptyset_i$ *make a decision*].

60 I$_i$ might [$_{clause}$ $\emptyset_i$ *do that tomorrow*].

61 You$_i$ must [$_{clause}$ $\emptyset_i$ *have been a very fast driver*].

Notice that it is possible for the bare infinitive verb to be realized as another auxiliary verb, as in (61), where it is the perfect auxiliary HAVE. (See section 8.6 for a discussion of sequences of auxiliary verbs.)

Dummy DO also occurs in this pattern, as in (62).

62 Poet Gavin Ewart said: 'In the old days [$_{NP}$ the Poet Laureate]$_i$ did [$_{clause}$ $\emptyset_i$ *write for royal weddings and birthdays*] and they were usually set to music.'

The modal verbs and dummy DO are analysed as raising verbs because the matrix clause Subject bears a semantic role vis-à-vis the verb in the subordinate clause (e.g. COME in (58)), not the matrix clause verb (CAN in (58)). Notice that we can paraphrase (58) as in (63).

63 It is possible [$_{clause}$ *for her to come with Anna and Peter*].

Verbs occurring in this pattern are shown in Table 8.12.

'NP$_i$ modal verb/dummy DO [$_{clause}$ $\emptyset_i$ bare infinitive...]'
The bare infinitive clause functions as Complement Clause; its Subject has been 'raised' from the bare infinitive clause to the matrix clause Subject position. The implicit Subject of the subordinate clause is understood as being coreferential with the matrix clause Subject.

CAN/could	WILL/would
MAY/might	MUST
SHALL/should	DO/did

Table 8.12: Verbs occurring in the pattern 'NP$_i$ modal verb/dummy DO [$_{clause}$ $\emptyset_i$ bare infinitive...]'

8.2.3 **Bare infinitive clauses functioning as Subject-related Predicative Complement: the pattern 'BE [clause Ø bare infinitive...]'**

Bare infinitive clauses can function as Subject-related Predicative Complement only with the verb BE. Here are some examples.

64 What you₍ᵢ₎ do is [clause Ø*ᵢ wear it like that*].

65 And all you₍ᵢ₎ have to do is [clause Ø*ᵢ write a rule that says PP goes to PNP*].

Notice that the bare infinitive clauses do not have their own Subjects, but we understand their implicit Subjects as being coreferential with a noun phrase higher up in the matrix clause.

8.3 ***-Ing* participle clauses**
. . . .

-Ing clauses can function as Subject, Direct Object, Complement Clause, Subject-related Predicative Complement, Object-related Predicative Complement, and Adjunct.

8.3.1 ***-Ing* participle clauses functioning as Subject**

-Ing participle clauses can occur with a Subject of their own (underlined), as in (66), or without, as in (67). In the latter case the referent of the implicit Subject is either recoverable from the context, or has a general interpretation ('for *people* to get aid through').

66 [clause <u>*Thurn and Taxis*</u> *having wrongful monopoly of the European postal system in the past*] caused Trystero to claim to have been disinherited.

67 [clause Ø *Getting aid through*] is a nightmare.

8.3.2 ***-Ing* participle clauses functioning as Direct Object**

-Ing participle clauses can function as Direct Object with or without their own Subject.

8.3.2.1   The pattern 'REMEMBER [$_{clause}$ Ø -*ing* participle...]'

In (68) below the -*ing* participle clause functions as Direct Object.

68 I$_i$ remember [$_{clause}$ Ø$_i$ *passing out in Sainsbury's once*].

In this case we again say that the subordinate clause has an implicit Subject which we interpret to be coreferential with the Subject of the matrix clause. In other words, the speaker is doing the remembering as well as the passing out. However, consider next the example in (69).

69 This role of corporation shouter is a long and honourable one, though probably not dating back to the days of Lord Reith, who discouraged [$_{clause}$ Ø *shouting at politicians*], even by reporters in evening dress.

Here the interpretation of the implicit Subject is not recoverable from the clause, but is interpreted as 'people in general'.

Other verbs occurring in the pattern under discussion are shown in Table 8.13.

'REMEMBER [$_{clause}$ Ø -*ing* participle...]'		
The -*ing* participle clause is the DO of the verb, and Ø is an implicit Subject coreferential with the matrix clause Subject, or the referent of the implicit Subject is unrecoverable from the clause.		
ACKNOWLEDGE	CONSIDER	NEGLECT
ADMIT	DENY	PREFER
ATTEMPT	DETEST	PROPOSE
AVOID	FINISH	QUIT
(NOT) BOTHER	HATE	REPORT
CAN'T BEAR	INTEND	RESENT
CAN'T STAND	LOATHE	RESIST
CONFESS	LOVE	RESUME

Table 8.13: Verbs occurring in the pattern 'REMEMBER [$_{clause}$ Ø -*ing* participle...]'

8.3.2.2   The pattern 'RECOMMEND [$_{clause}$ NP/NP's -*ing* participle...]'

In this pattern the -*ing* participle clause again functions as Direct Object. This time it takes either a regular noun phrase as its Subject, as in (70), or a genitive NP, as in (71).

70 The administrators recommended [clause *Jill carrying out this project*].

71 Other community countries would accept [clause *Britain's delaying a decision on joining a single currency until after the next election*].

Structures with genitival Subjects are not very frequent and considered formal. The genitive inflection *-'s* in (71) could be left out without a perceptible difference in meaning. We are regarding the NPs *Jill* and *Britain's* as being part of the subordinate clauses in (70) and (71), and not as Direct Objects of the verbs RECOMMEND and ACCEPT. This is because these NPs cannot become the Subject of a passive clause, as the ungrammaticality of (72) and (73) below shows.

72 *Jill was recommended carrying out this project by the administrators.

73 *Britain's would be accepted delaying a decision on joining a single currency until after the next election by other community countries.

Notice, however, that the *-ing* participle clause as a whole *can* become the Subject of a passive clause. This is a DO-like property.

74 [Jill carrying out this project] was recommended by the administrators.

75 [Britain's delaying a decision on joining a single currency until after the next election] would be accepted by other community countries.

A special construction appears in (76).

76 Bob, you need [clause *your head examining*].

The *-ing* participle clause in this infrequent construction has a passive flavour, given that *your head* is interpreted as the Direct Object of the verb EXAMINE: 'you need your head to be examined'.

Other verbs that pattern like RECOMMEND and ACCEPT are shown in Table 8.14.

8.3.2.3 The pattern 'CALL [clause NP/Ø *-ing* participle...] NP/AdjP/PP'

In this unusual pattern the *-ing* participle clause functions as Direct Object, and the following noun phrase, adjective phrase, or prepositional phrase functions as Object-related Predicative Complement. The subordinate clause can have an explicit or implicit Subject; the latter is interpreted as 'someone'.

'RECOMMEND [clause NP/NP's -*ing* participle...]'

The -*ing* participle clause is the DO of the verb, and NP/NP's is the Subject of the -*ing* participle clause which cannot become the Subject of a passivized matrix clause.

CAN'T BEAR	NEED
CAN'T STAND	PRECLUDE
CELEBRATE	PREFER
CONTEMPLATE	PREVENT
FORESEE	PROHIBIT
GET^{-G}	REMEMBER
HATE	RESENT
HAVE^{-G}	START^{-G}
KEEP^{-G}	STOP
LOATHE	TOLERATE
LOVE	WELCOME

Verbs marked '-G' cannot be followed by a genitive NP.

Table 8.14: Verbs occurring in the pattern 'RECOMMEND [clause NP/NP's -*ing* participle...]'

77 They do not regard [clause *John/John's fiddling with expenses*] [PP *as ethical*].

78 Do you call [clause Ø *doodling pictures on a wall*] [NP *art*]?

Notice that it is the Complement of the preposition *as*, not the PP as a whole, that ascribes a property to the situation described in the -*ing* participle clause in (77).

8.3.3 -*Ing* participle clauses functioning as Complement Clause

-*Ing* participle clauses can function as Complement Clause in a number of patterns.

8.3.3.1 The patterns 'PREVENT NP$_i$ [PP *from* [clause Ø$_i$ -*ing* participle...]]' and

'REGARD NP$_i$ [PP *as* [clause Ø$_i$ -*ing* participle...]]': raising to Object

In the first of these patterns the postverbal NP functions as the raised Object of the verb, whereas the PP headed by *from* functions as a Complement of the verb. The -*ing* participle clause functions as a Complement of the preposition *from*. The verbs in this pattern are often referred to as expressing 'negative causation'. (79) and (80) are analysed as in (81) and (82).

79 The state prevented you from teaching.

80 Other conditions prohibited him from entering any club or premises providing sporting facilities for women.

81 The state prevented [$_{NP}$ *you*]$_i$ [$_{PP}$ *from* [$_{clause}$ *$\emptyset_i$ teaching*]].

82 Other conditions prohibited [$_{NP}$ *him*]$_i$ [$_{PP}$ *from* [$_{clause}$ *$\emptyset_i$ entering any club*

or premises providing sporting
facilities for women]].

The NPs can become the Subject of a passive matrix clause, as (83) and (84) show.

83 You were prevented from teaching by the state.

84 He was prohibited from entering any club or premises providing sporting facilities for women by other conditions.

When the postverbal NP is headed by a pronoun that can have a case contrast it must take accusative case; genitive case is impossible.

85 The state prevented him from teaching.

86 *The state prevented his from teaching.

If we leave out the preposition *from*, the verbs occur in the pattern 'RECOMMEND [$_{clause}$ NP/NP's -*ing* participle...]', discussed in section 8.3.2.2, with NP/NP's functioning as the Subject of the -*ing* participle clause, and the clause as a whole functioning as DO. The meaning does not change.

87 The state prevented [$_{clause}$ [$_{NP}$ *you*] *teaching*].

88 Ballet dancing was her first choice of career, but a horse-riding accident prevented [$_{clause}$ [$_{NP}$ *her*] *pursuing that ambition*].

The verb KEEP is exceptional in this regard. Thus, omitting *from* in (89) leads to an opposite meaning in (90).

89 While the pilot quickly leveled the plane off after the bird strike to *keep it from stalling* and thought about where to land, the co-pilot kept trying to restart the engines.

90 While the pilot quickly leveled the plane off after the bird strike to *keep it stalling* and thought about where to land, the co-pilot kept trying to restart the engines.

Notice that the examples in (87) and (88) have no passive counterparts, as (91) and (92) show.

91 *You were prevented teaching by the state.

92 *She was prevented pursuing that ambition by a horse-riding accident.

Other verbs that pattern like PREVENT are shown in Table 8.15.

'PREVENT NP$_i$ [$_{PP}$ *from* [$_{clause}$ Ø$_i$ -*ing* participle…]]'

The NP is the raised Object of the verb, because it is not one of its semantic arguments; the -*ing* participle clause functions as Complement of the preposition *from*. The DO can become the Subject of a passive matrix clause. The implicit Subject of the -*ing* participle clause (indicated by 'Ø') is understood as being coreferential with the DO. The preposition *from* can be left out without a change in meaning, except in the case of KEEP.

KEEP	PROHIBIT	STOP

Table 8.15: Verbs occurring in the pattern 'PREVENT NP$_i$ [$_{PP}$ *from* [$_{clause}$ Ø$_i$ -*ing* participle…]]'

The second pattern discussed in this section is very similar to the pattern with PREVENT, except that the meaning of the verb does not involve 'negative causation'. It is fairly rare. Some examples are given in (93) and (94), and verbs occurring in the pattern are shown in Table 8.16.

93 However, the poor performance of Freshfields' junior recruits will amuse other sectors of the City that have long regarded [$_{NP}$ *lawyers*]$_i$ [$_{PP}$ *as* [$_{clause}$ Ø$_i$ *lacking commercial awareness*]].

94 Inge kept his professional attitude even though the Tigers treated [$_{NP}$ *him*]$_i$ [$_{PP}$ *as* [$_{clause}$ Ø$_i$ *being less than valuable last season*]].

'REGARD NP$_i$ [$_{PP}$ *as* [$_{clause}$ Ø$_i$ -*ing* participle...]]'

The NP is the raised Object of the verb, because it is not one of its semantic arguments; the -*ing* participle clause functions as Complement of the preposition *as*. The DO can become the Subject of a passive matrix clause. The implicit Subject of the -*ing* participle clause (indicated by 'Ø') is understood as being coreferential with the DO.

CONSIDER	REGARD	TAKE	TREAT

Table 8.16: Verbs occurring in the pattern 'REGARD NP$_i$ [$_{PP}$ *as* [$_{clause}$ Ø$_i$ -*ing* participle...]]'

8.3.3.2 The patterns 'FIND NP$_i$ [$_{clause}$ Ø$_i$ -*ing* participle...]' and 'DESCRIBE NP$_i$ [$_{PP}$ *as* [$_{clause}$ Ø$_i$ -*ing* participle...]]': object control

As with *to*-infinitive clauses we need to distinguish structures like (71), repeated here as (95), with a genitive Subject in the subordinate clause, from superficially similar structures like (96).

95 Other community countries would accept [$_{clause}$ *Britain's delaying a decision on joining a single currency until after the next election*].

96 Mary-Jane found [$_{NP}$ *me*]$_i$ [$_{clause}$ Ø$_i$ *lying on top of the bed*].

In (96) the noun phrase *me* is a semantic argument of the verb FIND, and functions as its Direct Object. It controls the reference of the implicit Subject of the -*ing* participle clause which functions as Complement Clause. The fact that *me* is a DO is clear from the fact that it is a pronoun carrying accusative case, and from the fact that this NP can become the Subject of a passive clause, as in (97). It cannot take genitive case.

97 I was found lying on top of the bed by Mary-Jane.

Other verbs like FIND are shown in Table 8.17.

Some verbs take an NP and PP as Complements. The Head of the PP is *as* which takes a subordinate clause with an implicit Subject as its Complement. Two examples are shown below.

98 Witnesses described [$_{NP}$ *it*]$_i$ [$_{PP}$ *as* [$_{clause}$ Ø$_i$ *being like a bayonet and up to 10in long*]].

'FIND NP$_i$ [$_{clause}$ Ø$_i$ -*ing* participle...]'
The NP is the DO of the verb, and the -*ing* participle clause functions as Complement Clause. The DO can become the Subject of a passive matrix clause. Ø is the implicit Subject of the -*ing* participle clause, coreferential with the DO.

CATCH	OBSERVE
DISCOVER	OVERHEAR
FEEL	PORTRAY
HEAR	SEE
NOTICE	WATCH

Table 8.17: Verbs occurring in the pattern 'FIND NP$_i$ [$_{clause}$ Ø$_i$ -*ing* participle...]'

99 A man who identified [$_{NP}$ *himself*]$_i$ [$_{PP}$ *as* [$_{clause}$ Ø$_i$ *having worn one of the costumes*]] sought to put the stunt in context in an interview with Roanoke's WSLS News (Channel 10).

This structure resembles the pattern in section 8.3.3.1, but it does not involve a raised Object. Participating verbs are shown in Table 8.18.

'DESCRIBE NP$_i$ [$_{PP}$ *as* [$_{clause}$ Ø$_i$ -*ing* participle...]]'
The NP is the DO of the verb, and the -*ing* participle clause functions as Complement of the preposition *as*. The DO can become the Subject of a passive matrix clause. Ø is the implicit Subject of the -*ing* participle clause, coreferential with the DO.

DIAGNOSE	RECOGNIZE
IDENTIFY	REMEMBER
PORTRAY	REPRESENT
PRAISE	SEE
QUOTE	

Table 8.18: Verbs occurring in the pattern 'DESCRIBE NP$_i$ [$_{PP}$ *as* [$_{clause}$ Ø$_i$ -*ing* participle...]]'

8.3.3.3 The pattern 'NP$_i$ BEGIN [$_{clause}$ Ø$_i$ -*ing* participle...]': raising to Subject

As we saw in section 8.1.3.4, *to*-infinitive clauses can function as Complement Clause in 'raising' constructions. The same is true for the -*ing* participle clause in the following example.

100 The company began grounding its planes last night.

We analyse this example as in (101).

101 [NP <u>The company</u>]ᵢ began [clause Øᵢ *grounding its planes last night*].

In this case the Subject of the matrix clause bears a semantic role vis-à-vis the lower verb GROUND, not the matrix verb BEGIN. For this reason we conceptualize the matrix clause Subject *the company* as having been 'raised' from the Subject position of the subordinate *-ing* participle clause, to the matrix clause Subject position. The fact that BEGIN is a raising verb becomes clear from the fact that it can take the meaningless word *there* as a Subject, as in *There began a party which lasted all night* (see section 11.6).

We will also regard the aspectual auxiliary BE in (102), analysed as in (103), as a raising verb, again because the matrix clause Subject bears a semantic role vis-à-vis the lower verb (ENTER), not the matrix verb.

102 America is entering an economic downturn.

103 [NP <u>America</u>]ᵢ is [clause Øᵢ *entering an economic downturn*].

The structure in (102) is the *progressive construction* (see sections 2.2.1.2, 3.6.3.3, and 9.3.2). Recall that it involves the aspectual auxiliary BE followed by a verb ending in *-ing*. The *-ing* participle clause again functions as Complement Clause.

Verbs that can take *-ing* participle clauses with a raised Subject are shown in Table 8.19.

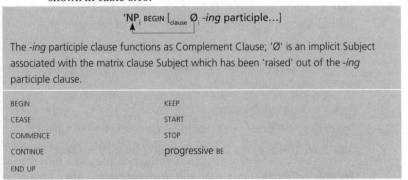

'NPᵢ BEGIN [clause Øᵢ *-ing* participle...]

The *-ing* participle clause functions as Complement Clause; 'Ø' is an implicit Subject associated with the matrix clause Subject which has been 'raised' out of the *-ing* participle clause.

BEGIN	KEEP
CEASE	START
COMMENCE	STOP
CONTINUE	progressive BE
END UP	

Table 8.19: Verbs occurring in the pattern 'NPᵢ BEGIN [clause Øᵢ *-ing* participle...]'

8.3.4   *-Ing* participle clauses functioning as Subject-related Predicative Complement

-Ing participle clauses can function as Subject-related Predicative Complement with or without a Subject of their own after the verb BE, as in (104) and (105), respectively. In (105) the referent of the Subject is not recoverable from the matrix clause, though it is likely to be interpreted as 'us'.

104 This is [clause *her being executrix to Pierce's will*].

105 The difficulty is [clause *Ø producing the quantity we may need at exactly the right moment*].

8.3.5   *-Ing* participle clauses functioning as Object-related Predicative Complement

In (106) *that* is an NP functioning as Direct Object, whereas the italicized clause, which lacks an overt Subject, functions as Object-related Predicative Complement. The referent of the implicit Subject is not recoverable from the matrix clause.

106 The Israelis call [NP *that*] [clause *Ø restoring the army's deterrent power*].

8.3.6   *-Ing* participle clauses functioning as Adjunct

In the examples below the italicized *-ing* participle clauses do not play a role as participants in the overall structures. Instead, they function as Adjuncts providing circumstantial information.

107 [clause *Egyptian archaeological sites being what they are*], Hekekyan came across some stone object or monument almost everywhere where he put in a drill.

108 We muddled through, [clause *him asking questions*], [clause *me answering the best I could*].

109 Every Tuesday I[i] stood there, [clause *Ø[i] waiting by the door*].

Notice that in (107) and (108) the *-ing* participle clauses have Subjects of their own, and can be paraphrased as 'in view of what we expect Egyptian archaeological sites to be like', 'while he was asking questions', and 'while I was answering the best I could', respectively. The clause in (109) does not have a Subject of its own, though it is inferrable from the matrix clause. It can be paraphrased as 'while I was waiting by the door'.

8.4 Past participle clauses
· ·

Past participle clauses can function as Direct Object, Complement Clause, and Adjunct. Model verbs will again be used to discuss the various patterns.

8.4.1 Past participle clauses functioning as Direct Object: the pattern 'HAVE [clause NP past participle...]'

In (110) the past participle clause functions as Direct Object, and occurs with a Subject of its own (underlined).

110 I had [clause _my tonsils_ removed].

The subordinate clause is passive, witness the fact that we can add a *by*-phrase.

111 Mr. Gombossy said he had [clause _the column_ approved by his editor].

The underlined NPs in (110) and (111) are not the DOs of the matrix clause verbs because they cannot become the Subjects of passive matrix clauses.

112 *My tonsils were had removed.

113 *The column was had approved by his editor by him.

Although the NP after HAVE can take accusative case if it is headed by a pronoun which can have a case contrast, as in (114), this is not a sufficient reason for assigning Direct Object status to it (cf. the treatment of WANT in section 8.1.2.1).

114 He was held for almost nine months while the US attempted to have [clause _him_ extradited].

The NPs *my tonsils* and *the column* in (110) and (111) are not semantic arguments of the verb HAVE, but arguments of REMOVE and APPROVE. The meaning of (110) is not 'I had my tonsils', but 'I brought about that my tonsils were removed'. Similarly, (111) does not mean that 'he had the column', but 'he brought about that the column was approved by his editor'. In the pattern discussed in this section the syntactic analysis matches the semantic analysis.

We can relate the pattern with HAVE discussed here to the pattern in section 8.2.1. If we passivize the subordinate clause in (115), we derive (116).

115 She… had [$_{clause}$ *the Queen open the refurbishment*]. (=(53))

116 She… had [$_{clause}$ *the refurbishment opened by the Queen*].

However, this does not work for all verbs. Compare (117) and (118).

117 Local activist Jerry Rubin got [$_{clause}$ *the order approved by a judge*] on behalf of Santa Monica Treesavers.

118 *Local activist Jerry Rubin got [$_{clause}$ *a judge approve the order*] on behalf of Santa Monica Treesavers.

We can 'salvage' (118) by adding *to*:

119 Local activist Jerry Rubin got [$_{clause}$ *a judge <u>to</u> approve the order*] on behalf of Santa Monica Treesavers.

Verbs that can take past participle clauses functioning as Direct Object are shown in Table 8.20.

'HAVE [$_{clause}$ NP past participle…]' The past participle clause functions as Direct Object.	
FEEL	OBSERVE
GET	ORDER
HAVE	SEE
HEAR	WANT
LIKE	WATCH
NEED	

Table 8.20: Verbs occurring in the pattern
'HAVE [$_{clause}$ NP past participle…]'

8.4.2 Past participle clauses functioning as Complement Clause

8.4.2.1 The pattern 'NP_i HAVE [_{clause} Ø_i past participle…]: raising to Subject

This pattern instantiates the perfect construction which was discussed in section 2.2.1.2. It involves the perfect auxiliary HAVE followed by a verb ending in *-ed* (or *-(e)n* for some verbs).

120 I have informed the police of the theft.

121 I_i have [_{clause} Ø_i *informed the police of the theft*].

We assign the function Complement Clause to the participle clause in this pattern. As with the progressive construction discussed in section 8.3.3.3, we regard the aspectual auxiliary in this construction as a raising verb, because the noun phrase Subject of the matrix clause bears a semantic role vis-à-vis the verb INFORM in the subordinate clause. See also sections 3.6.3.3 and 9.3.1.

8.4.2.2 The pattern 'NP_i BE/GET [_{VP} past participle _…]: special raising to Subject

The clauses in (122) and (123) are passive constructions, which were already discussed in sections 2.2.1.2, 3.6.3.4, and 4.1.3.1.4. Recall that such constructions involve the passive auxiliaries BE or GET followed by a verb ending in *-ed/-(e)n*.

122 <u>Her head</u> was buried _ in Tommy's neck.

123 <u>No one</u> got killed _.

As noted in section 3.6.3.4, the underlined Subject NPs are associated with the Direct Object positions of BURY and KILL, respectively, as indicated by the symbol '_'. We can now expand on this analysis by observing that the underlined NPs do not receive a semantic role from BE and GET, but from BURY and KILL. We accordingly analyse these constructions as involving an NP raised from the Direct Object position inside the verb phrase to the matrix clause Subject position, as indicated in (124) and (125).

124 [_{NP} <u>Her head</u>]_i was [_{VP} *buried _ in Tommy's neck*].

125 [_{NP} <u>No one</u>]_i got [_{VP} *killed _*].

This type of raising is different from the raising to Subject pattern we encountered earlier, for example in section 8.1.3.4, where a Subject is raised to a matrix clause Subject position from inside a subordinate clause. In this section we are concerned with a noun phrase that is raised from an Object position inside a VP to the Subject position of the same clause. The bracketed string in this pattern is not a subordinate clause because it cannot have a Subject.

8.4.3 Past participle clauses functioning as Adjunct

Past participle clauses functioning as Adjunct can occur with a Subject (underlined), as in (126), or without a Subject, as in (127).

126 Seven villagers were arrested, [clause _their feet_ bound together with rope], and they hung upside down for hours.

127 [clause Ø Dressed in civilian clothes] they gave the impression of being members of a rabble army.

8.5 Degrees of clause integration

We need to recognize that subordinate clauses are subject to _degrees of clause integration_. Subordinate clauses that function as Complements of a particular Head are more closely integrated into the structure of the phrase in which they occur than clauses that function as Adjuncts. To make this clear, consider first the examples below, repeated from Chapters 5 and 7.

128 I detect in the United States' latest position [NP a realisation [clause that it is important to keep the United Nations Security Council consensus]].

129 Successive surges of **violence** [clause _which swept through 18 jails on a single night in 1986_], have focused attention on living conditions.

As we have seen, in (128) the content clause functions as Complement of the noun _realisation_ inside a noun phrase. The clause is a Complement because we can relate the noun _realisation_ to the verb REALISE. Compare (128) with _(They) realised that it is important to keep_ *the United Nations Security Council consensus.* In (129) we have a non-restrictive relative clause (section 7.3.3.3) which is optional, and merely furnishes non-essential information about the Head *violence*. This relative clause functions as an Adjunct inside the NP.

Similarly, in (130) and (131) the clauses function as Complement and Adjunct, respectively.

130 I think [clause *that's fascinating*].

131 I was taking you to Newton Abbot [clause *to catch a train*].

In (130) the content clause is licensed by the verb: we cannot say *I think* without further specification. In (131) the subordinate clause is not syntactically licensed: the overall structure would make perfectly good sense without it. It merely specifies some further information, in this case a purpose.

Recall that when we say that a clause is optional, we mean 'grammatically optional', in the sense that leaving it out does not lead to an ungrammatical structure.

8.6 The structure of clauses with one or more auxiliary verbs

Recall from section 3.6.3 that English distinguishes the following types of auxiliaries: modal auxiliaries, aspectual auxiliaries, passive BE, and dummy DO. Each of these auxiliaries can occur on their own in a clause, followed by a lexical verb, as in (132).

132 The agents *will* book the tickets. [modal + lexical verb]

However, it is quite common for clauses in English to contain a sequence of auxiliaries. In the examples below the auxiliaries are italicized, and the lexical verbs are underlined.

133 The agents *will have* booked the tickets. [modal + perfect HAVE + lexical verb]

134 The agents *will have been* booking the tickets. [modal + perfect HAVE + progressive BE + lexical verb]

135 The tickets *will have been being* booked by the agents. [modal + perfect HAVE + progressive BE + passive BE + lexical verb]

The pattern in (135) is unusual, though perfectly grammatical.

In any sequence of two or more auxiliaries they will always occur in the order shown in (136).

136 modal—perfect—progressive—passive—lexical verb

It is important to see that auxiliaries, occurring on their own with a lexical verb, or in a sequence, always determine the form of the verb that follows them.

- Modal auxiliaries are always followed by a bare infinitive form.

- Dummy DO is also always followed by a bare infinitive form.

- The perfect auxiliary HAVE is always followed by a past participle, i.e. a verb form ending in -*ed* (-*(e)n* for some verbs, e.g. *been, broken, eaten, forgotten, grown, mown*).

- The progressive auxiliary BE is always followed by an -*ing* participle form.

- The passive auxiliary BE, like the perfect auxiliary, is always followed by a past participle.

It is possible for one or more of the 'slots' in (136) to be skipped, but the observations regarding the order and inflectional shape of the verbs still hold.

137 The agents *will be* <u>booking</u> the tickets. [modal + progressive BE + <u>lexical verb</u>]

138 The agents *have* <u>booked</u> the tickets. [perfect HAVE + <u>lexical verb</u>]

139 The agents *are* <u>booking</u> the tickets. [progressive BE + <u>lexical verb</u>]

140 The agents *have been* <u>booking</u> the tickets. [perfect HAVE + progressive BE + <u>lexical verb</u>]

141 The tickets *were* <u>booked</u> by the agents. [passive BE + <u>lexical verb</u>]

142 The tickets *will be* <u>booked</u> by the agents. [modal + passive BE + <u>lexical verb</u>]

143 The tickets *will be being* <u>booked</u> by the agents. [modal + progressive BE + passive BE + <u>lexical verb</u>]

144 The tickets *will have been* <u>booked</u> by the agents. [modal + perfect HAVE + passive BE + <u>lexical verb</u>]

145 The tickets *were being* <u>booked</u> by the agents. [progressive BE + passive BE + <u>lexical verb</u>]

146 The tickets *have been* <u>booked</u> by the agents. [perfect HAVE + passive BE + <u>lexical verb</u>]

147 The tickets *have been being* <u>booked</u> by the agents. [perfect HAVE + progressive BE + passive BE + <u>lexical verb</u>]

I will return to a discussion of the meanings of some of these combinations in Chapters 9 and 10.

The ordering restrictions on auxiliaries, and the fact that they determine the form of the verb that follows them, leads us to conclude that they behave syntactically like lexical verbs to the extent that lexical verbs also license the Complements they take (if any). Thus, as we have seen, intransitive verbs are followed by nothing; transitive verbs can be followed by a Complement in the shape of an NP, clause, etc., and linking verbs are followed by Predicative Complements (NP, AdjP, etc.). We can now say that auxiliary verbs are followed by Complements in the shape of non-finite clauses which function as Complement Clause.

We can represent structures like those in (132)–(147) by using labelled bracketings, as shown below for examples (132) and (133). Each nested bracketing is a non-finite subordinate clause with an implicit Subject (indicated by 'Ø'), which is interpreted as being coreferential with the highest Subject (underlined). Recall from section 8.2.2 that the matrix clause Subject is a raised Subject.

148 [<u>The agents</u>]ᵢ [$_{VP}$ will [$_{clause}$ Øᵢ [$_{VP}$ book the tickets]]].

149 [<u>The agents</u>]ᵢ [$_{VP}$ will [$_{clause}$ Øᵢ [$_{VP}$ have [$_{clause}$ Øᵢ [$_{VP}$ booked the tickets]]]]].

These structures can be understood more readily if we use tree diagrams (see section 4.4). The tree for (148) looks like (150). A triangle is used when the internal structure of a constituent can be surmised from other parts of the tree, or is not at issue.

150

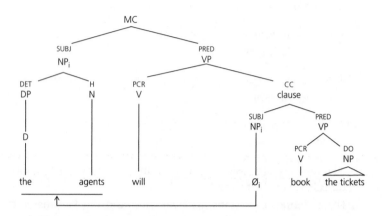

MC = matrix clause (here also a main clause); SUBJ = Subject; NP = noun phrase; DET = Determiner; DP = determinative phrase; D = determinative; H = Head; N = noun; PRED = Predicate; VP = verb phrase; PCR = Predicator; V = verb; CC = Complement Clause; DO = Direct Object

And here is the tree for (149).

151

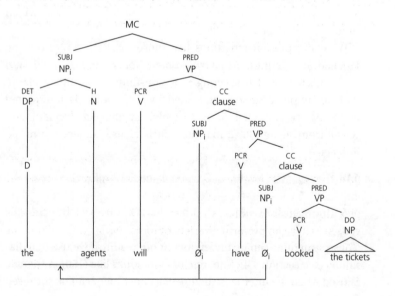

In these trees the verbs WILL and HAVE license a Complement Clause with an implicit Subject that is coreferential with the matrix clause Subject, whereas the verb BOOK takes a noun phrase as Direct Object.

8.7 Verbless clauses
. . . .

Consider the following examples which involve clauses without an overt verb.

152 She was born in 1896, daughter of a well-to-do and rigidly conventional family, [clause *her father* *a doctor*].

153 The atmosphere is that of a student house, with friends calling in and [clause *the teapot* *always full*].

154 The easiest way to remember correct roundabout procedure is to think of it as a crossroads with [clause *an island* *in the middle*].

155 "It's best for customers to enjoy their dinners while [clause Ø *at ease*]," said Takako Osuga, a restaurant manager who said she witnessed too many customers, especially old ones with brittle bones, having difficulty sitting on the floor.

156 No doubt Personnel will contact me if [clause Ø *necessary*].

157 Becket, [clause *himself* *a master of flamboyance and histrionics*], was actually killed in the north-west transept, on a spot called the Martyrdom.

In each of these cases we regard the italicized bracketed strings as clauses by virtue of the fact that the doubly underlined phrases within them function as Subject-related Predicative Complement which take the singly underlined phrases as their Subjects, or have an implicit Subject, as in (155) and (156). All these clauses are like complex intransitive structures (sections 4.1.3.3.1 and 5.4.1) involving the verb BE. They can perform a variety of functions such as Adjunct in (152), Complement of a preposition, as in (153)–(156), or parenthetical, as in (157). Although they have no verb, they are akin to non-finite clauses.

Part IV: Grammar and meaning

Chapter 9
Tense and aspect

In this part of the grammar I will discuss a number of topics that lie at the interface between grammar and meaning. In the present chapter I will discuss the notions of *tense* and *aspect* in sections 9.2 and 9.3, but we first turn to a very brief discussion of the notion of time.

9.1 Time

When we speak of time, we are talking about a real-world notion which we all experience as the hours, days, weeks, and years pass. It is defined by the *Concise Oxford English Dictionary* as 'the indefinite continued progress of existence and events in the past, present, and future, regarded as a whole'. As the *COED* definition indicates, we conceive of time as having three 'zones', past, present, and future, which we can represent on a 'timeline', as follows.

1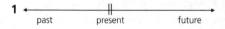

9.2 Tense

The term *tense* denotes a grammatical system which is used to locate *situations* in time. A situation is what a clause is about. As we will see in section 9.3.4.1, we can distinguish various types of situation, such as states, occurrences, processes, and achievements. The most basic distinction is between states and occurrences. States are unbounded, that is, they do not have a beginning and an end, whereas occurrences (which can be bounded or unbounded) are dynamic situations which come about. Languages locate situations in time most commonly by means of verbal inflections. Thus, when we read or hear (2), the past tense inflection on the verb indicates that the occurrence in question took place in the past. The Adjunct makes explicit exactly when the speaker arrived in Israel.

2 I *arrived* in Israel at two o'clock in the morning.

We can represent (2) as follows on a timeline.

3
arrival: 2 a.m.   present   future

It must be said at the outset that the inflectional system of tense in English is quite simple in allowing only a *present tense* and a *past tense*. English has no future tense, because it has no future tense inflections, in the way that many other languages do, nor any other grammatical form or combination of forms that can exclusively be called a future tense. This does not mean we cannot talk about the future: the English language offers various alternative ways of doing so, as we will see.

9.2.1 The present tense and its uses

In its basic use the English *present tense* encodes that a situation obtains at the present time, conceived of as the time of utterance. The present tense inflection is visible on lexical verbs in the third person singular, such as *walks*, *dances*, *falls*, *reads*, *leaves*, *hears*, as well as on the non-modal auxiliary verbs. Other present tense forms are in the plain present form. An exception is the verb BE, which has three distinct forms in its present tense paradigm (section 2.2.1.2).

In what follows we turn to the principal uses of the English present tense.

9.2.1.1 The 'state' use of the present tense

The present tense is often used to describe a situation that obtains within a span of time that includes the moment of utterance, and extends into the past and future.

4 I'*m* so tall and you'*re* so short.

5 This *means* that the amount of Family Credit you get *depends* on your normal net earnings.

6 He *speaks* 3 languages and *lives* all over Europe.

7 Well my cousin *is* housemaster at a private school.

8 It *faces* south and it *has* big rooms and it's a nice house.

So-called *psychological verbs*—verbs that describe cognitive states, such as THINK, BELIEVE, and KNOW—also often occur in the present tense.

9 I *think* those people are very quickly disabused of that notion.

10 This Government *believes* in the pound sterling.

11 He *knows* he will have only one chance.

12 I *wonder* if they've gone out.

The present tense is also commonly used to express a series of identical situations, that is, a habit.

13 She *wears* eight-inch, really high heels.

14 He *travels* to Manchester for music lessons.

In these cases the repeated situations can be viewed as making up a state.

The present tense can also describe a 'scientific truth', for example in mathematical formulae, or statements about the natural world, as in the examples shown below.

15 Seven times eight *makes* fifty-six.

16 Because of its salinity, seawater *freezes* at a slightly lower temperature than fresh water.

9.2.1.2 The 'instantaneous' or 'event' use of the present tense

The present tense forms of verbs can be used to describe an occurrence (event) that is simultaneous with the moment of speaking, for example in spontaneous commentaries on (sports and other) events, as in the examples below.

17 Carling *calls* for the ball inside his own half.

18 Tony Cotty *gets* his ninth goal of the season.

19 The band of the Scots Guards *continues* to entertain the crowd.

20 He *salutes* Her Majesty, *informs* her that the guards are ready to march off, and *trots* back to resume command of the parade.

21 And here *comes* the Northern Line.

Present tense verb forms are also often used for *performative verbs*, such as APOLOGIZE, NAME, and PROMISE. Such verbs can be used by speakers to perform the actions that the verbs denote.

22 I *apologise* for the very short notice.

23 I *name* this blog "An Editor's Blog".

24 I *promise* to think before I speak.

9.2.1.3 The historic present

In spontaneous speech, when recounting occurrences that happened in the past speakers can opt to portray those occurrences in a more lively way by using present tense verb forms, rather than past tense forms. This use of the present tense is called the *historic present*. In the example in (25) the speaker is describing occurrences as they unfold in a film, whereas in (26) the speaker recalls being told about the introduction of running contracts at the Bartlett. The verb form *tells* in (26) is equivalent to 'told me recently'. In both cases the use of a present tense form makes the reported occurrences sound more recent and relevant. We could say that in referring to past occurrences the present tense *recounts*, whereas the past tense *reports*.

25 He *goes* shooting off in the car up the road and he *has* to catch on to that electric bit, and then that flash of lightning *comes* and it *knocks* the thing down.

26 And Peter Lear from Personnel *tells* me that the Bartlett have introduced running contracts.

The examples above are from spoken English, but the historic present is also used in writing, both in more formal styles, as in (27), from an academic book entitled *Roman Imperial Themes*, and in informal styles, such as in the newspaper headline in (28).

27 Cicero constantly appealed to the sentiments of all Italy, and Virgil *celebrates* the prowess of the Italians who had resisted Aeneas, the prototype of the conquering Roman, and *looks* forward to the circumstances of his own day, when all had been reconciled and had become 'Latins of a single speech'.

28 Karpov *slips* up.

Notice how the author of (27) uses the past tense of the verb APPEAL to talk about Cicero, but present forms of the verbs CELEBRATE and LOOK to talk about Virgil. In setting up a contrast between Cicero and Virgil, the author seems to be more interested in Virgil, whose lasting legacy is the focus of interest here. In the newspaper headline in (28), the present tense form of the verb SLIP draws the reader into an account of a recent occurrence in a way that a past tense verb form could not do.

A variant of the historic present (arguably a separate use, sometimes called the *imaginary present*) is used in novels where present tense verb forms are often used to recount the occurrences as if they were happening right now. They make the writing more lively and direct. Some examples appear below.

29 Cathy *averts* her eyes from the tempting but calorie-laden toast and *picks* at the muesli.

30 She *rearranges* her nightdress and *falls* asleep almost immediately, thinking about how nice and safe she *is* lying here next to her husband.

Past tense forms of the italicized verbs would also have been perfectly possible in these examples.

9.2.1.4 The 'timeless' use of the present tense

In a number of contexts the present tense is used without referring to present time. These include general descriptions, descriptions of journeys or museum exhibits in travel guides, instructions in manuals, stage directions in plays, photo captions, and so on. Here are some examples.

31 A summary of the various operations involved in shaft construction is given in Table 1, which *shows* an anticipated project schedule extending for 34 weeks.

32 And then you *see* this beautiful marble statue of a naked Celt.

33 Gus *ties* his laces, *rises*, *yawns* and *begins* to walk slowly to the door, left. He *stops*, *looks* down, and *shakes* his foot.

34 Make sure it *sits* close to your body with the fastenings next to you.

9.2.1.5 The present futurate

In the following examples a present tense is used to refer to future time. We call this the *present futurate*.

35 I've decided to go back to college, so next week I *start* my degree course!

36 My sister *arrives* tomorrow from Venice.

37 'The Sportsman', Britain's first national daily for 20 years, *launches* next week.

It would have been possible to use other means of referring to the future in these examples, but with the present futurate the future situation is anchored in the present, and in some way scheduled to take place as a 'diaried occurrence' or as a natural occurrence. The use of the present futurate in speech makes the conversation more lively by bringing the anticipated situation to the fore. Notice that for these examples to be interpreted as futurate uses, a time specification is normally required.

In a subordinate clause a present tense verb can also refer to the future.

38 I'll tell you about it when I *see* you.

39 That will happen only if the Government *manages* to replace the poll tax with a more acceptable alternative.

In these examples the superordinate clauses have a marker of future time, such as WILL (underlined). The subordinate clauses can express a range of meanings, for example temporal meaning or conditional meaning. The future time reference of the present tense in the subordinate clause depends on the future time marker in the superordinate clause, which is generally not repeated. Thus (40) would be regarded as ungrammatical by most speakers.

40 *That *will* happen only if the Government *will* manage to replace the poll tax with a more acceptable alternative.

Logically, there is nothing wrong with (40) because both the matrix and subordinate clauses refer to future time. It seems that grammatically WILL is excluded from the subordinate clause because the matrix clause has already set up a future time sphere which extends into the subordinate clause, obviating the need for WILL to be repeated.

9.2.2 The past tense and its uses

The past tense is grammaticalized in English as a verb inflection on lexical verbs (*-ed*), or by other means, typically a vowel change (e.g. *sing–sang*). In sections 9.2.2.1–9.2.2.5 I discuss the principal uses of the past tense. The past tense forms of the auxiliary verbs will be discussed in section 9.2.3.

9.2.2.1 The past tense as used to refer to past situations

The *past tense* in its basic use encodes that a situation obtained at some point in the past, relative to the moment of utterance. There may be an explicit Adjunct locating the situation in time. Here are some examples, with the Adjuncts underlined.

41 When we *had* a head of departments' meeting <u>last week</u> I *circulated* a piece of paper and several people have returned it to me.

42 The meeting *finished* <u>at about 5 o'clock</u>.

43 <u>From 1974 to 1978</u> he *worked* for Granada Television in Manchester.

9.2.2.2 The past tense used for politeness

The past tense can be used for politeness, as in (44)–(46), which express requests.

44 We *wondered* whether you would like to have a go at your jigsaw puzzle.

45 I *wanted* to ask you a little about The Exorcist.

46 Sorry, *could* you start again?

These requests with past tense forms are more polite and self-effacing than their counterparts with present tense forms. The past tense distances the speaker from their request, which makes it easier for the addressee to turn it down.

9.2.2.3 The modal past tense

The past tense of verbs can be used to talk about modal situations, for example situations that are hypothetical or non-factual. For this reason we call it the *modal past tense*. Typically, the modal past tense occurs in clauses that express *remote conditions*, that is, conditions which are not likely to be fulfilled. They can be introduced by *if (only)*, *imagine if*, or *suppose/supposing*. Here are some examples. In each case the matrix clause (or an associated clause) contains a modal verb (in bold).

47 *If* you <u>turned</u> up for a day's shooting, the pheasants **would** die laughing.

48 *If* I <u>was</u> to go to Dubai, I **can** get things like electrical goods.

49 *If only* he <u>had</u> a darling, cuddly, relaxing dog, perhaps he **wouldn't** be such a miserable toad.

50 "… *Imagine if* you <u>portrayed</u> other police-state criminals in this way. There **would** be an outcry."

51 *Supposing* he <u>had</u> the management team who so intelligently advise Beckham; **might** it have made a difference?

We can turn the *if*-clause in an example like (47) into a clause expressing an *open condition*, that is, a condition that can realistically be fulfilled, by changing the past tense forms to present tense forms in both clauses.

52 *If* you <u>turn</u> up for a day's shooting, the pheasants **will** die laughing.

We also find the modal past tense after expressions like *it's time* and after verbs like WISH.

53 *It's time* people <u>knew</u> how their money was being spent.

54 I *wish* it <u>was</u> over now.

In (54) we can replace *was* by *were*. This possibility, which involves a subjunctive clause, will be discussed in section 10.3.2.

9.2.2.4 The past tense in indirect reported speech

The *direct reported speech* in (55) is rendered in (56) as *indirect reported speech*.

55 She said 'I *don't* know what it*'s* like to be husbandless but I *can* imagine.'

56 She said she *didn't* know what it *was* like to be husbandless but she *could* imagine.

The Subject pronoun *I* in (55) is changed to *she* in (56), and the auxiliary verbs and the verb BE (in the clause *what it's like*) have been *backshifted*, that is, turned into past tenses: *don't* becomes *didn't*, *'s* becomes *was*, and *can* becomes *could*. The non-backshifted version is shown in (57).

57 She said she *doesn't* know what it*'s* like to be husband-less but she *can* imagine.

This last possibility is more likely if the speaker knows at the time of utterance that the person referred to as 'she' still does not know what it is like to be husbandless, but can imagine it.

I will return to indirect reported speech in connection with *should* in section 9.2.3, and in connection with the past perfect in section 9.3.1.2.

9.2.2.5 The past futurate

The *past futurate* is a past tense that is used to talk about future situations viewed from the past (a 'future in the past'). Here are two examples.

58 When we last spoke, the meeting *was* to take place next week.

59 In 1956 Lumumba was a post office clerk; four years later he *would* be prime minister.

9.2.3 The past tense forms of auxiliary verbs

Progressive BE, perfect HAVE, passive BE, and the dummy auxiliary DO all have past tense forms. Examples are given below.

60 Their evidence suggested that the hole *was* growing bigger through time, and satellite surveillance confirmed the initial reports.

61 Cosmo thought her voice *had* not changed at all.

62 Suddenly the issue of ozone depletion *was* taken seriously.

63 And he says if civilians *did* die he's sorry.

Modal verbs, with the exception of MUST, have a morphological past tense form, as we saw in section 3.6.3.2. The forms *would, could, might,* and *should* are historically and morphologically past tense forms, and some can be used to denote past time. For example, in (64) the modal verb CAN expresses the semantic notion of 'ability' at the present time ('I am able to feel…'), whereas in (65) it expresses the same semantic notion in the past ('I was able to feel…').

64 I *can* feel you beginning to buckle under the weight of all this sincerity.

65 I *could* feel you beginning to buckle under the weight of all this sincerity.

However, in other cases the past tense forms cannot semantically be regarded as the past tense counterparts of the present tense forms, as (66) and (67) make clear.

66 We *shall* make up our mind when the IMF has reported.

67 We *should* make up our mind when the IMF has reported.

In (66) SHALL expresses an 'intention' to do something. However, (67) does not express an 'intention in the past', but rather 'obligation'.

For this reason some grammars argue that *should* is an entirely separate verb lexeme SHOULD.

Despite such semantic mismatches, in this grammar we will regard the past tense forms of the modals as the morphological past tense counterparts of the present tense forms. The reasons for this are twofold. First, we note that the past tense forms can be used with past tense meanings in conditional constructions (section 9.2.2.3). Consider first (68) with an open condition expressed in the subordinate clause.

68 *If* she *recommends* my book after that, I *shall* be very surprised.

If we turn this into a remote condition we obtain (69).

69 *If* she *recommended* my book after that, I *should* be very surprised.

The verb *should* in this example is semantically and grammatically a straightforward past tense form of SHALL. Put differently, the meaning expressed by *should* is the same as the meaning expressed by SHALL in (68), apart from the modal remoteness expressed by the past tense. It is therefore inappropriate to regard *should* as a separate lexeme SHOULD in this case.

Secondly, the past tense forms can be used in backshifted contexts. As we saw in section 9.2.2.4, these are contexts where a verb in a subordinate clause is 'shifted back in time' by taking on a past tense form. Consider (70) and its backshifted version in (71).

70 Mr Ghai said: 'I *shall* appeal until the very end, in the faith that my dying wish will not go unheard.'

71 Mr Ghai said he *should* appeal until the very end, in the faith that his dying wish would not go unheard.

Here the verb SHALL has been backshifted, resulting in *should*. This example shows that in this type of context too we must recognize *should* as a past tense form of SHALL. (The verb form *should* in (71) is actually ambiguous, because it can also carry the 'obligation' meaning.)

Further discussion of the meanings expressed by the auxiliaries will be presented in sections 9.3.3 and 10.3.4–10.3.8.

9.2.4 Other ways of referring to present, past, and future time

In English a variety of expressions can be used to refer to time. Here are some examples of different types of phrases referring to past, present, and future times.

72 [NP *Yesterday*] they went into game nine with the scores locked at 4-4 after a win apiece and six draws.

73 I'm going to be in Ramsford [NP *tomorrow*].

74 In [AdjP *recent*] years several schools of thought have emerged, each championed by leading exponents of the period.

75 What are your [AdjP *future*] study plans?

76 [PP *After he married*], he told his wife not to open the metal box because it belonged to a friend.

77 I do not need this lighthearted humour [PP *at the moment*].

78 There's no seats [PP *in the morning*].

79 I've tried to get in touch with Janet several times [AdvP *lately*] but I think she's moved.

To refer to future time we can also use the progressive futurate (section 9.3.2.4.4), WILL or SHALL followed by a bare infinitive (sections 10.3.4 and 10.3.5), or the modal lexical verb BE *going* [*to*] (section 10.3.11.3.3).

9.3 Aspect
. . . .

When we discussed time and tense earlier we saw that time is a real world notion, whereas tense is a grammatical notion: tense is the way a grammar allows speakers to encode the notion of time. In the same way, *aspectuality* is a notion which concerns how a situation is perceived to be unfolding in time in the real world (as completed, ongoing, or the like), whereas aspect is the way that a grammar encodes this. Many languages, especially the Slavic languages, have very rich aspectual systems. In these languages the way situations unfold can be encoded in verbal inflections. In English we recognize *perfect aspect* and *progressive aspect*. These are not encoded in verbal inflections, but as constructions.

9.3.1   Perfect aspect

In section 9.2.2 we saw that the principal way to refer to past occurrences is by using the past tense, and that the grammar of English encodes the past tense through the *-ed* ending in the case of regular verbs, and through a vowel modification in the case of many irregular verbs (e.g. *eat/ate*; see Appendix 1). English has a further means of referring to past time, namely the *perfect construction*, which combines the perfect auxiliary HAVE with a past participle form of a verb. We distinguish the present perfect construction from the past perfect and non-finite perfect constructions (see sections 2.2.1.2 and 3.6.3.3). They will be discussed in turn in sections 9.3.1.1–9.3.1.3.

9.3.1.1   The present perfect

The *present perfect* involves a present tense form of the auxiliary verb HAVE followed by a past participle.

80 I *have finished* the work that I had to do.

81 I *have been* unwell for the past 6 weeks.

As a general characterization of the English present perfect construction, we can say that it refers to a situation that happened or began in the past, and has relevance at the present moment. This is called *current relevance*. In (80), while the work in question was finished before the present moment, this is felt by the speaker to be relevant at the time of utterance, perhaps in indicating that he is now ready to do a new job. In (81) the perfect is used to indicate that the speaker has been unwell for some time, and this is in some way relevant at the moment of speaking, for example in an assessment of their performance at the present moment. We can represent the meaning of the present perfect on a timeline as in (82) for (80), and as in (83) for (81).

82

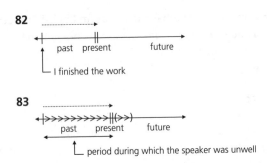

83

In both examples '|' indicates when the situation occurred or began in time. Current relevance is indicated by the dashed arrow. The time span of the situation denoted by (81) is indicated by angle brackets ('>') in (83). In this representation they go beyond the present moment to indicate that a situation can in some cases be interpreted to extend past the present moment (see also section 9.3.1.1.1). However, if an Adjunct like *until now* or *up to now* is used, as in (84), the situation explicitly extends only up to the present.

84 Estonia *has* <u>until now</u> *been* the calmest of the three Baltic republics.

The present perfect differs from the past tense; the latter is used to refer to situations that can be said to be 'over and done with'. While situations in the past can also be relevant at the present time, it is important to stress that the past tense does not *encode* current relevance, whereas the present perfect construction does. Compare (81) with (85), where a past tense is used. This means that the speaker was unwell last week which may or may not be relevant at the present moment.

85 I was unwell last week.

(85) can be represented on a timeline as follows.

86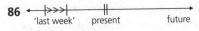

The present perfect in English is normally not compatible with a definite time reference, as (87) shows.

87 *I have been unwell last week.

The reason why (87) is ungrammatical is that there is a semantic clash between the meaning encoded by the present perfect, namely current relevance, and the meaning conveyed by *last week*, namely that the situation is perceived as being over and done with. However, English is showing signs of change in this respect. Many commentators have observed the phenomenon of the so-called *footballer's present perfect* which occurs with some frequency in the sports press, and in the spoken language used by footballers. It involves a present perfect construction, sometimes in combination with an explicit definite time reference, where one would normally expect a past tense. Here is an example.

88 The linesman*'s given* the decision, but what astounds me is that he *has sent* Taricco off <u>before he spoke to the linesman</u>.

It is possible that the restriction on the use of definite time Adjuncts in combination with the present perfect is being relaxed beyond the domain of sports. Here is an example of a present perfect construction combined with a definite time reference from an informal conversation.

89 I *have caught* up on a lot of sleep <u>when I was too ill</u>.

Consider now (90) and (91).

90 The mass media *have undergone* radical change <u>since then</u>.

91 <u>Over the past 15 years</u>, they *have become* the most riot-prone in the West.

Here we also have Adjuncts of time, namely *since then* and *over the past 15 years*, but, as in the case of (81), they do not cause ungrammaticality, because both Adjuncts are compatible with a current relevance reading: they indicate a period beginning in the past and leading up to the present, as can be seen in (92), which represents (90) and (91) diagrammatically.

92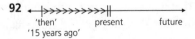

In the sections that follow I will give an overview of the principal uses of the English present perfect. In each case an element of current relevance can be detected, but in different ways.

9.3.1.1.1 The continuative present perfect

This use of the present perfect denotes a situation that began in the past and leads up to the present time, and possibly beyond. In addition to (81) some further examples follow below.

93 I *have lived* here eight or nine years and I would know if there was crack.

94 But the fact remains we *have been faced*, since the middle of January, with war.

95 In the Latvian capital Riga key buildings *have been blocked* off since the beginning of the week.

96 You *have been* there for me all through this crazy relationship with Colin.

The duration of the situation referred to, or its inception point, is usually indicated by an Adjunct of time. Adjuncts that convey 'continuation' cannot be used in the present perfect construction with verbs that are incompatible with that notion. Thus 'breaking the speed record' in (97) is an instantaneous occurrence without duration.

97 *I have broken the speed record ever since the summer.

The continuative perfect can also be used to refer to recurring or habitual situations in the past leading up to the present.

98 For centuries countless thousands of people *have arrived* in magical Provence for the sunshine and the quality of life that it provides.

99 And on occasion I *have lent* hardbacks and not got them back.

In (98) it is evident that the favourable conditions of Provence still obtain, and that up to the moment of speaking people have been going there. The link with the present is rather more implicit in (99), but becomes clear from what the speaker said immediately after uttering (99) in the same conversation, namely 'so I just don't lend hardbacks to anyone now'. In all these cases, except (94) and (95), a past tense would have been possible, but there would then be no suggestion that the situations referred to are relevant at the present time, and may continue to be relevant into the future.

9.3.1.1.2 The present perfect of the recent past

We can report situations that took place in the recent past using the present perfect construction, as the following examples make clear. In each case what is being said is in some way relevant at the present time. Adjuncts like *recently*, *of late*, and *just* are often used.

100 A financial adviser from Smith Jones Brown came to see me, and he *has* <u>recently</u> *sent* me his advice.

101 <u>Of late</u>, there *has been* research to indicate that procedural learning is retained in a great many contexts.

102 I *have* <u>just</u> *met* with Select who will be supplying us with our Box Office Computer.

This use of the present perfect is especially common in reportage. The following examples, from newspapers, report on occurrences in the recent past.

103 Police *have released* two women and two men, while two men who were found to have overstayed their immigration conditions are being dealt with.

104 Estate residents *have won* the first stage of their battle to stop developers demolishing family houses and building flats.

105 Investors are getting increasingly nervous about Murdoch, and News shares *have tumbled* to their lowest for six years.

Note that a past tense could have been used in these cases, but this would have had the effect of the reports losing their 'hot news' feel.

9.3.1.1.3 The present perfect of result

In the following examples the present perfect expresses a result.

106 Both of you *have recorded* quite a good deal of music.

107 The lesson the British *have learned* is not to appease dictators because they cannot be assuaged.

108 But we *have decided* that we will teach the fundamentals of ethics.

109 I *have found* out that I go on Monday 8th July, so maybe I'll have a chance to see you before I go.

110 The Moguls *have built* a bridge to get to the enemy.

In each case the results are identifiable, namely recordings of music, a learnt lesson, a decision, a piece of knowledge, and a bridge that has been built.

9.3.1.1.4 The experiential present perfect

The experiential present perfect is used to indicate that some situation obtained once or more than once during an indefinite period beginning in the past and leading up to the present. Here are some examples.

111 I *have toured* the Voronezh.

112 Well, these damn plants *have shot* up in price so much <u>over the last year or two</u>.

113 *Have* you *seen* it <u>before</u>, Caroline?

114 *Have* you <u>ever</u> *seen* 'Married with Children'?

Adjuncts compatible with this type of perfect construction (underlined in the examples above) indicate that the situation obtained in a period leading up to the present. Thus *before* in (113) can be glossed as 'at any point before now'.

9.3.1.2 The past perfect

Let's now turn to an example of the *past perfect* (sometimes called the *pluperfect*).

115 Sixteen years before, he *had married* Jessie, the pretty, musical, ambitious daughter of a Sheffield clergyman.

We understand the past perfect construction in this example to refer to a situation that took place sixteen years before an unspecified *reference point* in the past, as shown on the timeline in (116).

116

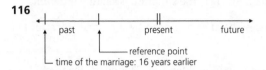

In this example the past perfect is like the past tense, except that the situation is viewed from a reference point in the past, rather than from the present (compare: *Sixteen years ago he married Jessie*). In such cases the past perfect, unlike the present perfect, is compatible with a definite time reference, as (117) and (118) additionally make clear.

117 <u>Even at the beginning of the century</u> political links *had had* tensions.

118 Checking marriage records, he found that Eugenie Loyer *had married* at St. Mary's Church, Lambeth, <u>on 10 April 1878</u>, her twenty-fourth birthday.

The first of these examples expresses that the tensions took place before the definite time reference ('the beginning of the century'), whereas in the second example Eugenie Loyer's marriage preceded the speaker's discovery of this fact.

Consider next (119), which involves a process lasting up to a reference point in the past.

119 Southern England *had become* a civilised area <u>by the second century</u>.

Here the process of Southern England becoming civilized started at some point in the indefinite past, and led up to the second century, which functions as a reference point in the past, as shown on the timeline below.

120

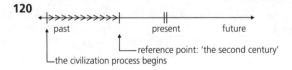

This example is like the continuative present perfect, except that again the situation is viewed from a reference point in the past, rather than from the present (compare: *Southern England has become a civilised area*). In (121) the situation is slightly different.

121 Margaret Thatcher *had been* <u>by that time</u> leader of her party for nearly four years.

Here the time span of Margaret Thatcher's leadership and its end point are explicitly mentioned.

122

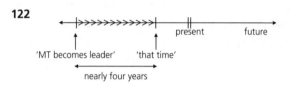

What we see here is that the time span shown in (92) for the present perfect has been shifted backwards in time in (120) and (122), such that the 'present' in (92) corresponds with the reference points 'the second century' and 'that time' in the case of the past perfect.

Consider also (123).

123 We set off for France on the evening of the 12th. We *had booked* ahead for a hotel, and stayed in Calais that night.

The past perfect construction in the second part of (123) is used here relative to the time of 'setting off' in the first part.

The past perfect can also be used to express a remote condition (section 9.2.2.3) in the past, as in (124) and (125).

124 If he *had been* a buyer I **would** have sent him a contract for buying.

125 Well, if I *had read* it I'm sure it **would** have been absolutely fascinating.

In these examples the past tense inflection on HAVE is a modal past tense (section 9.2.2.3), and the perfect construction indicates pastness.

Finally, in cases of indirect reported speech (see section 9.2.2.4), if the verb in the 'original' utterance was in the past tense or involved a perfect construction, a past perfect construction is used in the back-shifted version, as the following examples show.

126 He then said: 'I *hobbled* into work the next day.'

127 He then said he *had hobbled* into work the next day.

128 He said: 'I *have waited* nearly six years to find out what *happened* to my son.'

129 He said he *had waited* nearly six years to find out what *had happened* to his son.

9.3.1.3 The non-finite perfect construction

So far we have only looked at cases where the perfect auxiliary carries present or past tense. In the following examples we encounter non-tensed forms of HAVE.

130 Anyway, it's nice [clause to *have met* her].

131 She never married, claiming [clause never to *have been* in love].

132 I would like [clause to *have proposed* a motion to take industrial action].

133 So, [clause *having done* one year of planning], what made you decide to then go into the Architecture?

134 [clause *Having listened* to the Foreign Secretary], do you think that's his view too?

In (130) the *to*-infinitive clause is an extraposed Subject (sections 3.2.2.1.2 and 8.1.3.4), whereas in (131) and (132) the *to*-infinitive clauses are Direct Objects of the verbs CLAIM and LIKE, respectively (see section 8.1.2). In (133) and (134) the *-ing* participle clauses function as Adjuncts.

In its non-finite form the perfect construction signals a general meaning of 'pastness', and can correspond to the past tense or to the present perfect. To demonstrate this, consider first (135).

To demonstrate this, consider first (135), where an occurrence is reported.

135 The Iraqis claim to *have shot* down fourteen aircraft.

Here we interpret the perfect construction simply as referring to past time. It corresponds to the past tense (compare: *The Iraqis shot down fourteen aircraft*). As we saw above, the present perfect construction cannot normally be combined with a definite time reference (cf. (87)), but such Adjuncts *can* unproblematically occur in the nonfinite perfect construction, as (137) shows.

136 The Iraqis claim to *have shot* down fourteen aircraft <u>last week</u>.

Current relevance is not part of the meaning encoded by the nonfinite perfect. However, it is possible for an Adjunct accompanying this construction to express current relevance. Compare (136) with (137) and (138). Here we are dealing with situations in a period leading up to the present.

137 The Iraqis claim to *have shot* down fourteen aircraft <u>since the war began</u>.

138 Mr Bell, unmarried, is said to *have lived* alone since the death of his mother a year ago.

Notice that in (139) the matrix verb is in the past tense. In this case the shooting down of the aircraft should be understood to have taken place before the Iraqis made their claim.

139 The Iraqis <u>claimed</u> to *have shot* down fourteen aircraft.

The shooting down of the aircraft can even take place in the future, as in (140).

140 The Iraqis <u>aim</u> to *have shot* down fourteen aircraft <u>by the time the war is over</u>.

You can aim to do something only in the future, and we understand (140) to mean that the downing of the planes will have happened in the past relative to a future point in time ('when the war is over'). This is an example of the semantic notion of a *past in the future*. Further examples are shown below, involving WILL and MUST. In each case an explicit reference to future time is added (underlined).

141 However, about 75 per cent of those affected will *have stopped* having attacks <u>by the time they are twenty</u>.

142 Students must *have submitted* essays <u>by next week</u>.

In (141) the past is viewed from 'the time they are twenty', whereas in (142) the reference point in the future is 'next week'.

9.3.2 Progressive aspect

The progressive construction, briefly discussed in sections 2.2.1.2 and 3.6.3.3, is used in English to present a dynamic situation, which is not necessarily complete, as being in progress over a limited period. It has been part of the language since Old English times, but started to be used much more frequently in the 19th century, a trend that is continuing to this day. We distinguish the present progressive construction from the past progressive and non-finite progressive constructions (see section 3.6.3.3). They will be discussed in turn in sections 9.3.2.1–9.3.2.3. Other uses of the progressive will be discussed in section 9.3.2.4.

9.3.2.1 The present progressive

The *present progressive* is used to denote situations, typically activities, that unfold from some point in the past into the future, as in the examples that follow. We generally interpret the situation being described as having a restricted duration.

143 And he will now present her to those who *are waiting* inside the West Door of this great old church.

144 I'*m rambling*.

145 She *is wearing* a lime green suit, carrying a dark blue handbag, white gloves, and a pale hat.

We can represent the present progressive as follows on a timeline.

146

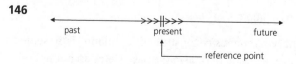

Here the present moment (indicated by '‖') functions as a reference point for the situation. There is no indication in (143)–(145) when the situations referred to started in the past, and no end point is being presented either.

Notice that the situation referred to using the progressive construction need not be taking place at the exact moment of speaking, but can take place in a more broadly conceived 'present time'. The situations in the next two examples clearly take a good deal of time, and will be interrupted by breaks, eating, sleeping, and so on.

147 I never read the classics or anything like that, and now I'*m reading* them.

148 And at the College of Speech Sciences I'*m putting* things in alphabetical order for them.

Typically, the progressive is used to denote temporary situations, but the example below makes clear that the situation does not have to be transient.

149 I'*m getting* old.

Here the process of getting old stretches into the (distant) future.

The progressive construction is generally not used with verbs that express a state, such as BELONG, CONTAIN, REMAIN, or so-called psychological verbs such as BELIEVE, KNOW, UNDERSTAND, WANT, and this is because in such cases there is a semantic clash between the meaning of the progressive construction ('unfolding situation') and the meaning of the verb. For this reason the following examples are odd, though not to the same extent for different people.

150 ?*I *am understanding* what you say.

151 ?*I *am believing* in God.

152 ?*This cat *is belonging* to me.

Exceptions to this generalization will be discussed in section 9.3.2.4.1.

9.3.2.2 The past progressive

In the *past progressive* construction a situation is presented as unfolding over a period of time in the past. Here's an example.

153 Warhol *was designing* shoes.

This can be represented as follows.

154

```
←→>>>>>>————||————————→
   past        present        future
```

Often, as in (153), there is no indication as to exactly when in the past a situation unfolded, although it may be implied in the context. It is possible, however, to specify a reference point. In (155) and (156) the underlined Adjuncts provide the reference point, whereas in (157) the reference point is an activity in the matrix clause.

155 I *was living* with Sarah <u>at the time you came to London</u>, but we split up at the beginning of December.

156 She *was spooling* the programme on to the tape machine <u>when the phone rang</u>.

157 When we *were walking* over the bridge Mary Jane <u>stopped</u> to take a shot of a woman on the other side of the road who was dragging a child along by the hand.

We can represent these temporal situations as follows on a timeline.

158

```
←→>>>|>>>————||————————→
  past   ↑    present        future
```
reference point: 'the time you came to London'/'the phone rang'/'Mary Jane stopped'

It is also possible to 'frame' the progressive situation by using an Adjunct that specifies the period within which it is contained.

159 We *were travelling* <u>in January</u>.

160 She was asked by the junior flying corps to come to the celebrations they *were holding* <u>that night</u>.

(159) and (160) can be represented as on the timeline below. Note that the situations expressed in (159) and (160) do not necessarily extend from the marked start point up to the end point.

161

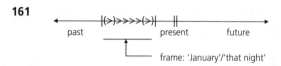

9.3.2.3   Non-finite progressive constructions

When progressive BE does not carry tense we speak of a *non-finite progressive*, as in (162) and (163) below.

162 It just didn't look good to *be living* it up at tax payers' expense.

163 The totals have *been growing* rapidly week in week out for more than a decade.

9.3.2.4 Further uses of the progressive

In the following sections I will discuss some additional uses of the progressive, other than the progressive of ongoing situations.

9.3.2.4.1 The progressive with state verbs

In section 9.3.2.1 we saw that the progressive typically does not combine with state verbs. There are, however, exceptions to this generalization, and these occur when we wish to indicate that a state verb is interpreted in a particular way, usually dynamically, and with an implication of temporariness, as in the following examples.

164 Maybe I *am being* fussy, but I don't want to spend my life as a secretary.

165 It sounds that you*'re wanting* to take care of yourself physically as well.

166 I have to say I*'m missing* all my friends.

167 The only thing I *am lacking* is a wardrobe.

168 I*'m* really *hoping* to clear some space in my life very soon to be able to do all that.

In (164) the speaker is saying that they are knowingly acting in a fussy manner. The same example without the progressive indicates a property ascribed to the referent of the Subject. Thus, *I am fussy* means that fussiness is part of my personality. In (165) the implication is that the addressee actively wants to take care of himself, while in examples (166)–(168) there is a sense of acuteness: in (166) the speaker misses their friends keenly, right now, while in (167) not having a wardrobe is strongly felt to be a problem at the moment of speaking. In the last example progressive HOPE expresses a wilful, determined desire 'to clear some space'. This is reinforced by the adverb *really*.

9.3.2.4.2 The interpretive progressive

Sometimes the progressive construction is used to indicate that a situation is interpreted in a certain way. This is called the *interpretive progressive*. (169) is an example.

169 Oh, you're *kidding*.

Here the speaker is saying 'I'm interpreting what you have just said as a joke'. The interpretive reading is not available in (170), where the speaker is telling you what they are doing, not interpreting their own words.

170 I'm only *kidding*.

However, compare (170) with (171), where the speaker is offering an interpretation of their own words.

171 When I said you were a hopeless case, I *was* only *kidding*.

The interpretive progressive also occurs in examples like the following.

172 If Nick says he'll repair the roof, he's *deceiving* you.

173 When John claimed he received a huge bonus, he *was exaggerating*.

In these cases the matrix clauses that contain the progressive construction offer an interpretation, explanation, or conclusion about whatever is expressed in the subordinate clauses.

9.3.2.4.3 The progressive of irritation

The progressive construction can be used to signal irritation, as in the following example.

174 She's <u>always</u> *poking* her damn nose in, isn't she?

The sense of irritation comes about through a combination of the discourse context, the verbal meaning, words expressing negative emotive force like *damn*, and the presence of Adjuncts like *always, forever, continually.*

9.3.2.4.4 The progressive futurate

When the present progressive is used to talk about future time we call it the *present progressive futurate*. It is exemplified in (175) and (176).

175 We *are leaving* the department at ten o'clock.

176 Tomorrow I'*m meeting* Sarah Duncan for lunch.

The use of the progressive in these examples indicates that a not-so-far-off future situation is thought of as an arrangement or plan on the part of a human agent. It often occurs with verbs of motion (COME, GO, LEAVE, etc.). It is important to be aware of the fact that this use of the progressive is not aspectual, that is, the situation is not regarded as unfolding over time.

The *past progressive futurate* in (177) expresses an arrangement in the past of a future situation, seen from a point in time in the past.

177 I *was going* Sunday night you see, but I'm not anymore.

The activity in question may or may not be actualized. In this particular example it will not be: the speaker explicitly says he will not leave on Sunday. The past progressive futurate is more common than the past futurate, discussed in section 9.2.2.5.

9.3.3 Perfect and progressive combinations

In section 8.6 we discussed the syntax of combinations of auxiliary verbs. The possible structures exemplified there include eleven with combinations of two or more auxiliary verbs. Of those, ten involve a perfect and/or progressive auxiliary verb. Examples of these combinations are repeated below. In many books on English grammar each combination is regarded as a separate tense. For example, the combination in (178) is often called the *modal perfect tense*, and the combination in (179) the *modal perfect progressive tense*. For reasons that were explained in section 9.2, we do not adopt this terminology. Instead we will speak of 'constructions', such that we have a *modal perfect construction* in (178), a *modal perfect progressive construction* in (179), and so on.

178 The agents *will have* <u>booked</u> the tickets. [modal + perfect HAVE + <u>lexical verb</u>]

179 The agents *will have been* <u>booking</u> the tickets. [modal + perfect HAVE + progressive BE + <u>lexical verb</u>]

180 The tickets *will have been being* <u>booked</u> by the agents. [modal + perfect HAVE + progressive BE + passive BE + <u>lexical verb</u>]

181 The agents *will be* <u>booking</u> the tickets. [modal + progressive BE + <u>lexical verb</u>]

182 The agents *have been* <u>booking</u> the tickets. [perfect HAVE + progressive BE + <u>lexical verb</u>]

183 The tickets *will be being* <u>booked</u> by the agents. [modal + progressive BE + passive BE + <u>lexical verb</u>]

184 The tickets *will have been* <u>booked</u> by the agents. [modal + perfect HAVE + passive BE + <u>lexical verb</u>]

185 The tickets *were being* <u>booked</u> by the agents. [progressive BE + passive BE + <u>lexical verb</u>]

186 The tickets *have been* <u>booked</u> by the agents. [perfect HAVE + passive BE + <u>lexical verb</u>]

187 The tickets *have been being* <u>booked</u> by the agents. [perfect HAVE + progressive BE + passive BE + <u>lexical verb</u>]

Some of these combinations are highly unusual. A construction like (180) hardly occurs, no doubt because language users are not likely to frequently find themselves in situations in which they want to express a combination of modal, perfect, progressive, and passive meanings at the same time.

The interpretations of the examples above are shown below.

188 'It is probable that the agents booked the tickets.' = (178)

189 'It is probable that the agents were in the process of booking the tickets.' = (179)

190 'It is probable that the tickets were in the process of being booked by the agents.' = (180)

191 'It is probable that the agents are in the process of booking the tickets.' = (181)

192 'In a period up to the present moment the agents were in the process of booking the tickets.' = (182)

193 'In the future the tickets will be in the process of being booked by the agents.' = (183)

194 'Before some point in the future the booking of the tickets by the agents will be completed.' = (184)

195 'At some point in the past the tickets were in the process of being booked.' = (185)

196 'In a period up to the present moment the tickets were booked by the agents.' = (186)

197 'In a period up to the present moment the tickets were in the process of being booked by the agents.' = (187)

In many cases these constructions combine the meanings of their individual components. For example, in (181) the modal verb introduces a semantic element of 'intention' (see section 10.3.4.2), whereas the progressive construction contributes an element of 'ongoingness'. Similarly, in (182) the current relevance meaning of the present tense perfect auxiliary is combined with a progressive element of meaning.

9.3.4   Aspect and lexical meaning

Apart from in the perfect and progressive constructions, aspectuality can also be expressed by the inherent meaning of verbs, or by a verb in combination with a dependent.

9.3.4.1 Situation aspect

Verbs and their dependents can express various types of situations. We refer to this phenomenon as *situation aspect*. (The terms *lexical aspect* and *Aktionsart* are also frequently used.) A situation is what a clause is about, as we have seen, and can be a *state* or *occurrence*. States denote situations that simply exist. They are unbounded, that is, they do not have a beginning and an end, and are internally undifferentiated (e.g. *The carpet is old*; *Unicorns exist*). By contrast, occurrences are dynamic situations which come about. They can be subdivided into *achievements*, which are punctual (e.g. *I spotted a fox in the garden*; *She blinked*), and *processes*, which have a duration. Among the processes we further distinguish between *activities*, which have no built-in end point (e.g. *They are watching football*), and *accomplishments*, which do have a built-in end point (e.g. *He is writing a text message*).

9.3.4.2 Aspectual lexical verbs

A small set of verbs in English carries meanings that can be said to be aspectual because together with their Complements they focus on the unfolding of situations in time. Examples of such *aspectual lexical verbs* (also called *aspectualizers*) are BEGIN, CEASE, CONTINUE, DISCONTINUE, FINISH, KEEP, PROCEED, QUIT, START, and STOP. Some examples follow.

198 Flowers *continued* <u>to arrive</u> at Downing Street this morning.

199 Can't you wait until everybody's *finished* <u>having their lunch</u>?

The aspectuality of these verb–Complement sequences comes about as a result of the inherently expressed aspectual meanings of the verbs in combination with the meanings expressed by the Complements, rather than situationally, as discussed in the previous section, or as a result of a combination of an auxiliary verb (HAVE/BE) and a lexical verb, as described in sections 9.3.1 and 9.3.2.

9.3.4.3 USED [*to*]

The combination of the past tense form of the verb USE with a *to*-infinitive clause (indicated by '[*to*]') expresses a habitual situation in the past, and as such is aspectual. The fact that this verb takes a *to*-infinitive clause as Complement makes it like a lexical verb.

200 Steven Winyard *used* <u>to be</u> a croupier in Nassau.

201 Yeah, we *used* <u>to buy</u> Mum a vase every year for her birthday.

In interrogative structures USED [*to*] normally takes DO-support (section 3.6.3.5), which is also a property of lexical verbs. Some examples are shown below.

202 <u>Didn't</u> John *used* <u>to deal</u> with divorce in his earlier days?

203 <u>Didn't</u> there *used* <u>to be</u> deer in Richmond Park?

USED [*to*] cannot occur in combination with core modal auxiliaries, and has no present tense forms (*uses to/*use to*) or participle forms. Morphologically it is a past tense form. For some speakers inversion without DO-support and negative contraction are possible, as in (204) and (205). These are characteristics of auxiliary verbs, and for this reason some grammars classify USED [*to*] as a marginal auxiliary verb. It should be noted, however, that structures such as these are very rare.

204 *Used* they <u>to walk</u> home at night?

205 There *used*<u>n't</u> to be anything there in my young days, I'm sure.

It is important to distinguish USED [*to*] from the verb USE in the example below.

206 The motion of the platform is *used* to build up a continuous image by careful synchronization of subsequent pulses with platform velocity.

The analysis of this example involves the lexical verb USE followed by a *to*-infinitive clause functioning as an Adjunct expressing a purpose. When uttered it is pronounced with a [z], and there is a very short pause after it. We can reorder (206) as in (207), in which the *to*-infinitive clause has been fronted from the position indicated by '_'.

207 <u>To build up a continuous image by careful synchronization of subsequent pulses with platform velocity</u>, the motion of the platform is *used* _.

Chapter 10
Mood

In the previous chapter we discussed the grammatical notions of tense and aspect, and the associated semantic notions of time and aspectuality. In this chapter we look at *mood*.

10.1 Mood and modality

The term 'mood' refers to the way in which the grammar of a language encodes *modality*, a concept which is concerned with such semantic notions as 'possibility', 'probability', 'necessity', 'obligation', 'permission', 'intention', and 'ability'. These are called *modal meanings*. What unites these seemingly unconnected notions is that they are all used to talk about situations that are not factual or not actualized. As an example, if we talk about a situation as being 'possible', it is not known to be the case at the moment of speaking, but it could come about. Similarly, if I am obliged to do something, then I am compelled to bring it about (to actualize it). For example, (1) below, which contains the modal verb MAY (section 3.6.3.2), can be paraphrased as 'it is *possible* that she is thin-skinned', and the second clause in (2), with the modal verb MUST, can be paraphrased as 'he is *obliged* to act now'.

1 She *may* be thin-skinned.

2 There is a crisis, and he *must* act now.

A clause that contains a modal expression is said to be *modalized*. In Old English (spoken between approximately AD 450 and 1100) modal meaning could be conveyed through inflectional endings on verbs (the 'subjunctive mood'). In present-day English it does not make sense to speak of a subjunctive mood, as we saw in section 2.2.1.3. How, then, are modal meanings expressed in the language as it is spoken today? It is useful to think of English as displaying a system of *analytic mood*, that is, a grammatical system of mood in which the meanings typically expressed by inflectional endings on verbs in older forms of English are carried by a *construction*, such as the combination of a modal verb followed by a lexical verb, or a clause type.

In the remainder of this chapter I will discuss three types of modality (section 10.2), and the various ways in which modality in English can be expressed (section 10.3).

10.2   Three types of modality in English

We distinguish between three types of modality in English: *deontic modality*, *epistemic modality*, and *dynamic modality*.

Deontic modality is concerned with getting people to do things or (not) allowing them to do things, that is, with such notions as 'obligation' and 'permission', as in the examples below.

3 Well, you *must* be slightly more succinct then.

4 You *may* voluntarily give up your right to reduced liability.

Epistemic modality is concerned with 'knowledge' and/or 'inference'. Here are two examples that make this clear.

5 'He *must* be here somewhere,' Anne said.

6 You *may* be left out of it because you are a freelancer.

In both cases the speaker has some evidence for the conclusion they are drawing. In the first example, Anne has some knowledge which allows her to make an inference about the whereabouts of the person she is talking about, while in (6) the conclusion that it is possible that the addressee will be left out is based on the knowledge that they are a freelancer.

In the case of deontic and epistemic modality the 'source' of the obligation, permission, or knowledge is typically the speaker. For example, in (3) it is the speaker who is imposing an obligation on the addressee, and in (5) and (6) the person drawing the conclusion is also the speaker.

Deontic and epistemic modality are closely related. For example, if I draw a certain conclusion on the basis of my knowledge of the world, then I am *obliged* to draw that conclusion, sometimes even *logically* obliged (e.g. *John killed the fly* entails *The fly must be dead*). It has been suggested that historically, epistemic modality developed from deontic modality, and this explains why the same modals can be used to express both types of modality (e.g. MUST can express 'obligation' and '(logical) conclusion').

Dynamic modality typically concerns 'ability' and 'volition', and these semantic notions relate to the Subject of the clause that contains the modal verb, rather than to the speaker. Thus in (7), the individuals referred to as *we* have the 'ability' to speak their native language, while in (8) WILL signals 'volition' on the part of the referent of the Subject of the clause, namely *you*. We can give an approximate paraphrase of (8) as 'If you are willing to go downstairs,...'.

7 In two or three years of learning that language we're never going to be able to speak it to the same standard we *can* speak our native tongue.

8 So if you *will* go downstairs, and then you could look through these two postgraduate guides.

Dynamic modality also covers neutral circumstantial meanings relating to 'possibility' and 'necessity', as expressed for example by CAN (e.g. *You can buy newspapers here*) and MUST (e.g. *The envelope must be sealed before being posted*). Here the source of the modality is the way the world is organized, that is, circumstances.

10.3 The expression of modality in English
. . . .

Modality is expressed in a number of ways in English, as we will see in the sections that follow.

10.3.1 The modal past tense

The modal past tense was discussed in section 9.2.2.3. Here are some further examples.

9 If organisations *operated* according to classical free-market theory, there would be no organisational problem.

10 If I *had* a recording of them would I be able to understand it?

In each case the past tense signals that the situation expressed in the conditional clause is not likely to happen or to be the case: it is an improbable, doubtful possibility. Alternatively, the situation expressed by the conditional clause is known not to be the case.

10.3.2 Subjunctive clauses

In many languages modality is expressed through verbal inflections. Compare the following examples from Spanish.

11 Juan siempre   trae un regalo.

Juan always bring-3RD-PS-SG-PRES-IND a present

'Juan always brings a present'

12 Espero   que Juan traiga   un regalo.

hope-1ST-PS-SG-PRES-IND that Juan bring-3RD-PS-SG-SUBJVE a present

'I hope that Juan brings a present'

PS = person; SG = singular; PRES = present; IND = indicative; SUBJVE = subjunctive

In the first example Juan's always bringing a present is presented as a fact. The statement is therefore *unmodalized*. In the second example, however, the speaker is expressing the hope that Juan will bring a present, and is for that reason talking about a particular type of modal situation, namely a 'hoped-for situation'. This time we have a present subjunctive verb form (*traiga*), which is quite different from the regular indicative present tense form (*trae*). As we saw earlier, Old English also had subjunctive verb forms, but the verbal paradigms of English changed over time, such that Modern English does not have a subjunctive mood to speak of. It therefore makes little sense to speak of the 'present subjunctive' forms of English verbs, simply because they cannot be distinguished from the plain forms, as in (13), where the verb URGE triggers the presence of the plain form of the passive auxiliary BE. In American English this is the default option. However, as (14) shows, a plain form is not always used: here we have *are*, a present tense verb form, rather than *be*. This construction is barely used in American English, but quite common in British English. Recall from section 2.2.1.3 that we refer to the bracketed clause in (13) as a *subjunctive clause* which expresses modal meaning. More specifically, we will refer to it as a *mandative subjunctive* clause which expresses a directive meaning.

13 I <u>urged</u> in my previous letter [that these research staff *be* treated as their present colleagues].

14 Some water boards <u>insist</u> [that all cold water taps in the house *are* taken from the rising main].

In section 10.3.5.2.3 I will discuss a special type of mandative clause which involves the modal verb *should*.

English also does not have past subjunctive verb forms, as we saw in section 2.2.1.3. The only exception is the verb BE which has the past subjunctive form *were* for the first and third person singular, as in (15) and (16). This is the only true remnant of a subjunctive verb form in English.

15 If I *were* you, I'd apply for the York position just for the experience.

16 Asked whether he would accept the Everton job if he *were* offered it, he replied: "I never comment on hypothetical situations."

The simple past tense form *was* would be used by many speakers in these examples. In this connection consider the example in (17). Here the speaker uses *were* after the Subject *he* in the first *if*-clause, but *was* after the Subject *I* in the second one.

17 I wouldn't be surprised if he *were* found hanging on the end of that phone very shortly, so I'd dial quickly if I *was* you.

Given that they express conditions, that is, hypothetical possibilities, *if*-clauses typically create modal, non-factual contexts. Conditional meaning can also be signalled by inversion, as in (18).

18 *Were this a Yoshizawa book*, the designs would be yet more beautiful, but western writers are not usually permitted to publish the very best of his work.

Other expressions that create modal contexts include *as if* and *as though*.

19 Well, I suppose if I lived each year *as if* it *were* my last I could enjoy myself, couldn't I?

20 It's *as though* there *were* a garden round him with coolness and roses.

In the following example, the expression *as it were* is fossilized.

21 In one leap, *as it were*, the unravelling of that frustrating knot made the law approachable for them.

In the next section we turn to a discussion of the core modal verbs.

10.3.3   The core modal verbs

As we have seen, the core modal verbs in English are WILL/*would*, CAN/*could*, MAY/*might*, SHALL/*should*, and MUST. Recall from section 9.2.3 that the forms *would*, *could*, *might*, and *should* are shown in italics because they can have specialized uses in which they do not behave as past tense forms of WILL, CAN, MAY, and SHALL.

As one might expect, the different modals do not occur in equal measure. Table 10.1 shows the frequencies of the modal auxiliaries in the ICE-GB corpus per million words, differentiated by medium.

present form	spoken	written	past form	spoken	written
will/'ll	1,883/1,449	3,284/361	*would/'d*	2,581/795	2,533/182
won't	232	80	wouldn't	394	87
can	2,652	2,533	*could*	1,339	1,353
can't	792	222	couldn't	231	90
cannot	80	316			
may	646	1,898	*might*	670	600
mayn't	2	-	mightn't	3	0
shall	196	217	*should*	861	1,192
shan't	5	0	shouldn't	71	26
must	472	857	-	-	-
mustn't	24	0	-	-	-

Table 10.1: Frequencies of the English core modal auxiliaries per million words in the ICE-GB corpus

The table shows some striking differences in the use of the modals in English. *Will* and *can* and their past tense counterparts *would* and *could* far outnumber the other modals. As might be expected, *shall* is very infrequent. Recent research has shown that it is declining in use, possibly because it is perceived to be rather formal. MUST is also not very common, and again research has shown that its use is declining. Perhaps this is because it is perceived as being authoritarian.

The modal verbs are syntactically characterized by the NICE properties which they share with the larger set of auxiliaries (see section 3.6.3.1), but they also have a few properties that only pertain to them.

First, modal verbs are always followed by a bare infinitive verb form, which can be a lexical verb, as in (1) and (2) above, or another auxiliary verb, as in (22)–(24), repeated from section 8.6.

22 The agents [modal auxiliary verb *will*] [progressive auxiliary verb *be*] [lexical verb *booking*] the tickets.

23 The tickets [modal auxiliary verb *will*] [passive auxiliary verb *be*] [lexical verb *booked*] by the agents.

24 The tickets [modal auxiliary verb *will*] [perfect auxiliary verb *have*] [passive auxiliary verb *been*] [lexical verb *booked*] by the agents.

Secondly, modal auxiliaries are always tensed. There are therefore no modal participles or modal infinitives (*has mayed*, *are musting*, *to shall*). If there is a modal verb in a clause, it must always be placed before any other verb.

Finally, modal verbs are said to be *defective*: although they have past tense forms (with the exception of MUST), and negated forms, they do not take a third person singular present tense *-s* ending.

25 *He *cans* do it.

26 *She *wills* attend the conference.

An overview of the properties of the modal verbs is given in Table 10.2.

Modal verbs...
• can have 'unpredictable' meanings when they occur in their past tense forms;
• conform to the NICE properties;
• are always followed by a bare infinitive verb form;
• do not have non-tensed forms (*mayed, *musting, etc.);
• have invariant present tense forms, i.e. do not have third person singular present tense endings (*he mays, *she musts, etc.).

Table 10.2: The morphosyntactic properties of the modal verbs

In the following sections I will discuss the meanings of the core modal verbs in turn. As we will see, each modal has more than one meaning. It is important to be aware of the fact that very often it is not clear in a particular clause which meaning a modal verb expresses, and very often meanings overlap. We will also see (in section 10.3.13.1) that contextual or discourse factors frequently affect the interpretation of modal verbs.

10.3.4 Will/*would*

In the sections below I will outline the uses of WILL and *would*.

10.3.4.1 Epistemic modality: futurity and evidence-based predictions or conclusions

The most common use of WILL followed by an infinitive verb form is to refer to future time. Often this verb expresses the epistemic meaning of 'prediction', based on circumstantial knowledge. Here are some examples.

27 I suggest you wait till September when it *will* be much, much cooler.

28 Winds *will reach* gale force.

29 This treatment *will* make you a lot more comfortable.

The situations referred to in these examples may or may not come about.

The modal WILL can in addition express evidence-based predictions or conclusions, also a typical epistemic use, as in (30) and (31). Notice that this use of WILL may concern present time, as in (30), or past time, as in (31), where WILL is followed by the perfect auxiliary HAVE.

30 Moments later, the doorbell rings. "That'*ll* be the girls!" shouts Paloma, as she skips off down the hallway before returning with Claire, a smartly dressed brunette, and Bianca, an elfin figure with long auburn hair.

31 You *will* have gathered from the above that I, for one, do not intend to re-apply.

The preceding examples involve a conclusion which the speaker bases on previous knowledge and/or experience. In some cases predictions are based on the speaker's knowledge of an existing schedule or a statutory course of events, as in (32)–(34).

32 Practically all the children that I coach *will* be off that week.

33 And in a few moments we *will* hear the trumpeter on his grey horse sound the command to trot.

34 If approved, the proposed Council decision *will* authorise Community membership of the EBRD.

Consider next (35), which is slightly different, because it involves a conditional clause.

35 If you have two identical twins and one of them is schizophrenic there is a fifty per cent chance that the other *will* be schizophrenic.

In this example the speaker draws a conclusion on the basis of medical knowledge. The modal verb expresses a meaning that might be paraphrased as 'scientific prediction'. Importantly, it does not refer to future time here.

Finally, in (36) the verb *would* expresses a past futurate (section 9.2.2.5): the future is viewed from a point of view in time fifteen years before the Berlin wall fell.

36 Fifteen years later he *would* play Bach in thanksgiving again – amid the rubble of the newly demolished Berlin Wall.

10.3.4.2 Dynamic modality: volition

WILL can carry the dynamic modal meaning of 'volition', though pure examples of this are hard to find. An example was given in (8) above, and another example is given in (37).

37 If you sell your vehicle through a motor auction, please ask whether the auctioneer *will* complete the notification of sale on your behalf. If they *will* not, you should tell DVLA in writing that you have transferred the vehicle to the auction firm.

In the next two examples the past tense form *would* expresses volition.

38 I *would* not live anywhere else in England.

39 She *wouldn't* go to sleep, she *wouldn't* eat, she *wouldn't* do anything.

Volitional meaning is particularly clear when the modal verb is stressed, as in *I will go to New York, even if you don't approve.*

Another meaning signalled by WILL is 'intention', which is a weaker kind of volition, as in the examples that follow.

40 Well, we *will* have dips and crisps and things like that.

41 The statement also said that he *would* be sending a personal envoy to Baghdad for a meeting with the Iraqi leader.

10.3.4.3 Dynamic modality: predisposition

In some cases WILL expresses a predisposition on the part of the referent of the Subject.

42 A new book by Ms Holland, We Don't Play with Guns Here, urges early-years centres to reconsider the ban on "war, weapon, and superhero play", arguing that boys *will* be boys.

43 A solvent is a substance, usually liquid, that *will* dissolve another substance.

After (42) we might add 'that's what they are like', and after (43) 'that is its nature'.

10.3.4.4 Deontic modality: obligation

In (44) below the speaker is directing the addressee to do something, so that the modal verb in this example (which has stress on it) clearly expresses deontic meaning.

44 You *will* do as I tell you.

The uses of WILL and *would* are summarized in Table 10.3.

The uses of WILL/*would*
epistemic modality: futurity and evidence-based predictions/conclusions
dynamic modality: volition
dynamic modality: predisposition
deontic modality: obligation

Table 10.3: The uses of WILL/*would*

10.3.4.5 WILL + infinitive is not a future tense

In some grammars the WILL + infinitive combination is regarded as a future tense. We do not take this view here. The reason is that WILL almost never refers purely to future time, typically contributing a modal dimension of meaning. It therefore semantically belongs with the modal verbs. Syntactically, too, it belongs with the modals (see section 10.3.3 for an overview of the syntactic properties of the modals).

10.3.4.6 WILL/SHALL + progressive

Consider the example below.

45 And you'll start by riding around a small circuit under close observation from your instructor who *will be monitoring* your progress, as you learn to control your bike.

In this example the modal auxiliary WILL combines with the progressive auxiliary BE and the lexical verb MONITOR. (With first person Subjects SHALL is also possible.) As we saw in section 9.3.2, the progressive construction expresses that a dynamic situation is in progress over a certain period of time. In (45) the ongoing monitoring 'frames' the process of learning to ride a bike.

Consider now (46)–(48) which also contain WILL + progressive BE + a lexical verb, but lack the semantic element of 'unfolding' over time.

46 My right honourable friend *will be making* that clear in his own statement.

47 Following a fatal accident the inspector *will be making* a report to the Coroner.

48 I regret to now inform you that we *will be terminating* all our contracts with you as of Monday 22nd of July 1991.

In these examples we have a combination of the arrangement meaning of the progressive futurate, discussed in section 9.3.2.4.4, and the future meaning of WILL. This special meaning has been glossed as 'future as a matter of course'. What this means is that the future events referred to are in some way expected to take place, given what the speakers know about the present circumstances. Thus in (46) the speaker, a Member of Parliament, knows that his colleague is due to make a clarificatory statement of his own in the pre-scheduled parliamentary proceedings, while (47) carries the implication that 'a fatal accident normally entails an inspector's report'. In (48), from a letter, the word *now* is significant. The letter in question is being written as a result of some unmentioned event that took place earlier, resulting in the impending termination of the contracts. We can paraphrase (48) as follows: 'now that X has taken place it follows that contracts will be terminated'. As noted already, the future events in these examples are not viewed as unfolding over time, as is the case with the 'regular' progressive, and hence they are not aspectual. This is the reason why this construction is discussed in this chapter.

10.3.5 SHALL and *should*

In section 9.2.3 we saw that the verb *should* is the past tense form of SHALL despite the fact that the relationship between these verbs is mostly not a matter of tense. We will regard *should* as being idiomatic. For this reason I will treat SHALL and *should* separately.

10.3.5.1 SHALL

10.3.5.1.1 Futurity

As with WILL, the main use of SHALL is to refer to future time.

49 I *shall regret* this for the rest of my life!

50 We *shall arrive* on Monday 18 March and leave on Thursday 2 May.

51 Whatever it is, we *shall* not have that kind of quality, if we do not have a prosperous economy founded on a quality workforce.

In these examples WILL is also possible, and in fact much more likely to occur. The difference between the two verbs is that SHALL is rather formal-sounding, and a little old-fashioned. What's more, it is mostly used in British English, and normally only with first person singular or plural Subjects. Recent research has shown that the use of SHALL is declining rapidly both in the UK and in the US.

10.3.5.1.2 Deontic modality: rules and regulations, asking for instructions, self-imposed obligation

Subjects other than first person singular and plural are possible with SHALL in written language, especially in 'rules and regulations', as in (52)–(54). This is not a future time use.

52 The committee *shall have* the power of consultation with appropriate experts not being members of the Central Activity or School in question.

53 The time spent on private clinical practice *shall* not exceed the equivalent of one half day per week.

54 Professors and readers *shall* retire at the age of 65.

In interrogative clauses (section 6.2) SHALL carries deontic meaning because the speaker is asking the addressee for instructions.

55 *Shall* I keep it here till the summer?

Finally, a somewhat marked use of deontic SHALL occurs in (56).

56 You *shall* go to the show.

Here the speaker promises the addressee that a particular event will happen by imposing an obligation on himself to bring it about. The verb will normally carry heavy stress.

10.3.5.1.3 Dynamic modality: volition

In the following examples SHALL expresses 'volition', more specifically 'intention', which is typically a dynamic concept because it relates to the Subject of the clause.

57 I *shall* bear that in mind for future reference.

58 We *shall* make up our mind when the IMF has reported.

Table 10.4 provides an overview of the uses of SHALL.

The uses of SHALL
futurity
deontic modality: rules and regulations, asking for instructions, self-imposed obligation
dynamic modality: volition

Table 10.4: The uses of SHALL

10.3.5.2 *Should*

10.3.5.2.1 Deontic modality: necessity

Should can be used to express deontic meaning, as in (59)–(62).

59 I think she *should* wait at the airport.

60 And of course as a learner you *should* be extra careful.

61 A theorem *should* come to your mind like a flash of lightning.

62 The main focus of economic planning *should* be on meeting the medium-term impact of the recession, particularly on employment.

This use of *should* is concerned with the way the world must be constituted, as perceived by the speaker, or as dictated by circumstances. There is no expectation that the situation that is expressed in the Complement Clause ('wait at the airport', 'be careful', etc.)

will come about. This use of *should* is interchangeable with OUGHT [*to*], discussed in section 10.3.9.2.

10.3.5.2.2 Epistemic modality: evidence-based supposition

The epistemic use of *should* occurs when a speaker or writer makes a supposition about a future situation on the basis of knowledge or experience they possess. The situation in question may not be actualized in the way that is anticipated.

63 On Saturday I'm off to a fireworks & classical music evening at Leeds Castle which *should* be good.

64 Well, I'm having Gay put out a reminder slip at the moment which *should* be in your pigeon-hole before ten-thirty.

The knowledge on which the suppositions are based can vary in strength. In the first example the speaker is led to the conclusion that the forthcoming event will be good on the basis of what she knows is on offer at Leeds Castle. In the second example the conclusion is based on a knowledge of circumstances, for example how quickly the person referred to as *Gay* usually dispatches messages. Arguably also epistemic are the following, perhaps somewhat mannered, locutions where *I should think* and *I should have thought* are more tentative and speculative than *I would think* and *I would have thought*.

65 I *should* think the number of people who would actually run a process like this would be really quite small.

66 I *should* have thought he'd've had one before now.

Epistemic *should* is weaker than epistemic MUST (discussed in section 10.3.8.2).

10.3.5.2.3 Mandative and putative *should*

Certain verbs, adjectives, and nouns trigger the use of *should*. Here are some examples.

67 It also <u>recommended</u> [that the service *should* have at least 240 lines, which happened to be the limit for the Baird system at the time].

68 It was in nineteen hundred and six that the Queen's great-grandfather King Edward the Seventh <u>decreed</u> [that privates in the Household Cavalry *should* henceforth to be known as troopers].

69 It is <u>important</u> [that all randomised clinical trials *should* be published irrespective of their results].

We refer to *should* in the *that*-clauses as *mandative <u>should</u>*, and to the clauses themselves as *mandative <u>should</u> clauses*. These express a directive meaning. When the subordinate clause contains only a plain form of the verb we speak of *mandative subjunctive clauses*, which express the same directive meaning, as we saw in section 10.3.2. In (67)–(69) the trigger word (underlined) is 'forward-looking' (i.e. modal), in the sense that what is recommended, decreed, or important has not (yet) been brought about. Notice that the matrix clause verb can be in the past tense, as in (67) and (68). Other triggers for mandative *should* include the verbs BEG, DEMAND, ENTREAT, INSIST, ORDER, RECOMMEND, SUGGEST; the nouns *decision, demand, intention, recommendation, order, proposal, request*; and the adjectives *advisable, desirable, essential, necessary, preferable, urgent*, and *vital*, among others.

When the *that*-clause expresses an evaluative, reflective, attitudinal or emotive meaning we speak of *putative <u>should</u>*, as in (70)–(72). The bracketed clauses are called *putative <u>should</u> clauses*.

70 It is <u>disappointing</u>, therefore, [that the submitted design *should* fall far short of its clearly stated goal].

71 It seems <u>amazing</u> now [that somebody I remember as so conventional *should* have been so ahead of her time in female rights].

72 There were good <u>reasons</u> [why the Commonwealth *should* not have been popular with the English and Welsh in general].

Should is not required in the examples above, as (73)–(75) show. Here the bracketed clauses are unmodalized.

73 It is <u>disappointing</u>, therefore, [that the submitted design falls far short of its clearly stated goal].

74 It seems <u>amazing</u> now [that somebody I remember as so conventional was so ahead of her time in female rights].

75 There were good <u>reasons</u> [why the Commonwealth was not popular with the English and Welsh in general].

Other triggers for putative *should* include *good, incredible, sad, surprising, remarkable, a pity,* and *a shame.* Mandative and putative *should* are a feature of British English, and not used frequently in American English.

10.3.5.2.4 *Should* in conditional and purposive clauses

Should can also occur in conditional clauses where a certain amount of doubt is expressed as to the actualization of the situation referred to. Thus in (76) the speaker probably thinks it unlikely that the addressee will run into him, or will have further queries, in the case of (77).

76 I'll accept cash if you *should* run into me.

77 *Should* you have any further queries please do not hesitate to contact me.

In (78) *should* is used in a clause that expresses 'purpose'.

78 There was a deliberate effort to make it appear surgical, and almost consequence-free in order that public opinion at home *should* not be eroded.

Table 10.5 gives an overview of the uses of *should*.

The uses of *should*
deontic modality: necessity
epistemic modality: evidence-based supposition
mandative/putative uses
conditional use
purposive use

Table 10.5:The uses of **should**

10.3.6 Can/*could*

We distinguish dynamic, deontic, and epistemic meanings for can/*could*, discussed in the following sections.

10.3.6.1 Dynamic possibility: neutral possibility, ability, and existential meaning

The core meaning of CAN is 'possibility', exemplified in (79)–(82), paraphrasable as 'It is possible for…'. We regard this neutral type of modality as dynamic because it concerns circumstances in general, not the speaker.

79 I don't understand why the service sector *can* show any optimism.

80 When those resolutions are fulfilled or are in the process of being fulfilled then operations *can* cease.

81 For example, one *could* record every minute of the operation and gain an enormous amount of data.

82 You *could* walk to our cabins, and not meet a soul.

In the examples above *could* is more tentative, or expresses a theoretical, rather than a real, possibility.

Another type of dynamic possibility is 'ability', as exemplified in the examples below.

83 Though dolphins *can* sense an oil-slick and will move away from it, the size of the current spill guarantees that it will catch some animals.

84 Pete *could* do basic things on a computer, but it wasn't enough.

Finally, the 'existential' meaning of *can* typically concerns a property that is ascribed to some members of a particular set of individuals, animals, or the like, or a property that applies to a referent at certain times. In (85)–(87) the properties of 'being aggressive', 'being fatty', and 'being brave' are ascribed to the Subjects of the clauses, and for this reason the modal verbs express dynamic modality. The example in (88) with *could* refers to past time, and can be paraphrased as 'It was possible for her to be negative about him'.

85 Don't blame breed, all dogs *can* be aggressive.

86 Lamb *can* be fatty when you buy it so make sure you trim off any obvious and excessive chunks of fat before putting the meat in for mincing.

87 The public, which has a clear view of what it expects from the police, understands the need for measured police responses and knows that individual police officers *can* be outstandingly brave.

88 Given a little bit of an excuse she *could* be negative about him.

10.3.6.2 Deontic possibility: permission

A less common meaning for CAN is deontic possibility, that is, 'permission'. Examples are shown in (89) and (90).

89 You *can* only have showers on week-days after supper.

90 You *cannot* dump them in here.

It is not always possible to distinguish the 'possibility' and 'permission' senses of CAN. In the example below, both readings are possible: 'Is it possible to change my flight?' or 'Am I permitted to change my flight?'

91 *Can* I change my flight to the eight forty one on Thursday evening?

If *could* had been used in this example, the request would have been more tentative and polite. Attested examples of *could* in its permission sense are hard to find. Two candidates are shown in (92) and (93). The first of these examples is likely to mean 'Are we permitted to have our *Locoscript 2* disc back?' The 'possibility' sense is unlikely, given that the clause begins with *if possible*, and the notion of possibility would then be expressed twice. Example (93), like (91), is ambiguous: both 'possibility' and 'permission' are possible interpretations.

92 If possible, *could* we please have our *Locoscript 2* disc back?

93 *Could* we have an indie disco on the third floor?

It should be stressed that in many cases the discourse context makes clear which meaning was intended.

Prescriptivists and schoolteachers have in the past frowned upon the 'permission' use of CAN, and have argued that speakers should use MAY instead, but in fact the permission sense is well established, and poses no communicative problems.

10.3.6.3 Epistemic necessity: knowledge-based conclusion

In the following example the speaker concludes, on the basis of his knowledge of Simon, that he is not any older than the people referred to as 'us'. The verb CAN clearly expresses epistemic meaning here. It can only be used with this sense when it is negated.

94 Actually, Simon *can't* be too much older than us.

Table 10.6 summarizes the uses of CAN / *could*.

The uses of CAN/*could*
dynamic possibility: neutral possibility, ability, and existential meaning
deontic possibility: permission
epistemic necessity (in negative contexts): knowledge-based conclusion

Table 10.6: The uses of CAN/*could*

10.3.7 MAY/*might*

In the following sections we look at the epistemic, deontic, and formulaic meanings of MAY/*might*.

10.3.7.1 Epistemic possibility: knowledge-based supposition

The modal verb MAY, with its past tense form *might*, commonly expresses epistemic possibility, paraphrasable as 'It is possible that…'.

95 I appreciate that it *may* be too late, or not desirable to make any change, but I just thought I would send you this anyway.

96 It *may* mean he's not normal.

97 She *might* be coming to Clare's party.

98 You said to me once you *might* come to London to visit.

These examples express epistemic meanings, because the speakers have some knowledge or evidence for their assumptions, though this evidence is likely to be weak.

How does *may* differ from *might*, and how does it differ from CAN expressing 'possibility'? The answer to the first question is that a speaker expresses a higher degree of uncertainty when using *might* than when using *may*. The past tense form *might* seems to distance the speaker further from the non-factuality of the clause than does *may*. Put differently, the *strength* of the modal meaning is lessened in the case of *might*. In an example like (97) this means that the speaker is less committed to the possibility that Clare will come to the party than if *may* had been used. As for the second question, if we look at an example like (96) MAY can be said to express a 'real' possibility, unlike CAN, which would express a more remote or theoretical possibility. A therapist not wanting to influence her colleagues' views when discussing with them the possible diagnoses for a patient's problems might utter (96) using CAN.

In the following examples, we can paraphrase the clauses containing MAY (called *concessive* MAY) by using an unmodalized clause introduced by *(al)though*.

99 It *may* be good for you, but it's not very good for the black people in South Africa. > 'Although it is good for you, it's not very good for the black people in South Africa.'

100 It *may* be bad for the earth's climate, but in the short term it's good for Brazil's economy. > 'Although it is bad for the earth's climate, in the short term it's good for Brazil's economy.'

10.3.7.2 Deontic possibility: permission

A less common meaning for MAY is 'permission'.

101 *May* I point out they need trade as much as they need aid?

102 *May* I also ask if you would send me deadline dates for when the Journal goes into six issues a year?

103 If you are excepted you *may*, if you wish, pay Class 2 contributions voluntarily to keep up your right to the benefits they provide.

We saw in section 10.3.6.2 that it is also possible to use CAN to express 'permission'. How do CAN and MAY differ in this regard? In general, MAY is much more formal, and a speaker who grants permission using this verb is more likely to be in a role of authority. Conversely, a speaker who asks for permission using MAY can be perceived to be overly polite.

The permission meaning of *might* is rare. An example is shown below.

104 When she decided that the Shah – himself a chain-smoker – was saying nothing of interest, she stopped taking notes and asked whether she *might* smoke.

10.3.7.3 Formulaic MAY

In main clauses MAY can be used formulaically to express a wish, as in (105). In many languages a subjunctive verb form is used here.

105 Long *may* they fail.

Table 10.7 summarizes the uses of MAY/*might*.

The uses of MAY/*might*
epistemic possibility: knowledge-based supposition
deontic possibility: permission
formulaic use

Table 10.7: The uses of MAY/*might*

10.3.8 MUST

MUST can express deontic, epistemic, or dynamic necessity.

10.3.8.1 Deontic necessity: obligation

The core meaning of MUST is deontic necessity, that is, 'obligation'.

106 You seem to be seeking to destroy yourself in some way, but you *must* not include me in your plan of action.

107 She *must* not put him through that agony again.

108 You *must* keep them moist.

120 I <u>don't</u> even *dare* <u>to write what the best and the worst I can expect is</u>.

121 You <u>don't</u> *need* <u>to bother</u>.

122 Why <u>did</u> they *dare* <u>to rob the Northern Bank of more than £26 million</u>?

123 Why <u>do</u> you *need* <u>to chop them down</u>?

The *to*-infinitive clause can have a Subject of its own, as in (124) and (125) (section 8.1.2.1), though for DARE this involves a different meaning ('challenge').

124 I *dare* <u>you to visit Johannesburg</u>, the city for softies.

125 I *need* <u>you to do me a huge favour</u>.

Lexical DARE can also take a bare infinitive Complement, as in (126) below. In this example it is preceded by a modal verb, and cannot therefore itself be modal.

126 He wouldn't *dare* <u>take it from you</u>.

In addition, NEED can take a noun phrase as Direct Object, as in (127).

127 They don't *need* <u>any more business</u>.

As modal verbs, DARE and NEED take a bare infinitive Complement in negated and/or inverted structures. They do not have third person singular forms.

128 Or *daren't* you <u>ask</u>?

129 You *needn't* <u>read every chapter</u>.

130 And *dare* I <u>suggest that that is the match-winner</u>?

131 Nor *need* I <u>look further than my own city of Sheffield</u>.

As a marginal modal verb NEED has no past tense: we cannot say for example *He needed read every chapter*. It expresses 'necessity' which is clearly a central modal meaning. DARE is not obviously modal from the point of view of meaning, though it is 'forward-looking', and is sometimes regarded as instantiating dynamic modality, due to the fact that the act of daring relates to the Subject of a clause.

10.3.9.2 Oᴜɢʜᴛ [*to*]

Syntactically, ᴏᴜɢʜᴛ is followed by a *to*-infinitive (indicated by '[*to*]'), and it is this fact that makes ᴏᴜɢʜᴛ a marginal modal, because core modals are followed by bare infinitives. Here are some examples.

132 Oh well, I suppose I *ought* <u>to go to bed</u>, as it's work tomorrow.

133 Do you think we *ought* <u>to bring some wine</u>?

134 I think Carol *ought* <u>to leave at this point</u>.

ᴏᴜɢʜᴛ resembles ᴍᴜsᴛ in having no past tense form.

For some speakers ᴏᴜɢʜᴛ [*to*] can take ᴅᴏ-support (section 3.6.3.5), a property of lexical verbs, though this is non-standard.

135 Bristol was built on the slave trade, *didn't* we *ought* <u>to flatten it</u> just to show how sorry we are?

Interrogative and negative structures with ᴏᴜɢʜᴛ [*to*], exemplified below, are rare. Notice that in inverted structures the *to*-infinitive is separated from the verb.

136 *Ought* the doctor <u>to have intervened as he did</u>?

137 Peter Jackson confirmed at Comic-Con that his eagerly-anticipated two-part Hobbit film is still some way off, but that *oughtn't* <u>to stop us speculating about casting</u>.

Some grammarians have noted that ᴏᴜɢʜᴛ can be followed by a bare infinitive in American English in interrogative and negative structures, as in (138) and (139).

138 But, *ought* I <u>deceive you</u>?

139 This *oughtn't* <u>be a one-time thing</u>.

The infinitival marker *to* does not belong with ᴏᴜɢʜᴛ, because it can be separated from it, as in (136) above, and in (140) below where an adverb is placed between ᴏᴜɢʜᴛ and *to*.

140 But we need to get out of this war into a peace which the Arabs themselves have to make and anything which suggests that the Western Christian world is imposing its own values on the Muslim world is something which we *ought* **now** <u>to avoid</u>.

OUGHT [*to*] mainly carries the same deontic meaning as *should* (discussed in section 10.3.5.2.1), which is concerned with the way a speaker believes the world must be constituted. As with *should*, there is no expectation that the situation expressed in the Complement Clause will be actualized. Almost always *should* can be substituted for OUGHT [*to*].

10.3.10 Modal idioms

Modal idioms are idiosyncratic verbal formations which consist of more than one word and which have modal meanings that are not predictable from the constituent parts (compare the non-modal idiom *kick the bucket*). Under this heading we include HAVE *got* [*to*], *had better/best*, *would rather/sooner/as soon*, and BE [*to*].

10.3.10.1 HAVE *got* [*to*]

We regard HAVE *got* [*to*] as idiomatic, because the element *got* is fixed, and because it derives its meaning from the combination as a whole (often shortened as *gotta*). In this connection note that the meaning of *got* is 'bleached' (i.e. has lost its original meaning), and does not carry the meaning 'possess'.

The verb HAVE within the combination HAVE *got* behaves like an auxiliary verb because it can invert with a Subject and can be negated, as in (141) and (142), but cannot be preceded by other auxiliary verbs, modal or otherwise, as (143) and (144) show. In this respect it behaves like the core modals. Also like the core modals, HAVE *got* is always tensed (it almost always occurs in the present tense); but unlike the core modals, it can agree with a Subject, as in (145), and it is followed by a *to*-infinitive (indicated by '[*to*]'). In this respect it resembles the modal lexical verbs (section 10.3.11.3), though not sufficiently to put it in that class.

141 *Have* you *got* to pay for Betty to go?

142 Are you sure you just *haven't got* to send it off to the American address?

143 *Each of us will have got to do it three times.

144 *Each of us is having got to do it three times.

145 Each of us *has got* to do it three times.

The verb HAVE can be attached to the Subject in shortened form, as in (146) and (147), or left out, as in (148).

146 You*'ve got* <u>to keep it there</u>.

147 It*'s got* <u>to sound as though it fits in somehow</u>, hasn't it?

148 You *got* <u>to have the money</u>, though, haven't you?

We know that HAVE is left out in (148) because of the presence of the interrogative tag *haven't you?* Interrogative tags always 'pick up' the verb in the matrix clause (see section 4.1.1.8).

HAVE *got* [*to*] is used in informal settings, mostly in British English, and can express the deontic meaning of necessity (i.e. 'obligation'), as in (149). It is very often interchangeable with MUST, though it expresses an objective necessity, rather than a subjective one.

149 You *have got* <u>to work hard</u>, you *have got* <u>to perform well</u>.

With HAVE *got* [*to*] the source of the obligation is often not the speaker, but external circumstances such as regulations, procedures, etc., as in (150) and (151). The idiom then expresses dynamic meaning.

150 "You*'ve got* <u>to get a form, a complex form</u> – the government's good at complex forms; you *have got* <u>to get a photograph</u>."

151 "It*'s got* <u>to be the same</u> whether you're a back bencher, or whether you're the chancellor of the exchequer, the same rules *have got* <u>to apply to you</u>," she added.

Less commonly HAVE *got* [*to*] expresses epistemic meaning, as in (152).

152 These girls are having a lot of pressure put on them – it *has got* <u>to be excruciatingly difficult</u>.

We must distinguish HAVE *got* [*to*] from HAVE *got* (= 'possess'), as in (153), and HAVE *got to do* [*with*] (= 'relate to'), as in (154).

153 I'm deliberately taking this out of order because we *have got* a nomination for Secretary.

154 So you might wonder what this *has got to do with* climate.

I will discuss the modal lexical verb HAVE [*to*] in section 10.3.11.3.2.

10.3.10.2 Had better/best and would rather/sooner/as soon

We regard *had better/best* and *would rather/sooner/as soon* as idiomatic, because they contain fixed, semantically bleached components. Syntactically, these modal idioms are followed by a bare infinitive, a property of the core modals.

155 We *had better* <u>keep our feet on the ground</u>.

156 I *would rather* <u>spend the money on something else</u>.

157 "I *would sooner* <u>die in jail</u>," Gilfoyle told *The Times* in an exclusive interview this week.

158 Sometimes you happen on an area you *would as soon* <u>keep to yourself</u>.

The idioms with *would* can also be followed by a finite clause, as in the example below.

159 If you feel you're in danger, remember that BR *would rather* <u>your train were delayed than that you became the victim of a crime</u>.

Notice the occurrence of *were* in the Complement Clause.

Morphologically, these idioms resemble the core modals: there are no third person singular present tense forms (*has better, **wills rather/sooner*), and no non-tensed forms (*having better), although *had* and *would* can be attached to a preceding Subject, as in (160) and (161), or even left out, as in (162).

160 You*'d better* not let Jo get hold of this.

161 Well I*'d rather* a friend picked their ear personally.

162 I think I *better* show you.

The first element of these combinations behaves like an auxiliary because inversion and negation are possible.

163 So *had* I *better* shut up concerning them?

164 *Would* I *rather* drink tea than water?

Two types of negation are attested: one with *hadn't* or *wouldn't*, the other with the word *not* following the idiom.

165 I *hadn't better* ask him again in case somebody here notices.

166 Poor wholesome Todd *had better not* let the side down or Sarah'll get her gun.

167 People used to ask him sometimes if he *wouldn't rather* have had a son, and he used to say that Amanda was a son as well as a daughter.

168 We *would rather not* use animals and we try hard to find alternatives.

The negated structures are interchangeable in the case of *had better*, but this is not always so for the other idioms. Thus, *wouldn't rather have had a son* in (167) does not mean the same as *would rather not have had a son*.

Had better expresses deontic necessity, which is very similar to the meaning expressed by *should* and OUGHT [*to*]. The idioms containing *would* express the dynamic meaning of 'preference'.

10.3.10.3 BE [*to*]

The combination BE [*to*] is idiomatic because the verb BE is used with a specialized modal meaning. Like the core modals it is always tensed, and hence cannot be preceded by other auxiliary verbs. As (169) and (170) show, inversion and negation are possible for BE; this is an auxiliary-like property. However, modal BE is always followed by a *to*-infinitive (indicated by '[*to*]'), and can agree with a Subject, as shown in (171)–(173). In this respect it resembles modal lexical verbs (section 10.3.11.3). However, as with HAVE *got* [*to*], discussed in section 10.3.10.1, this is not sufficiently the case to assign it to this class.

169 *Are* we <u>to start</u>?

170 The group began devising some form of punctuation to mark posts that *weren't* <u>to be taken seriously</u>.

171 He *is* <u>to hold talks on the Gulf crisis with the Prime Minister</u>.

172 Judges *are* <u>to take far less account of the offender's past record</u>.

173 The peoples of Europe *are not* <u>to be formally consulted at any point, by referendum or otherwise</u>.

BE [*to*] can express the deontic meanings of 'obligation' and 'necessity', as in (169) and (170), or can be used to express future arrangements, plans, and so on, as in (171). The examples in (172) and (173) are ambiguous: the former can mean either 'judges must take far less account of the offender's past record' (the most likely reading), or 'judges will be taking far less of the offender's past record'. (173) can mean either 'the consultation must not take place' or 'the consultation is not planned to take place'.

In the past tense BE [*to*] can express an arrangement in the past or a 'future in the past'.

174 And these buildings *were* <u>to be the home of Ordnance Survey for the next one hundred years</u>.

175 Living with her family in Oxford, she had set herself to learn Latin and Greek as a girl, later attending St Anne's College of which she *was* <u>to become an honorary fellow</u>.

10.3.11 Lexical modality

Modal meanings can be expressed lexically by nouns, adjectives, verbs, adverbs, and particles. These trigger (or 'govern', as traditional grammar has it) a *modal context*, usually in the shape of a subjunctive clause (sections 10.3.2 and 10.3.5.2.3).

10.3.11.1 Modal nouns

Examples of modal nouns include *condition, decree, demand, necessity, order, requirement, request, resolution,* and *wish*. In the example below the modal noun *intention* creates a modal context which contains the modal verb *should*.

176 So I drew the inference that the *intention* was <u>that the media *should* reproduce the programme</u>.

Notice that *should* in this example is mandative *should* (section 10.3.5.2.3). In (177) the verb *be* in the subjunctive clause is 'governed' by the modal noun *insistence*. This example contains two further modal expressions: *were* in the *if*-clause, and *would* in the matrix clause.

177 And yet if it <u>were</u> not for Mrs Thatcher's *insistence* <u>that the 12 water businesses of England and Wales *be* made economically healthy</u>, the Lowermoor plant <u>would</u> have had someone on duty on the day the aluminium sulphate was dumped into the wrong tank.

Another example of a modal noun is *wish*, illustrated by the example below, in which it licenses a subjunctive clause.

178 We respect the judge's *wishes* <u>that we not raise the temperature further</u>.

10.3.11.2 Modal adjectives

Examples of modal adjectives include *able, advisable, anxious, bound, concerned, crucial, desirable, essential, fitting, imperative, important, likely, necessary, possible, supposed, sure, vital,* and *willing.* These create modal contexts to varying degrees, often depending on how the speaker or writer views the situation expressed by the Complement.

179 Survivors are *likely* <u>to experience adverse physical and psychological effects</u>.

180 There are *bound* <u>to be guards at the checkout</u>, whether the alarm is out for us or not.

181 It would be *desirable* <u>to have as much analysis as possible done automatically</u>.

182 I mean as councillors we are legally *obliged* <u>to try and ensure that our expenditure matches our income</u>.

183 It is therefore *necessary* <u>to encourage the operators to take short breaks to keep them properly alert</u>.

In the examples above the Complements are viewed as non-actualized, potential situations in the future.

Notice that *should* in (184) and (185) is mandative *should* (section 10.3.5.2.3), whereas (186) involves a mandative subjunctive clause (section 10.3.2).

184 He was *anxious* <u>that arguments within the Community *should* not leave Britain isolated</u>.

185 It is *desirable* that the robot *should* be deflected when it is kicked so that the cow is not harmed.

186 It is *imperative* that a new maturity *be* achieved in domestic and international communications.

10.3.11.3 Modal lexical verbs

10.3.11.3.1 Modal lexical verbs taking a Direct Object

We have already come across examples of modal lexical verbs, namely URGE in (13) and DECREE in (68). Others include ADVISE, INTEND, PROPOSE, RECOMMEND, REQUIRE, SUGGEST, and WISH. These verbs can license mandative *should* clauses or mandative subjunctive clauses.

187 We *intend* that this bank *should* provide the stimulus for private investment in Eastern Europe.

188 We *recommend* that front brake pads *be* checked for wear at least every 12,000 miles or 12 months.

189 Both divisions *suggest* that treatment *be* directed towards the cause underlying the disease rather than the symptoms.

10.3.11.3.2 HAVE [*to*]

Unlike the core modal auxiliaries, modal lexical HAVE can take inflectional endings, and licenses a *to*-infinitive clause as Complement (indicated by '[*to*]').

190 You *have* to pay for these.

Although it readily takes DO-support, as in (191), inversion and negation, as in (192) and (193), are barely possible for most speakers.

191 Do we *have* to take a bottle of wine?

192 *Have* we to consider the alarming possibility that the British just don't have the tennis gene?

193 "We *haven't* to get worried after this because we played well and we need to remember we were playing away to Milan, who are a pretty strong side."

HAVE [*to*] can occur as a non-tensed form, and can be preceded by an auxiliary verb, modal or non-modal, as (194) and (195) demonstrate.

194 But I'<u>ll</u> *have* <u>to drive</u>.

195 At the moment the Gunners <u>are</u> *having* <u>to defend</u> as Savavakos brings that up.

Like the core modal verb MUST, and like HAVE *got* [*to*], the combination HAVE [*to*] can express 'obligation'. The latter is more formal than HAVE *got* [*to*]. However, unlike with MUST, but like with HAVE *got* [*to*], the obligation is imposed by someone other than the speaker. For example, in (190), the requirement to pay is imposed by the seller, not by the speaker. Recall that MUST has no past tense form (sections 10.3.3 and 10.3.8). To express past obligation HAVE [*to*] is used instead, as in (196).

196 I *had* <u>to get down there by nine</u>.

Another meaning expressed by HAVE [*to*] is dynamic necessity. In (197) the obligation of checking on the babies is imposed on the nurse by hospital regulations.

197 Twenty babies have been born overnight and she *has* <u>to check they're all healthy</u>.

Finally, HAVE [*to*] can express epistemic meaning, as in (198), though this is more common in American English.

198 It *has* <u>to be true</u>; they must be putting something in the water.

Notice that this sentence also contains an example of epistemic MUST.

10.3.11.3.3 BE *going* [*to*]

BE *going* [*to*] is an idiosyncratic, idiomatic combination, which resembles other verbs and verbal constructions in a number of ways, as we will see.

Firstly, BE in this combination can take a full range of inflectional forms, including non-finite forms. For example, in (199) BE takes a bare infinitive form, placed after the modal *will*.

199 The admissions process for entry in 2007 begins when the schools go back this month, although children will only find out in March which schools they *will* <u>be going</u> to attend.

Examples like this make clear that in this respect BE *going* [*to*] behaves like a lexical verb, and cannot syntactically be regarded as a core modal verb, because sequences of two or more modal auxiliaries are not possible in Standard English (though they are attested in the southern US, in Tyneside, and in Scotland). This example is particularly interesting because it combines two future time markers.

Secondly, BE *going* [*to*] takes a *to*-infinitive clause as Complement (indicated by '[*to*]'), which is again a property of lexical verbs. However—and in this sense BE *going* [*to*] is idiosyncratic—within this combination BE behaves like an auxiliary verb (the progressive auxiliary BE) which conforms to the NICE properties (section 3.6.3.1), as (200)–(203) show.

200 John Brown *isn't* going <u>to be there</u>. [Negation]

201 *Is he* going <u>to come back here</u>? [Inversion]

202 He isn't going <u>to come back</u>, and neither is she. [Code]

203 He is going <u>to come back</u>. [Emphasis]

On the basis of the data presented above we conclude that on balance BE *going* [*to*] behaves like a lexical verb with a modal meaning. Its idiomatic nature is reflected in the fact that the element *going* is semantically bleached. However, we do not regard BE *going* [*to*] as a modal idiom (section 10.3.10), because the members of that class behave like the core modals to a much greater extent.

BE *going* [*to*] is common in spoken informal English, and is used to refer to future time. Despite our analysing it as modal, it also has aspectual qualities by virtue of the presence of the progressive auxiliary BE, and because it has 'current orientation'. This means that it often conveys a sense of immediacy, or the currency of present purpose, as the examples below show.

204 Right, I'*m going* <u>to dish this up now</u>.

205 Oh God I'*m going* <u>to stop for a minute</u>.

206 I'*m going* <u>to be in Ramsford tomorrow</u>.

By contrast, the verb WILL, which is also used to refer to future time, has a more neutral future meaning. Very often BE *going* [*to*] and WILL are interchangeable, though not always. Thus in (207) WILL cannot replace BE *going* [*to*].

207 If I'm *going to* (*will*) make such a meal out of every exercise, I'll never complete the course.

Here BE *going* [*to*] occurs in a conditional subordinate clause where WILL is rare, and only occurs in restricted circumstances, for example when it expresses volition. A volitional reading is excluded in (207), because one would not normally willingly 'make a meal out of every exercise'. However, consider next (208) where a volitional reading is plausible ('If they are not willing to...'). Here BE *going* [*to*] would sound odd.

208 Please ask whether the auctioneer will complete the notification of sale on your behalf. If they *will* not (?*are not going to*), you should tell DVLA in writing that you have transferred the vehicle to the auction firm.

In (209), too, the most likely reading for WILL is 'volition'. If we substitute *isn't going to* for *will not*, the *if*-clause will express 'intention' (i.e. it will mean 'if Parliament doesn't have the intention to restrain its law-making zeal').

209 If Parliament *will* not restrain its law-making zeal, it should at least have addressed this state of affairs by making legal advice and assistance available to the myriad caught in its tentacles.

BE *going* [*to*] can also express epistemic meaning, as in the following example.

210 I think that there's *going* to be incompetence in every profession.

The meaning conveyed here is 'prediction' based on general knowledge.

The past tense forms *was/were going* [*to*] express a past futurate (section 9.2.2.5), as exemplified in (211).

211 Bob *was going* to try and find him today.

10.3.11.4 Modal adverbs

Among the modal adverbs in English we find *arguably*, *probably*, *maybe*, *possibly*, *perhaps*, and *surely*. Here are some examples.

212 The age of total war is a recent phenomenon, *arguably* dating from the Thirty Years War.

213 I thought *maybe* you'd come round.

214 They may *possibly* increase the capacity of an individual organism to track or avoid change.

215 The teachers aren't *perhaps* aware of how they can work with the disabled student.

216 *Probably* the worst thing that one can have is a large, south facing window glazed with reeded glass which can disperse the sun's rays in all directions.

Notice the positional versatility of modal adverbs, and that in (214) modality is doubly encoded: here we have a modal verb, as well as a modal adverb, both expressing the meaning 'possibility'.

10.3.12 Hedges

Hedges are expressions that qualify a statement with regard to its truth. Some can add an element of modal meaning (e.g. doubt) to an utterance, as in (217)–(220).

217 So you would actually say, *I would have thought*, within your executive summary, something to the effect that the detailed design work you've done has been focused on the key element of the process.

218 But I mean it's working extremely well, and *I think* hopefully that will continue.

219 Well we're *sort of* working towards our first performance.

220 I used to *kind of* say you know please, please God get me out of this.

10.3.13 Other issues pertaining to modality

10.3.13.1 Contextual influences on the interpretation of modal verbs

The way we interpret modal expressions, especially modal verbs, often depends on the discourse context in which a particular verb is used. As an example, consider (221).

221 *May* I put it in a different way?

If this is uttered by someone who is asking for permission to make a point differently, then there is nothing remarkable about it, apart from the fact that CAN is more usual in such requests. However, imagine now the director of a big company uttering (221) at an important meeting. In such a situation, depending on how it is uttered, this person may simply be expressing an intention, namely 'I'm going to put it in a different way'. By uttering (221) containing the over(t)ly polite MAY, a certain degree of deliberately understated authority can be conveyed. Using the modals in this way to convey a particular stance in a conversation is extremely common, as a few further examples will make clear.

The interpretation of (222) in a particular context depends on interpersonal relationships, conversational setting, and so on. For example, if (222) is uttered by a friend it is likely to constitute a piece of advice, but if it is uttered by one's grandfather it might be a strong exhortation, or perhaps even an order.

222 You *should* keep your ancestral paintings.

Similar considerations apply to (223) and (224). These are not examples of speakers imposing their demands, but rather the sort of things we say to each other in friendly, polite interchanges. The most likely reading for (223) is that it is an offer, while (224) is an invitation.

223 Ah, you're exquisite; you *must* let me paint you.

224 However, the important thing is that we are having a house warming party and you *must* come.

Finally, consider the examples in (225), from a training video on how to ride a motorbike, and (226), from a cookbook.

225 You *can* now let go of the front brake.

226 You *can*, if you like, add some anchovy in a pattern between the eggs.

While ostensibly expressing 'permission' or 'possibility', it is possible to interpret the first use of CAN as an instruction, whereas the second use is likely to be understood as a suggestion. Notice the parenthetical *if you like*.

10.3.13.2 Indeterminate meanings

Modal expressions can be semantically indeterminate: it is not always possible to detect one clear meaning in a particular example. We came across a few instances of ambiguities in earlier sections. As an additional example, consider (227), from a sports commentary. Here we can perceive the meanings of 'ability' and 'possibility'. Of course, these meanings are closely related, because if someone is able to do something it is generally possible for them to do it (circumstances permitting).

227 Now Paul Allen *can* run at those Arsenal defenders.

Where more than one meaning is applicable to a particular verb we speak of *semantic merger*.

Chapter 11

Information structuring

This chapter discusses the syntactic choices speakers have in presenting information to their addressees.

11.1 Introduction

When we communicate with others there are various ways in which we can convey a particular message in speech or in writing. For example, if we want to make a statement about a particular state of affairs in the world which we believe to be true, we normally use a declarative clause (see section 6.1), as in example (1).

1 Pete married a strong woman.

The constituent order here is Subject–Predicator–Direct Object. We can embed an example like (1) in the conversational situation in (2).

2 Jim: Pete married a strong woman.

Meg: How come Pete married the wrong woman?

Jim: A **strong** woman Pete married _, not the **wrong** woman.

In this mini-interchange Meg mishears Jim. To set this right, Jim reorders the information conveyed in his original utterance by displacing the Direct Object from its original position following the verb MARRY (indicated by '_') to an initial position, thus deriving the order Direct Object–Subject–Predicator. In addition, the words *strong* and *wrong* are stressed, as indicated by the bold typeface. It is very common for users of English to highlight certain parts of the content of a clause in this manner, and in this chapter we will look at a number of ways in which speakers and writers can do so. This is called *information structuring*.

Before we proceed we need to distinguish between two types of meaning: *propositional meaning* and *non-propositional meaning*. The former is a semantic notion, concerned with what is expressed by the verb and its arguments, as well as any Adjuncts, abstracting away from a particular context of use. In the case of an example like (1) the propositional meaning roughly equates to 'x marry y (at some point t in the past)', with the values for x and y fixed as 'Pete' and 'a strong woman', respectively. By contrast, when we speak of non-propositional meaning we are talking about how processes such as information structuring can affect interpretation. As a rule of thumb, if the constituents in a clause are reordered by an information structuring process, the propositional meaning of the clause does not change, but the non-propositional meaning does.

We could say that the meaning of an utterance on a particular occasion is the sum total of its propositional meaning and its non-propositional meaning. Returning to (1) and Jim's second utterance in (2), their propositional meaning is the same, namely 'x marry y (at some point t in the past)', again with the values for x and y fixed as 'Pete' and 'a strong woman'. However, Jim's second utterance in (2), with a displaced Direct Object, has an added layer of non-propositional meaning, namely the information structuring effects of displacing and stressing the Direct Object. In this particular conversational setting, the information structuring effect amounts to correcting a wrong assumption on the part of Meg that Pete married the wrong woman.

Presenting information differently can be done in many ways, for example by displacement and stress, as above, but also by non-linguistic means such as accompanying an utterance with facial expressions, gestures, and so on. In this chapter I will focus only on the different *syntactic* possibilities of expressing a proposition in different ways.

11.2   Two principles of information structuring

Information structuring is 'regulated' by a number of principles, chief among them the *Given-Before-New Principle* and the *Principle of End Weight*. The former stipulates that speakers and writers, in composing their messages, will tend to place given information before new information. We understand given information to be information that is 'known' in the previous situational or linguistic context, that is, shared between interlocutors. New information has not become known in this way. By contrast, the Principle of End Weight stipulates that 'heavy' constituents, in the sense of units containing many words, tend to be placed at the end of a message. We will come across examples of these two principles in what follows. As we will see, both principles can be overridden.

11.3   Movement

In section 11.1 we saw that we can highlight information by displacing a particular unit in a clause. As in previous chapters, there is no suggestion here that we should regard displacement as a process that happens in the mind; making use of the notion of displacement is merely a convenient way of describing the structures we are dealing with.

We need to distinguish *obligatory movement* from *optional movement*. The former is exemplified by open interrogative clauses such as (3) (see section 6.2.1).

3 <u>What</u> did you say _?

Here the Direct Object of SAY has been displaced from the position indicated by '_' to the beginning of the clause. To form an open interrogative clause a speaker *must* move the *wh*-phrase to a clause-initial position, as well as implement Subject–auxiliary inversion (see section 11.7 below). By contrast, when movement is effected for information structuring reasons, it is normally optional, as we will see. We distinguish *leftward movements* from *rightward movements*.

11.3.1   Leftward movements

Displacements to the left are typically regulated by the Given-Before-New Principle, or they are motivated by a desire on the part of a speaker to establish a contrast between constituents in different clauses.

11.3.1.1 Preposing

Consider the following fragment from a conversation.

4 I go in Waterstones, or wherever, and buy paperbacks and read them and probably cast them aside or give them or lend them to someone else, and forget who you've lent them to. But hardbacks I wouldn't lend to anyone.

Notice that in the second sentence the Direct Object of the verb LEND, *hardbacks*, is not placed in its canonical position after the verb, but at the beginning of the clause. We can represent this displacement as in (5).

5 <u>Hardbacks</u> I wouldn't lend _ to anyone.

This type of *preposing* is called *topicalization*. This is because the first slot in a clause is often occupied by a string of words that specifies what the clause is about; it is the *topic* position. Topics characteristically represent given information in clauses, and usually function as Subject. In (4) the topic NP *hardbacks* represents given information because the conversation is about books. The preposed phrase establishes a link with a similar phrase (*paperbacks*) earlier on in the discourse. Here is a further example from a novel.

6 She was prevented from meeting a man with whom she was infatuated, a man who spent every day of the week three hundred yards from her own house by the proprieties, by those absurd social conventions which dictated what was becoming a lady of her position, and furthermore by *duty to King and country*. She shuddered as she remembered her prejudices which amounted to spurning with contumely and disgust the enemy at her door. *Her duty to her husband*, fighting on foreign field for his and her freedom, she did not consider at all.

The second part of this fragment is analysed as in (7).

7 [_{NP} <u>Her duty to her husband, fighting on foreign field for his and her freedom</u>], she did not consider _ at all.

The preposed phrase clearly establishes a link with the phrase *duty to King and country* in the preceding context.

Although it is rare, Indirect Objects can also be preposed, as in the example shown below.

8 Well I've been doing a lot of research into this, and [NP everybody that cooks] I ask [clause how they make pastry].

The clause introduced by *how* functions as Direct Object (see section 7.3.1.2.5).

Other types of phrases with different functions can also be preposed, as in the examples below.

9 [AdjP Horrible] it is _.

10 [PP To Rockefeller] it's rational economic planning _.

11 [AdvP Carefully] he _ lifted the lid of the cistern and dropped the wreckage of the mobile phone into the still filling waters.

In (12) and (13) we have a variant of preposing. It involves the displacement of a constituent, typically an adjective phrase, from inside a *though*-clause to the left.

12 Excellent though they both are _, they may not be enough.

13 Tempting though it is _ to link rising crime and the economic downturn, factors such as inequality play a far greater role.

The versions of these examples without displacement are shown in (14) and (15).

14 Though they both are excellent, they may not be enough.

15 Though it is tempting to link rising crime and the economic downturn, factors such as inequality play a far greater role.

Displacement from clauses with *as* is also possible.

16 My retail job, crazy as it is _, keeps me sane.

However, here a version without displacement is not possible.

17 *My retail job, *as it is crazy*, keeps me sane.

As with the earlier examples of preposing, the displaced phrases represent given information, and often establish a link with the preceding context. The following passage makes this clear.

18 At the start, the author appears to be going through the same agonies as the reader. Why spend time thinking about people who spend their lives regularly eating against the clock? 'Competitive eating', writes Fagone, 'was a symbolic hairball coughed up by the American id. It was meaningful like a tumour was meaningful.' In other words, *horrible though it is*, competitive eating is worth writing about, as a sign of the worst aspects of human nature.

In this passage the adjective *horrible* can be regarded as given information, because it is linked in the preceding text with something that is unpleasant, namely competitive eating.

Finally, in the following example the preposing of the noun phrase sets up a contrast. Consider again Jim's response in (2), repeated in (19).

19 [NP A strong woman] Pete married _, not the wrong woman.

As we have seen, Jim is correcting a wrong assumption on the part of Meg that Pete married the wrong woman.

11.3.1.2 Left dislocation

Consider the examples shown in (20) and (21).

20 *The colleague I mentioned to you*, I married *her*.

21 *Your mother*, *she* was just misunderstood.

In both cases a noun phrase has been preposed, but a 'copy' is left in the regular position of the NPs in the shape of a pronoun. In the first example, a Direct Object is copied; in the second example, a Subject. This process is called *left dislocation*. In speech there is often a short pause after the left-dislocated phrase, which usually represents given information. The pragmatic effect of left dislocation is that it creates discourse cohesion or textual cohesion. Notice that in (20) the dislocated NP conveys given information, witness the presence of the definite article *the*, which signals that the colleague in question is identifiable from the preceding discourse or represents shared knowledge. As we have seen, given information tends to precede new information. Example (21) is from a novel. The phrase *your mother* is used in the immediately preceding text (not shown here), and hence represents given information. By placing it in clause-initial position a textual link between the two instances of the phrase is created.

11.3.2 Rightward movements

Displacements to the right are characteristically regulated by the Principle of End Weight, introduced in section 11.2.

11.3.2.1 Postposing

As an example of *postposing*, consider (22).

22 She calls [NP writing paper] [NP notepaper].

Recall that we functionally analysed an example like this as involving a Subject (*she*), a Predicator (*calls*), a Direct Object (*writing paper*), and an Object-related Predicative Complement (*notepaper*) in a complex transitive complementation pattern (see section 4.1.3.3.2). Consider next the same example with a lengthened DO.

23 She calls [NP any kind of paper that can be used for correspondence] [NP notepaper].

Because the addressee will have to wait a long time before the Object-related Predicative Complement comes along, (23) is hard to process, and for this reason the DO will tend to be postposed rightwards, as in (24).

24 She calls _ [NP notepaper] [NP any kind of paper that can be used for correspondence].

This displacement, called *Heavy Noun Phrase Shift*, is in accordance with the Principle of End Weight: because the Direct Object NP is heavy it is moved to the end of the clause resulting in the order Subject – Predicator – Object-related Predicative Complement – Direct Object. The lengthier an unmoved Direct Object is, the harder it is to process the containing clause, and the more likely it is that it will be moved 'across' the Object-related Predicative Complement. The following example makes this particularly clear.

25 He lays 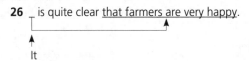 [_AdjP_ bare] [_NP_ <u>the mechanisms that construct a narrative whose secondary revisions are attempts to deny the very desire which it expresses, a desire which is nonetheless readable by the analyst who knows how to unscramble the code of the dream unconscious, where persons are interchangeable, the time is always the present, where positives may signify negatives and vice versa</u>].

Here the constituent order is Predicator (*lays*) + gap + Object-related Predicative Complement (*bare*) + Direct Object (*the mechanisms … versa*). The bracketed DO is a very long and complex noun phrase, and has been postposed to the right from the position indicated by '_' in conformity with the Principle of End Weight. Had the DO stayed in its regular position, the clause would have been virtually impossible to process.

11.3.2.2 Extraposition

As we saw in sections 3.2.2.1.2, 7.3.1.1, and 7.3.1.2, when a clause is moved and anticipatory *it* is substituted for the displaced clause as a place-holder, we speak of *extraposition*. Here are some further examples.

26 _ is quite clear <u>that farmers are very happy</u>.

It

27 _ seemed to me <u>that they weren't getting any better</u>.

It

28 Rajiv found _ frustrating [_clause_ <u>that his policies made little impact on poverty</u>].

it

In (26) and (27) the Subjects of the clauses have been displaced to the right. By contrast, in (28) a Direct Object has been moved to the end of the clause. In all these cases the displaced clauses are heavy, and therefore prefer to come last, in accordance with the Principle of End Weight. Extraposition is optional for (26), as its counterpart in (29) shows.

29 [That farmers are very happy] is quite clear.

By contrast, it is obligatory for (27) and (28), as can be seen below, where the displaced units have been 'put back' into the Subject and Direct Object positions, respectively.

30 *[That they weren't getting any better] seemed to me.

31 *Rajiv found [that his policies made little impact on poverty] frustrating.

However, notice in (32) that preposing of the content clause to a clause-initial position without inserting *it* is possible for (28).

32 [That his policies made little impact on poverty] Rajiv found _ frustrating.

Extraposition is also obligatory in (33), which, like (28), involves a complex transitive pattern with a *that*-clause functioning as Direct Object. Here the dummy pronoun *it* is possible in the position indicated by '_', but its omission facilitates the 'flow' of the clause.

33 He made _ clear [_clause_ that the nature of a future watchdog for the European banking industry within the single market should not be neglected].

11.3.2.3 Right dislocation

Consider (34).

34 I married *her, the woman I mentioned to you*.

This is the mirror image of (20), repeated here as (35).

35 *The colleague I mentioned to you*, I married *her*.

In (34) the Direct Object is displaced to the right, with a 'copy' in the shape of a pronoun in the 'regular' Direct Object position. This process is called *right dislocation*. When uttered there is normally a short pause after the pronoun. This pattern can be used in a situation in which the speaker thinks that the hearer may not be sure who the pronoun *her* refers to. For clarity the full referential NP is spelled out. This pattern is noteworthy because the right-dislocated constituents represent given information, and the Given-Before-New Principle is thus overridden.

11.4 Passivization

Recall that syntactically passive clauses involve the passive auxiliary BE followed by a past participle and an optional *by*-phrase. Less commonly the passive construction contains the verb GET (section 3.6.3.4). The Subject position of passive clauses is characteristically filled by a noun phrase that carries the semantic role of Patient or Theme. Here is an example.

36 The process was devised in 1795 by a man called Conté.

The active counterpart of this example is shown in (37).

37 A man called Conté devised the process in 1795.

Notice that the Direct Object of the active clause (*the process*) is the Subject of the passive clause. As we have seen, English also has passive structures in which the Subject corresponds to an Indirect Object or the Complement of a preposition in an active clause, as (38) and (39) show.

38 Parliament was given the best estimate.

    Cf. The committee gave <u>Parliament</u> the best estimate.

39 The problem was dealt with.

    Cf. The police dealt with <u>the problem</u>.

Passive clauses have the same propositional meaning (section 11.1) as their active counterparts. However, (36) and (37) convey subtly different *non-propositional* meanings. As we have seen, by virtue of being positioned at the beginning of a clause the Subject is said to be the topic, and because the active and passive clauses above have different Subjects, we can say that they focus on different topics.

Thus (36) can be said to be about 'the process', whereas (37) is about 'a man called Conté'. The order of the constituents in (36) is in conformity with the Given-Before-New Principle. The 'process' referred to in (36) constitutes given information because it is identifiable to the addressee from the preceding text, shown in (40), which makes reference to a process of 'firing'.

40 Pencil "lead" today is composed of less pure graphite – mostly from Mexico – and Bavarian clay, fired like porcelain in a kiln.

Notice also that the NP *the process* in (36) is definite. Because the passive clause conforms to the Given-Before-New Principle it is more natural than its active counterpart in (37) which has new information (the phrase *a man called Conté*) placed clause-initially. Having the new information in clause-final position in (36) makes Conté, and his role in devising the firing process, more focal.

The *by*-phrase, which typically expresses the semantic role of Agent in the passive versions of active clauses that express an action, can generally be left out. When this is done we speak of an *agentless passive*. Leaving out the Agent can be done for a number of reasons. One reason could be that the Agent is already known. Another might be that the speaker does not want to draw attention to the Agent, or does not know who the Agent is. Notice that if we leave out the Agent in (36) the addressee's attention is focused on the action of devising a process. Omitting the Agent is not always possible. If we remove the *by*-phrase from (41) we derive (42) which is ungrammatical.

41 The gum infection is caused by two germs that live together.

42 *The gum infection is caused.

11.5 The Indirect Object – Prepositional Phrase as Complement alternation

In the following example we have a ditransitive complementation pattern (see section 4.1.3.2), involving an Indirect Object and a Direct Object.

43 In September 1921, the British newspapers gave <u>one story prominence</u> – Lansbury was in Brixton prison.

An alternative (attested) constituent order is shown in (44).

44 In September 1921, the British newspapers gave <u>prominence</u> <u>to one story</u> – Lansbury was in Brixton prison.

In this version the NP *one story*, which is the Indirect Object in (43), functions as Complement of the preposition *to*. It is no longer an IO. At clause level the PP *to one story* functions as a Complement of the verb (section 4.1.3.2.1). Notice that (43) is less natural than (44), given that the Principle of End Weight is not respected: a heavier unit consisting of two words precedes a light unit consisting of just one word. In (44) the information flow is optimal, because the Principle of End Weight is respected, and because the content of the story, which is specified after the dash, is directly juxtaposed to the noun phrase *one story*.

Consider next (45).

45 They gave <u>me</u> <u>a lotion that wasn't as good as the cream</u>.

Notice that this example conforms to both the Given-Before-New Principle and the Principle of End Weight: the NP *a lotion that wasn't as good as the cream* carries new information (witness the indefinite article), comes last, and is also a heavy phrase. The IO is a personal pronoun, which conveys given information because the person referred to is identifiable by the addressee. An alternative constituent order for (45) is shown in (46).

46 They gave <u>a lotion that wasn't as good as the cream</u> <u>to me</u>.

This order is less natural than (45), given that both ordering principles are not respected: new information precedes old information, and a heavy unit precedes a light unit.

The next example conforms to the Given-Before-New Principle (the restaurant is known to the addressee), but the Principle of End Weight does not apply, given that both the IO and the DO have the same length, measured in number of words.

47 We need to give <u>the restaurant</u> <u>a ring</u>.

Example (48) is unusual in having definite NPs functioning as IO and DO. Both express identifiable information, so the Given-Before-New Principle is not relevant. A violation of the Principle of End

Weight explains why (49) sounds odd. (In addition, notice that the pronoun *they* is followed by its antecedent.)

48 It *gives* [the people of our country] [the opportunities for employment and for earnings which they want].

49 ?It *gives* [the opportunities for employment and for earnings which they want] [to the people of our country].

11.6   The existential and presentational constructions

Existential constructions involve clauses that are introduced by *existential there* (section 3.2.2.1.3) followed by the verb BE or one of the raising-to-Subject verbs (APPEAR, SEEM, etc.; section 8.1.3.4). We distinguish *bare existentials* from *extended existentials*. In the *presentational construction* the noun *there* is followed by a verb from a small set of verbs of 'appearance', such as APPEAR, ENTER, and EMERGE.

11.6.1   The bare existential construction

Bare existentials conform to the template below.

Bare existential

There + BE / raising verb + **semantic Subject** (+ Adjunct(s))

There is the *grammatical Subject*, which fills the Subject slot and is meaningless. The *semantic Subject* is the constituent in the clause that has a semantic role to play vis-à-vis the verb (section 4.2). Here are some examples, in which the semantic Subject is in boldface type. The underlined Adjuncts in (51) can (by definition) be omitted without affecting the grammaticality of the clauses. Bare existentials do not have a non-existential counterpart.

50 *There* is **a crisis**.

Cf. *A crisis is.

51 *There* is **a shortage of accommodation** here due to the impending Olympics.

Cf. *A shortage of accommodation is here due to the impending Olympics.

52 *There* seems to have been **some sort of interruption**.

Cf. *Some sort of interruption seems to have been.

53 *There* appears to be **a Barcelona equivalent of Camden Market**.

Cf. *A Barcelona equivalent of Camden Market appears to be.

11.6.2   The extended existential construction

The extended existential conforms to the template below.

Extended existential

There + BE/raising verb + **semantic Subject** + <u>extension</u>

Extended existentials have a non-existential counterpart, and involve a locative, temporal, predicative, infinitival, or participial extension which typically cannot be left out without a radical change in meaning. As before, the semantic Subjects in the examples that follow are in bold; the material that belongs to the extension is doubly underlined.

54 *There* were **two men** <u>inside the five yard area</u>.

Non-existential version: Two men were inside the five yard area.

Cf. *There were two men. (This can be acceptable, but with a different meaning.)

55 *There* are **bits** <u>missing</u>.

Non-existential version: Bits are missing.

Cf. *There are bits. (Acceptable with a different meaning.)

56 *There* is **a case** <u>to be made</u>.

Non-existential version: A case is to be made.

Cf. *There is a case. (Acceptable with a different meaning.)

57 Well *there* were **so many Dutch people** <u>wanting to come here</u>.

Non-existential version: So many Dutch people were wanting to come here.

Cf. *There were so many Dutch people. (Acceptable with a different meaning.)

11.6.3 The presentational construction

When *there* is followed by one of a small set of verbs of 'appearance', 'emergence', and the like (e.g. APPEAR, ARISE, ARRIVE, BEGIN, COME, DEVELOP, EMERGE, ENTER, ESCAPE, EXIST, LIVE, LOOM, OCCUR, REMAIN, STAND), we speak of *presentational <u>there</u>* introducing the *presentational construction*.

Presentational construction
There + verb of 'appearance' + **semantic Subject** + (<u>Adjunct(s)</u>)/
(<u><u>extension</u></u>)

As before, in the following examples the semantic Subject is in bold. The presentational construction can be of the bare type with an optional Adjunct (underlined), or of the extended type with an extension (doubly underlined) which is typically optional. The latter can be placed before the Subject, as in (62). An adjunct may also occur.

58 In all that dreary wilderness there was not a light to be seen until, beyond a wood, *there* appeared **a tiny golden cube that seemed magically suspended in air**.

59 *There* began **an 11-year stint during which he let his ambition run wild, sometimes against the advice of his bosses**.

60 In all walks of life *there* exist **people who feel it necessary to take on the role of the typical school bully, prepared to isolate and exploit others**.

61 *There* remain **five bridges across the Tigris** <u>in the downtown area alone</u>, <u><u>all intact</u></u>.

62 This flat was by no means dark; large windows in all four of its rooms admitted both morning and afternoon light, and <u>on each of the window-ledges</u> *there* stood **a well-tended box of brightly coloured flowers – pansies, trailing aubretia, rare summer-flowering crocuses**.

Typically the existential and presentational constructions involve a semantic Subject that is new to the addressee, and hence occurs more naturally later in the clause in accordance with the Given-Before-New Principle. To make this clear, compare (58) with (63).

63 In all that dreary wilderness there was not a light to be seen until, beyond a wood, *a tiny golden cube that seemed magically suspended in air* appeared.

The semantic Subject in (58), the NP *a tiny golden cube that seemed magically suspended in air*, contains new information (witness the indefinite article), and for that reason is more naturally placed further to the right. Notice also that (58) satisfies the Principle of End Weight. In (63) the heavy Subject (in italics) is positioned awkwardly before the verb.

11.7   Inversion

Inversion involves constituents exchanging places in a clause, sometimes involving minor syntactic adjustments. We need to distinguish *obligatory inversion* from *optional inversion*. The former occurs, for example, in closed interrogative clauses (e.g. *Did you call him?*; see section 6.2.2), where the Subject and the auxiliary verb DO are inverted. Crucially, speakers have no choice as to whether or not to apply inversion: if they wish to use a closed interrogative clause they *must* apply it. By contrast, inversion that is applied for information structuring purposes is optional, with one or two exceptions.

Consider first the examples in (64) and (65), and their uninverted counterparts in (66) and (67).

64 [_Adjp_ *Imperative too*] is [_NP_ *the need to economise at the Home Office*].

65 [_Adjp_ *Most relevant*] was [_NP_ *a dramatized version of how the news of the Battle of Trafalgar was brought to London*].

66 The need to economise at the Home Office is imperative too.

67 A dramatized version of how the news of the Battle of Trafalgar was brought to London was most relevant.

In (64) and (65) the italicized Subject noun phrases have been inverted with the adjective phrases, which function as Subject-related Predicative Complements. (66) and (67) display the unmarked (i.e. expected) constituent order. Notice that the motivation for the inversion is the length of the Subjects in (66) and (67): moving them to the end of the clause satisfies the Principle of End Weight. In addition, in both cases the adjective phrases supply old information, witness the presence of the words *too* and *most*, and hence placing them in clause-initial position satisfies the Given-Before-New Principle. In the example below, the heaviness of the Subject (italicized) is particularly clear.

68 Besides favourite books, [$_{AdjP}$ *essential*] seemed to be [$_{NP}$ *a literary landscape (Leeds?), a knowledge of metre and scansion and (this was the clincher) a passion for the Icelandic sagas*].

The examples in (69)–(72) are slightly different because in these cases the inversion involves a preposed locative or temporal expression.

69 And [*here*] comes [*the Northern Line*].

70 [*Then*] came [*Allan Smith's equaliser*].

71 And then suddenly [*from the bottom*] appears [*a motor car*].

72 [*Below*] is suggested [*a more sophisticated approach to this problem*].

Consider next (73)–(75).

73 [*Backing it*] was [*a massive 6-speed ZF gearbox*].

74 [*Running along a strip just above the keyboard*] are [*some familiar features of digital parameter access: an Exit button, a data entry slider and increment/decrement buttons, a two-digit LED display for the currently-selected program number, two backlit LCD windows, Page up/down and Cursor left/right buttons, an Int/Card selector button, eight Bank and eight Number buttons for Patch selection, and buttons providing direct access to Compare, Copy, Manual, Write and Data Transfer functions*].

75 [*Tucked away in the upper left-hand corner of the main editing panel*] are [*four sliders collectively known as the Palette*].

In these examples the Complements of BE (*backing it, running along a strip just above the keyboard*, and *tucked away in the upper left-hand corner of the main editing panel*) have been preposed, and this is accompanied by postponement of the Subject. In (73) an NP carrying new information occurs in clause-final position in accordance with the Given-Before-New Principle. Example (74) is especially noteworthy: had its extremely long Subject appeared in the regular Subject position, the clause would have been very hard to comprehend. In (75) it might appear at first sight that the constituent order is unexpected, since the sequence *tucked away in the upper left-hand corner of the main editing panel* is 'heavier' than the italicized Subject, and there is thus a violation of the Principle of End Weight. To explain this we need to look at what precedes (75) in the text in which it appears, namely (76).

76 Incidentally, all your front-panel synthesis edits can optionally be transmitted via MIDI as SysEx data, and so recorded into a MIDI sequencer for subsequent playback.

The technical content of this example need not concern us here. What is important is that mention is made of some sort of 'panel for editing'. Since such a panel has now been introduced into the discourse, it is no longer new information, and the word order in (75) is therefore in harmony with the Given-Before-New Principle. We thus see that, in information processing terms, the inversion serves to make the text flow better, and aids textual cohesion. We also see that a principle like the Principle of End Weight can be overridden by the dynamics of other information processing concerns.

11.8 Clefting

Clefting is a procedure which divides a clause into two parts for information highlighting purposes. We distinguish *it-clefts* from *wh-clefts*. The latter are also called *pseudoclefts*.

11.8.1 *It*-clefts

Consider the examples below.

77 Simioni has gone down.

78 Ancient history attracted me.

79 You need exercise.

80 The young Dutchman first fell in love here.

81 I'd wanted to work in the theatre for some time.

82 I consulted with the chairman of the Select Committee on this matter.

These clauses have an unmarked (i.e. regular) clause structure where none of the items occurs in an informationally privileged position. We can form *it*-cleft versions of these clauses using the template below, as in (83)–(88).

> ### *It*-cleft
> *It* + BE + {focus} + <u>relative clause</u> (*who(m)/that/Ø/which …*)

83 *It* is {Simioni} <u>who's gone down</u>.

84 *It* was {ancient history} <u>that attracted me</u>.

85 *It* is {exercise} <u>you need</u>.

86 *It* was {here} <u>that the young Dutchman first fell in love</u>.

87 *It* was {the theatre} <u>that I'd wanted to work in for some time</u>.

88 *It* was {this matter} <u>on which I consulted with the chairman of the Select Committee</u>.

It is important to stress that particular clauses can have more than one cleft version. For example, (78) also has (89) as a possible cleft, and (80) has (90) as an alternative cleft.

89 *It* was {me} <u>who was attracted to ancient history</u>.

90 *It* was {the young Dutchman} <u>who first fell in love here</u>.

The Subject position of the *it*-cleft template is filled by the pronoun *it* (called *cleft <u>it</u>*, section 3.2.2.1.2), which is followed by a form of the verb BE. This in turn is followed by the *focus position* which allows speakers to highlight a constituent. The relative clause, introduced by *who(m)*, *that*, *Ø*, or *which*, provides further information about the element in the focus position. Unlike the relative clauses that were discussed in section 7.3.3, relative clauses in cleft constructions do not form a constituent with an antecedent. Thus, in (83) *Simioni* and *who's gone down* do not form an NP.

Different items are in the focus position in (83)–(88) above: the Subjects of (77) and (78), the Direct Object of (79), an Adjunct in (80), and the Complement of a preposition in (81) and (82). Almost any type of constituent can occur in the focus position, though not verbs and verb phrases, as (91) shows.

91 *It was *attract me* that ancient history did.

The focus position is usually occupied by units that provide foregrounded information: it highlights a constituent which merits special attention. Thus in (83), which is from a commentary on an incident in a football match in which it was not immediately clear to the commentator who fell to the ground, Simioni is finally identified as the person who went down. In (84), from an interview with a novelist, ancient history is contrasted with other topics that are mentioned in the preceding discussion. The relative clause can specify either old or new information, but in any case provides information that is not under primary consideration: it is backgrounded.

11.8.2 *Wh*-clefts (or pseudoclefts)

Consider the following examples.

92 I saw one of the most impressive government policies in years.

93 You wear it like that.

94 They actually sent 6 huge C.I.D. men to say that I'd accused her of stealing the video and that I was no friend of hers.

95 I sent a complaint to Radio 2.

96 You'll find that people who are nearer the camera will be bleached out.

97 I didn't like leaving my mum.

The *wh*-cleft versions of these clauses have a structure involving a clause-initial *wh*-item, usually *what* (though *where* and *when* are also possible), followed by a Subject, a Predicator, and other possible elements of clause structure. Together these form a free relative clause (section 7.3.3.5) which is followed by a form of the verb BE and the focus position, as shown in the template below.

Wh-cleft

[free relative clause *wh*-word + SUBJ + PCR + (…)] + BE + {focus}

Notice that in *wh*-clefts the focus position is at the end of the clause. As the examples below show, a wide range of constituents can occur here, for example noun phrases, as in (98), verb phrases, as in (99)–(101), and clauses, as in (102)–(103). The constituent that fills the focus position identifies whatever it is that the free relative clause specifies as requiring identification. Thus in (98) the NP in focus position identifies what the speaker saw.

98 [free relative clause What I saw] *was* {one of the most impressive government policies in years}.

99 [free relative clause What you do] *is* {wear it like that}.

100 [free relative clause What they actually did] *was* {send 6 huge C.I.D. men to say that I'd accused her of stealing the video and that I was no friend of hers}.

101 [free relative clause What I did] *was* {send a complaint to Radio 2}.

102 [free relative clause What you'll find] *is* {that people who are nearer the camera will be bleached out}.

103 [free relative clause What I didn't like] *was* {leaving my mum}.

As with the *it*-clefts, more than one *wh*-cleft version is usually possible. For example, (95) also has (104) as a possible cleft.

104 [free relative clause What I sent to Radio 2] *was* {a complaint}.

When the free relative clause and the focus are reversed we speak of a *reversed wh-cleft*.

105 {One of the most impressive government policies in years} is [what I saw].

106 {Send a complaint to Radio 2} is [what I did].

Not all *wh*-clefts have an uncleft counterpart. Thus (107) does not have (108) as its non-cleft version.

107 [What I found happening over the period of study] was {that I began to bring those two areas together}.

108 *I found that I began to bring those two areas together happening over the period of study.

The fact that not all *wh*-clefts have a non-cleft counterpart is one of the main reasons why some grammars speak of *pseudo*clefts, rather than real clefts.

The free relative clause in *wh*-clefts provides backgrounded information: it is information that is somehow known by the interlocutors, or information which somehow played a role in the preceding discourse. As with *it*-clefts, the focus position is occupied by constituents that provide foregrounded information.

Appendix 1: English irregular verbs

Forms preceded by the superscript symbol '⁺' are alternative forms which are restricted in use (e.g. to particular senses). The abbreviation 'arch.' indicates an archaic form, and the annotations 'GB' and 'US' indicate British and American usages, respectively.

plain form	*past tense form*	*past participle*
a		
abide	abode, abided	abode, abided
arise	arose	arisen
awake	awoke	awoken
b		
be	was / were	been
bear	bore	borne
beat	beat	beaten
become	became	become
befall	befell	befallen
beget	begot, arch. begat	begotten
begin	began	begun
behold	beheld	beheld
bend	bent	bent
beseech	beseeched, besought	beseeched, besought
beset	beset	beset
bespeak	bespoke	bespoke, bespoken
bet	bet, betted	bet, betted
bid	bade, bid	bidden, bid
bind	bound	bound
bite	bit	bitten
bleed	bled	bled
blow	blew	blown
break	broke	broken
breed	bred	bred

plain form	*past tense form*	*past participle*
bring	brought	brought
broadcast	broadcast	broadcast
browbeat	browbeat	browbeaten
build	built	built
burn	burned, GB burnt	burned, burnt
bust	bust, GB busted	bust, GB busted
buy	bought	bought
c		
cast	cast	cast
catch	caught	caught
choose	chose	chosen
cleave	cleft, cleaved, clove	cleft, cleaved, cloven
cling	clung	clung
come	came	come
cost	cost, ‡costed	cost, ‡costed
creep	crept	crept
crow	crowed, arch. crew	crowed
cut	cut	cut
d		
deal	dealt	dealt
dig	dug	dug
dive	GB dived, US dove	dived
do	did	done
draw	drew	drawn
dream	dreamed, GB dreamt	dreamed, GB dreamt
drink	drank	drunk
drive	drove	driven
dwell	dwelt	dwelt
e		
eat	ate	eaten
f		
fall	fell	fallen
feed	fed	fed
feel	felt	felt
fight	fought	fought
find	found	found

plain form	*past tense form*	*past participle*
flee	fled	fled
fling	flung	flung
floodlight	floodlit	floodlit
fly	flew	flown
forbear	forbore	forborne
forbid	forbade, forbad	forbidden
forecast	forecast, forecasted	forecast, forecasted
foresee	foresaw	foreseen
foretell	foretold	foretold
forget	forgot	forgotten
forgive	forgave	forgiven
forsake	forsook	forsaken
forswear	forswore	forsworn
freeze	froze	frozen

g

gainsay	gainsaid	gainsaid
get	got	got, US gotten
give	gave	given
go	went	gone
grind	ground	ground
grow	grew	grown

h

hamstring	hamstrung	hamstrung
hang	hung, ‡hanged	hung, ‡hanged
have	had	had
hear	heard	heard
heave	heaved, ‡hove	heaved, ‡hove
hew	hewed	hewn, hewed
hide	hid	hidden
hit	hit	hit
hold	held	held
hurt	hurt	hurt

i

inlay	inlaid	inlaid
inset	inset	inset
interweave	interwove	interwoven

plain form	*past tense form*	*past participle*
k		
keep	kept	kept
kneel	knelt, US kneeled	knelt, US kneeled
knit	knitted, knit	knitted, knit
know	knew	known
l		
lay	laid	laid
lead	led	led
lean	leaned, GB leant	leaned, GB leant
leap	leaped, GB leapt	leaped, GB leapt
learn	learned, GB learnt	learned, GB learnt
leave	left	left
lend	lent	lent
let	let	let
lie	lay	lain
light	lit, ‡lighted	lit, ‡lighted
lose	lost	lost
m		
make	made	made
mean	meant	meant
meet	met	met
miscast	miscast	miscast
misdeal	misdealt	misdealt
mishear	misheard	misheard
mislay	mislaid	mislaid
mislead	misled	misled
misread /-ri:d/	misread /-red/	misread /-red/
misspell	misspelled, GB misspelt	misspelled, GB misspelt
misspend	misspent	misspent
mistake	mistook	mistaken
misunderstand	misunderstood	misunderstood
mow	mowed	mowed, mown
o		
outbid	outbid	outbid, US outbidden
outdo	outdid	outdone
outgrow	outgrew	outgrown
output	output, outputted	output, outputted

plain form	*past tense form*	*past participle*
outrun	outran	outrun
outsell	outsold	outsold
outshine	outshone	outshone
overbid	overbid	overbid
overcome	overcame	overcome
overdo	overdid	overdone
overdraw	overdrew	overdrawn
overeat	overate	overeaten
overfly	overflew	overflown
overhang	overhung	overhung
overhear	overheard	overheard
overlay	overlaid	overlaid
overlie	overlay	overlain
overpay	overpaid	overpaid
override	overrode	overridden
overrun	overran	overrun
oversee	oversaw	overseen
overshoot	overshot	overshot
oversleep	overslept	overslept
overtake	overtook	overtaken
overthrow	overthrew	overthrown

p

partake	partook	partaken
pay	paid	paid
plead	pleaded, US pled	pleaded, US pled
prove	proved	proved, proven
put	put	put

q

quit	quit, quitted	quit, quitted

r

read /riːd/	read /red/	read /red/
rebuild	rebuilt	rebuilt
recast	recast	recast
redo	redid	redone
rehear	reheard	reheard
remake	remade	remade
rend	rent	rent

plain form	*past tense form*	*past participle*
repay	repaid	repaid
reread /-riːd/	reread /-red/	reread /-red/
rerun	reran	rerun
resell	resold	resold
reset	reset	reset
resit	resat	resat
retake	retook	retaken
retell	retold	retold
rewrite	rewrote	rewritten
rid	rid	rid
ride	rode	ridden
ring	rang	rung
rise	rose	risen
run	ran	run

s

saw	sawed	sawed, GB sawn
say	said	said
see	saw	seen
seek	sought	sought
sell	sold	sold
send	sent	sent
set	set	set
sew	sewed	sewn, sewed
shake	shook	shaken
shear	sheared	shorn, ‡sheared
shed	shed	shed
shine	shone, ‡shined	shone, ‡shined
shit	shat	shat
shoe	shod	shod
shoot	shot	shot
show	showed	shown, showed
shrink	shrank	shrunk, shrunken
shrive	shrived, shrove	shrived, shriven
shut	shut	shut
sing	sang	sung
sink	sank	sunk
sit	sat	sat
slay	slew	slain
sleep	slept	slept

plain form	*past tense form*	*past participle*
slide	slid	slid
sling	slung	slung
slink	slunk	slunk
slit	slit	slit
smell	smelled, GB smelt	smelled, GB smelt
smite	smote	smitten
sow	sowed	sowed, sown
speak	spoke	spoken
speed	sped, ‡speeded	sped, ‡speeded
spell	spelled, GB spelt	spelled, GB spelt
spend	spent	spent
spill	spilled, GB spilt	spilled, GB spilt
spin	spun, arch. span	spun
spit	spat	spat
split	split	split
spoil	spoiled, GB spoilt	spoiled, GB spoilt
spotlight	spotlit, spotlighted	spotlit, spotlighted
spread	spread	spread
spring	sprang	sprung
stand	stood	stood
stave	staved, stove	staved, stove
steal	stole	stolen
stick	stuck	stuck
sting	stung	stung
stink	stank, stunk	stunk
strew	strewed	strewed, strewn
stride	strode	stridden
strike	struck	struck
string	strung	strung
strive	strove	striven
sublet	sublet	sublet
swear	swore	sworn
sweep	swept	swept
swell	swelled	swollen, swelled
swim	swam	swum
swing	swung	swung

t

take	took	taken
teach	taught	taught

plain form	*past tense form*	*past participle*
tear	tore	torn
tell	told	told
think	thought	thought
thrive	thrived, throve	thrived, arch. thriven
throw	threw	thrown
thrust	thrust	thrust
tread	trod	trodden

u

underbid	underbid	underbid
undercut	undercut	undercut
undergo	underwent	undergone
underlie	underlay	underlain
underpay	underpaid	underpaid
undersell	undersold	undersold
understand	understood	understood
undertake	undertook	undertaken
underwrite	underwrote	underwritten
undo	undid	undone
unfreeze	unfroze	unfrozen
unlearn	unlearned, GB unlearnt	unlearned, GB unlearnt
unstick	unstuck	unstuck
unwind	unwound	unwound
uphold	upheld	upheld
upset	upset	upset

w

wake	woke	woken
waylay	waylaid	waylaid
wear	wore	worn
weave	wove, weaved	woven, weaved
wed	wedded, wed	wedded, wed
weep	wept	wept
wet	wet, wetted	wet, wetted
win	won	won
wind	wound	wound
withdraw	withdrew	withdrawn
withhold	withheld	withheld

plain form	*past tense form*	*past participle*
withstand	withstood	withstood
wring	wrung	wrung
write	wrote	written

Appendix 2: The structure of the ICE-GB corpus

ICE-GB is the British component of the *International Corpus of English*. It contains one million words of fully grammatically analysed texts, almost two thirds of which is spoken. The material is searchable with the innovative ICECUP software (International Corpus of English Corpus Utility Program).

The structure of the corpus is shown below. Each text in the corpus contains 2,000 words.

Text Categories

Spoken (300 texts)
 Dialogue (180)
  Private (100)
   direct conversations (90)
   telephone calls (10)
  Public (80)
   classroom lessons (20)
   broadcast discussions (20)
   broadcast interviews (10)
   parliamentary debates (10)
   legal cross-examinations (10)
   business transactions (10)
 Monologue (120)
  Unscripted (70)
   spontaneous commentaries (20)
   unscripted speeches (30)
   demonstrations (10)
   legal presentations (10)
  Scripted (50)
   broadcast news (20)
   broadcast talks (20)
   non-broadcast talks (10)

Written (200 texts)

    Non-printed (50)

        students' untimed essays (10)

        students' examination scripts (10)

        social letters (15)

        business letters (15)

    Printed (150)

        Informational writing (100)

            academic (40)

            popular (40)

            press reports (20)

        Instructional writing (20)

            administrative/regulatory (10)

            skills and hobbies (10)

        Persuasive writing (10)

            press editorials (10)

        Creative writing (20)

            novels and stories (20)

For more information, see www.ucl.ac.uk/english-usage and www.ucl.ac.uk/english-usage/projects/ice-gb/index.htm.

Notes and further reading

Chapter 1: An overview of English grammar
· ·

For general introductions to English linguistics, see Crystal (2003), and the chapters in Aarts and McMahon (2006). On grammar and grammar writing, see Leitner (1986), Michael (1970), and Linn (2006). On the history of prescriptivism, see Crystal (2006). Apart from Quirk *et al.* (1985) and Huddleston and Pullum *et al.* (2002), some well-known modern grammars of English are Jespersen (1909–1949), Poutsma (1914–1929), H. E. Palmer (1924), Kruisinga (1932), Zandvoort (1945), Curme (1947), Fries (1952), Long (1961), Stockwell, Schachter, and Partee (1973), Huddleston (1984), Givón (1993), McCawley (1998), and Biber *et al.* (1999).

On English usage, see Peters (2004, 2006).

For more information on the British component of *The International Corpus of English*, see Appendix 2 and Nelson, Wallis, and Aarts (2002).

Chapter 2: Word structure and word-formation
· ·

On morphology, see Spencer (1991), Carstairs-McCarthy (2002), Bauer (2003, 2004), Katamba and Stonham (2006), and Booij (2007). On word-formation, see Marchand (1969), Bauer (1983), Adams (2001), and Plag (2003). On compounding, see Bauer (1998, 2006). On inflection and derivation, see Blevins (2006).

In many accounts of English grammar the notion 'finite' is equated with 'tensed'. This is not entirely unproblematic, especially regarding the subjunctive and imperative in English which most grammars claim involve finite verbs. If we recognize a 'present subjunctive' and 'past subjunctive' there is no problem, but if we say, as do Huddleston and Pullum *et al.* (2002: 88), that 'subjunctive verbs' involve the plain form of the verb in the case of the 'present subjunctive', and that we have a 'subjunctive construction', rather than a subjunctive verb form, then it is hard to see why a 'subjunctive verb' should be regarded as tensed or finite. It is for this reason that 'subjunctive verbs' are *not* tensed or finite for Huddleston and Pullum *et al.* (*ibid.*: 85, 87). The same applies to 'imperative verbs'. These authors also argue that there is no 'past subjunctive' verb form in English, because it would be indistinguishable from the past tense form. (They regard *were*, as in *If I were you*, which they call *irrealis were*, as being exceptional.) Nevertheless, Huddleston and Pullum *et al.* (*ibid.*: 90) say that subjunctive constructions, as opposed to verb forms, *are* finite because their syntax resembles that of tensed clauses for three reasons: they have an obligatory subject, they take the same subordinators as do tensed declarative clauses, and they can alternate with tensed constructions.

Chapter 3: Word classes and simple phrases
. . . .

On word classes in general see Aarts and Haegeman (2006). On English verbs see Palmer (1987) and Leech (2004), and on auxiliaries in particular, see Warner (1993). On personal pronouns, see Wales (1996). On gradience between word classes, see Taylor (2003), Aarts *et al.* (2004), and Aarts (2007).

There are many disagreements about the assignment of a great number of elements to the various word classes. It would take up too much space to list them all here. What follows below is a brief overview of the major differences between grammatical frameworks, especially Quirk *et al.* (1985) and Huddleston and Pullum *et al.* (2002).

In Quirk *et al.* (1985: 335 f.) pronouns are treated as a separate word class. For Huddleston and Pullum *et al.* (2002: 425 f.) they are a subclass of nouns. The latter recognize five classes of pronouns: personal, reciprocal, interrogative, relative, and temporal. Reflexive pronouns are included within the class of personal pronouns. Temporal pronouns are words like *today* (analysed as nouns in the present book). Huddleston and Pullum *et al.* (2002: 1461) recognize a category of pro-forms which overlaps with the pronouns.

In many frameworks, if a particular word has a dependent and an independent use, it is assigned to different word classes, as has been done in this grammar for *these* in *I like these books* and *I like these*, where in the former example *these* is a determinative, while in the latter it is a pronoun. In Huddleston and Pullum *et al.* (2002) both instances of *these* are determinatives, but with different functions (Determiner and Fused Determiner-Head, respectively). In Huddleston and Pullum's grammar the indefinite pronouns listed here in Table 3.10 would be treated as fused Determiner-Head constructions. For these grammarians 'there is no interrogative pronoun *which*' (2002: 422). Instead *which* in e.g. *Which did you buy?* is a determinative, functioning as fused Determiner-Head (*ibid.*: 398, 410 f.).

Table 3.11 is based on Huddleston and Pullum *et al.* (2002: 356, 373 f.). On *many* as an adjective, see Spinillo (2004).

Chapter 4: Grammatical functions, semantic roles, and tree diagrams
. . . .

On grammatical functions and their realization see F. Aarts and J. Aarts (1982). On semantic roles see Saeed (2009).

Chapter 5: Complex phrases and coordination

On phrase structure, see Aarts (2008). On coordination, see Huddleston and Pullum (2006).

I largely follow Huddleston and Pullum *et al.*'s (2002) account of noun phrase structure, though there are some differences between the two analyses. For example, I prefer to use the functional label Adjunct inside phrases, rather than Modifier. Another difference is that for Huddleston and Pullum *et al.* there are two types of *external modifiers* for noun phrases: *predeterminer modifiers* (*predeterminers* for short) and *peripheral modifiers*. In this grammar I also use the function label Predeterminer, but I use the label *External Adjunct* instead of peripheral modifier.

In this book I am assuming two levels within phrases: the phrase level and the lexical level. The *X-bar syntax* framework recognizes so-called *bar-level categories* which are intermediate between the phrase and word. Some evidence for this intermediate level inside noun phrases comes from *one*-substitution data. Thus, in the sentence *I like the big brown dog, but not the small one* the word *one* refers back to *brown dog* which is clearly not a full noun phrase, but also not just a noun. Similarly, in the NP *the real edge-of-your-seat action* the string *edge-of-your-seat* is something less than a full NP, but more than a bare noun. The label *N-bar* is used for such strings, or sometimes *Nom(inal)*, as in e.g. Huddleston and Pullum *et al.* (2002). See Aarts (2008) for further discussion.

In many grammars sequences like *come in* and *cut back* NP/*cut* NP *back* in constructions 1 and 2 in Table 5.10 are called *intransitive phrasal verbs* and *transitive phrasal verbs*, respectively, i.e. they are regarded as verbs consisting of more than one word. The verbs in construction 3 (Type 1, e.g. *rely on* NP, *account for* NP) are referred to in the literature as *intransitive prepositional verbs*, while those in construction 4 (Type 2, e.g. *blame* NP *on* NP, *do justice to* NP) are called *transitive prepositional verbs*. Finally, in constructions 5 (Type 1) and 6 (Type 1) sequences like *put up with* NP and *fob* NP *off with* NP are often called *intransitive phrasal-prepositional verbs* and *transitive phrasal-prepositional verbs*, respectively. In this grammar these labels have not been adopted. Instead, the verbs in these constructions license particular PPs/NPs as Complements.

Chapter 6: Clause types and negation

On clause types, see Collins (2006). The classical references for speech acts are Austin (1962/1975) and Searle (1969). Other books that discuss speech acts include Levinson (1983) and Leech (1983).

Chapter 7: Finite subordinate clauses
....

In many grammars (e.g. Quirk *et al.* 1985) content clauses are called *nominal clauses*, though these also comprise non-finite structures. Such clauses are said to be like NPs. See Huddleston and Pullum *et al.* (2002: 1014 ff.) for arguments against this analysis.

In Huddleston and Pullum *et al.* (2002: 1018–1019) reasons are put forward for not analysing postverbal content clauses as Direct Objects, though note that they make one exception to this, namely when a content clause in a complex transitive clause is pre-posed, as in *That he lost his temper I find odd* (Huddleston and Pullum *et al.* 2002: 1022).

In Quirk *et al.* (1985) the word *that* in relative clauses is analysed as a Subject in e.g. *The book that fell on the floor was already soiled*, and as Direct Object in e.g. *The book that I bought _ was expensive*.

Free relative clauses are called *nominal-relative clauses* in Quirk *et al.* (1985), whereas in Huddleston and Pullum *et al.* (2002) they are called *fused relative constructions*, and are analysed as noun phrases.

Chapter 8: Non-finite and verbless subordinate clauses
....

Some of my non-finite Complement Clauses are called *Catenative Complements* in Huddleston and Pullum *et al.* (2002). As with content clauses, in Huddleston and Pullum *et al.* (2002: 1206 ff.) arguments are put forward for not analysing postverbal non-finite clauses as Direct Objects, though they recognize that *-ing*-participle clauses do behave like DOs if there is a following Objective Predicative Complement, as in the example *I would call eating raw meat inadvisable*.

The analysis of many of the patterns discussed in this chapter is controversial. To take just one example, the raising to Object pattern 'INTEND NP$_i$ [$_{clause}$ Ø$_i$ *to*-infinitive...]' is analysed in the Chomskyan tradition as involving a single clausal Complement: 'INTEND [$_{clause}$ NP *to*-infinitive...]'. In this pattern the postverbal NP is regarded as the Subject of the subordinate clause, principally because there is no thematic relationship between the matrix clause and the NP. For a detailed discussion of this analysis, see Aarts (2008).

The treatment of auxiliary verbs as main (catenative) verbs is adopted by Huddleston and Pullum *et al.* (2002: 1214 ff.), but not by Quirk *et al.* (1985) who follow the traditional analysis of auxiliary verbs as 'helping' verbs, i.e. verbs that are dependent on the lexical verb that they accompany. In some frameworks each of the verbs in tree diagrams like (150) and (151) takes a VP Complement. I have not adopted this analysis. For discussion, see Aarts and Meyer (1995).

In some frameworks the postverbal NP in a sentence like *I find it fascinating*, where there is no semantic relationship between the verb and the NP in question, is regarded as the Subject of a verbless clause, often called a *small clause*: *I find* [$_{SC}$ *it fascinating*]. See Aarts (1992).

Chapter 9: Tense and aspect

On tense, see Comrie (1985) and Michaelis (2006). On aspect, see Comrie (1976) and Binnick (2006).

Many grammars, especially school textbooks, regard the progressive and perfect constructions as tenses, and thus recognize a *present/past progressive tense* (also called the *present/past continuous tense*) and a *present/past perfect tense*. As noted, in this grammar these constructions are not regarded as separate tenses.

Some grammars, e.g. Huddleston and Pullum *et al.* (2002), regard the perfect as a (secondary) tense rather than as an aspectual construction. One reason for doing so is that arguably only the present perfect construction is aspectual due to its 'current relevance' meaning. Other uses of the perfect (the past perfect and the non-finite perfect) are principally used to refer to past time. In this grammar we take the present perfect construction to be the most frequent, and hence basic use of the perfect construction, and for that reason regard the perfect construction in general as being aspectual.

The term 'current orientation' as applied to BE *going* [*to*] is due to Palmer (1990: 144). He discusses the interesting idea that BE *going* + *to*-infinitive mirrors the present perfect construction which has 'current relevance'.

The footballer's perfect is discussed in Walker (2008).

On issues of meaning with respect to English verbs and verbal constructions, see Leech (2004).

On short-term changes in the syntax of English verbal constructions, see Mair and Leech (2006), Leech *et al.* (2009), and Aarts *et al.* (forthcoming).

Chapter 10: Mood

In Table 10.1 all numbers have been rounded up. Analytic negations (e.g. *will not, could not*) have not been counted separately, because they were included in the counts for the unnegated verbs in question. It should be borne in mind that it is impossible to reliably distinguish the spoken instances of *cannot*. The instances of *can, might,* and *will* as homonymous nouns or verbs were excluded. Although some scholars claim that *'ll* can represent WILL or SHALL it was counted as WILL. The contraction *'d* was counted as *would*, except where it was a contraction of *had* (as in e.g. *I'd been there an hour*; S1A-082 119). I excluded *'d better* and the following 'mention' use of *must: This is another 'must' for you* (W1B-005 008).

There is a lot of confusing terminology in the domain of modality which is often the result of authors not keeping the syntax and semantics of the various verbs and verbal patterns apart. On mood and modality in general, see Coates (1983), Palmer (1990), Depraetere and Reed (2006), and Collins (2009). The term *analytic mood* is due to Huddleston (1984).

The 'dynamic possibility' meaning for the modal verb CAN can be found in Palmer (1990: 83 f.), and in Huddleston and Pullum *et al.* (2002: 184–185).

The difference between MAY and CAN expressing 'possibility' is characterized in Leech (2004: 82–83) as being one of 'factual possibility' vs 'theoretical possibility'.

Some linguists (e.g. Coates 1983) distinguish between *epistemic modality* and *root modality*, where the latter category subsumes all types of modality that are not epistemic.

With regard to the non-existence of a future tense in English, Palmer (1990: 140) writes, 'In general, however, WILL seems to be used where there is reference to a general envisaged, planned, intended, hoped for, etc. state of affairs, as opposed to a statement that a specific event or specific events will in fact take place. It is in this sense that it indicates a "modal" rather than a real ("tense") future.' By contrast, Declerck (1991) and Salkie (2010), among others, argue that English does have a future tense.

The term *semi-auxiliary verb* is used in Quirk *et al.* (1985: 143 f.) for such combinations as BE *able to*, BE *bound to*, BE *going to*, BE *likely to*, BE *obliged to*. These can carry modal or aspectual meanings. In this grammar these combinations are not viewed as units.

Strength and degree of modality are discussed in Huddleston and Pullum *et al.* (2002: 175 ff.).

Mergers are discussed in Coates (1983).

Chapter 11: Information structuring

General studies on information structuring include Taglicht (1984), Lambrecht (1994), and Birner and Ward (1998, 2006). On existential constructions, see Lumsden (1988). On cleft constructions see Collins (1991).

List of sources of examples

The following is a list of sources for all authentic examples given in the text and tables. Items such as 'S1B-036 010' are identifiers for examples taken from the ICE-GB corpus (described in Appendix 2); those beginning with 'S' and 'W' come from spoken and written texts respectively. The dates of newspapers are given in abbreviated form in the order day, month, year (e.g. 4/7/93 for 4 July 1993). Examples for which no source is listed were constructed for illustrative purposes.

Chapter 1

(2) S1A-032 215
(11) S1B-069 002
(12) W2F-011 088
(13) S2A-031 015
(14) S1A-011 140
(15) S1B-036 010
(17) S1B-049 049
(18) S1A-082 023
(19) S1B-025 078
(20) W1B-009 107

Chapter 2

(1) *The Independent*, 28/2/09
(2) S1A-080 160
(3) S2A-042 034
(6) *The Independent*, 4/7/93
(10) *The Guardian*, 12/6/06
(11) W2F-008 076
(12) W2B-010 108

Table 2.4
(a) *The Times*, 30/1/08
(b) S1B-039 074

(c) W2C-017 042

Table 2.6
(a) S1A-046 415
(b) W2B-023 078
(c) S1B-022 052
(d) S1A-011 140
(e) S2A-020 119

Chapter 3

(5) W2B-009 032
(7) S1A-076 067
(8) S1A-007 072
(9) S2A-050 137
(10) S1A-017 215
(11) S1B-041 192
(12) S1B-043 058
(13) S1B-037 068
(14) S1A-015 216
(15) S2A-014 196
(16) S1B-048 194
(17) S1A-073 053
(18) *Daily Telegraph*, 18/10/01
(19) S1A-019 017
(20) S2A-021 105
(21) S1A-040 235/8

(22) S1A-083 057/8
(23) S2A-014 004
(24) W2A-001 096
(25) W1B-006 069
(27) W2F-010 115
(28) S1A-030 242
(29) W2F-011 108
(30) *New York Times*, 14/12/09
(31) *The Guardian*, 22/9/08
(32) S1A-094 079
(33) S1A-017 265
(34) W2A-024 069
(36) W1B-007 099
(37) W2F-013 047
(38) *The Guardian*, 29/6/2002
(39) W2D-001 016
(40) *The Independent*, 3/6/2009
(41) *The Independent*, 23/1/2007
(42) *Daily Telegraph*, 3/11/2007
(43) S1A-004 087
(44) S1A-077 012
(45) *The Independent*, 25/8/10
(46) S1A-069 183
(47) W2F-010 083
(48) S1A-012 096
(49) *The Times*, 29/1/2006
(50) *The Independent*, 29/5/2007
(51) *The Independent*, 10/3/2002
(52) *The Guardian*, 6/10/02
(53) S1B-049 068
(54) *The Independent*, 21/4/95
(55) *The Times*, 26/5/06
(56) S1A-043 098
(57) S1A-007 197
(58) S1B-068 042
(59) S1A-032 133
(60) S1A-008 127
(61) S1A-038 001
(62) S1A-001 042
(63) S1B-047 112
(64) S1A-019 071

(65) W2F-014 053
(66) S1A-011 101
(67) S1B-036 062
(68) W2C-016 022
(69) W2B-004 089
(70) S1A-019 342
(71) S1A-020 001
(72) S2A-059 011
(74) S2A-060 049
(75) S1B-008 039
(77) W1B-008 204
(78) W1B-007 086
(79) S1B-046 096
(80) *Washington Post*, 3/6/06
(81) BBC News, 31/5/02
(82) *The Guardian*, 22/11/09
(83) W2C-002 007
(84) S1A-096 063
(85) S1A-001 090
(86) S1A-023 164
(87) W1B-028 032
(88) S1A-081 024
(89) W2B-021 005
(90) S1A-021 031
(91) W1A-017 033
(92) S1A-054 118
(93) S1A-008 127
(95) S1A-002 138
(98) W2F-018 134
(125) S1A-001 090
(126) S1A-073 027
(127) S1B-079 060
(129) W1B-014024
(130) S1A-020 277
(131) S1A-001 056
(132) S1B-015 003
(137) S1A-011 135
(138) S2A-024 013
(139) W1B-025 106
(140) S1A-019 189
(141) W1B-007 142

(142) S1A-001 035
(143) W1B-008 039
(144) S1A-013 101
(145) W1B-014 069
(146) S1A-099 120
(147) S1A-014 220
(148) W1B-020 083
(149) S1A-005 236
(150) W2D-012 005
(151) W1B008- 115
(152) S1A-004 104
(153) *The Guardian*, 19/10/08
(154) BBC News, 4/11/06
(155) S1B-022 003
(156) W1A-007 064
(157) *The Guardian*, 4/9/09
(158) W2B-019 101
(159) S1A-005 212
(160) W1B-001 004
(161) S2B-006 032
(162) S1A-095 159
(163) S1B-029 050
(164) S2B-006 032
(165) S1A-004 091
(166) S1B-016 097
(167) S2B-029 128
(168) W1A-018 119
(169) W1B-015 005
(170) S1A-062 155
(171) popsong lyric, *The Guardian*,
      17/3/06
(172) S1A-009 257
(173) S1A-094 006
(174) S1A-007 127
(175) S1A-100 088
(176) S1A-052 148

Table 3.10
(a) W1A-009 062
(b) S2B-024 007
(c) BBC News, 3/6/09

(d) S1B-029 030
(e) S1A-019 081
(f) W1B-013 007
(g) S2A-028 117
(h) *Daily Telegraph*, 8/6/08
(i) S2B-006 117

Table 3.11
(a) S2A-014 158
(b) S2B-007 087
(c) S1A-004 133
(d) S2B-005 091
(e) S1A-037 073
(f) S1A-013 147
(g) S1A-005 087
(h) S1B-031 042
(i) W2F-007 079
(j) S1A-019 193
(k) S1A-010 042
(l) S1B-008 039
(m) S1A-011 144
(n) S1A-005 239
(o) S1A-099 286
(p) *The Times*, 18/12/06
(q) S1A-016 176
(r) *Daily Telegraph*, 24/2/06
(s) *Washington Post*, 3/6/06
(t) BBC News, 31/5/02
(u) *The Guardian*, 22/11/09
(v) S1A-093 273
(w) S2B-025 084

Table 3.18 ('basic' version sentence)
S1A-045 267

Chapter 4
. . . .

(1) *The Guardian*, 24/10/08
(2) S1A-077 077
(3) BBC News, 12/09/08

Chapter 5
. . . .

(13) W2A-019 064

(14) W2A-005 058

(15) S1A-060 124

(16) S1B-049 068

(17) *The Times*, 21/1/06

(18) *The Times*, 20/1/09

(19) *The Independent*, 26/6/08

(20) headline, *BBC News*, 13/1/98

(21) *Daily Telegraph*, 20/9/01

(22) S1A-013 004

(23) W1B-021 053

(24) *The Guardian*, 1/3/09

(25) S1B-058 056

(26) *The Guardian*, 10/6/07

(27) *Daily Telegraph*, 16/3/09

(28) W2B-036 098

(29) S2B-022 075

(30) *The Independent*, 3/6/07

(31) S1A-007 182

(32) S1B-036 091

(33) W2B-006 022

(34) W2B-035 079

(35) W1A-010 121

(36) W2A-031 032

(37) W1B-026 152

(42) S2B-001 084

(43) S1A-002 144

(44) S1B-035 016

(45) W2C-009 097

(46) S1B-035 095

(47) W2E-005 049

(48) W2C-020 097

(53) W2B-020 013

(54) S2A-023 004

(55) W2E-003 092

(56) BBC News, 24/11/09

(57) W1B-016 075

(58) W2C-006 067

(59) W2F-004 130

(60) W2C-020 057

(61) S2A-067 162

(62) S1A-010 185

(63) W2A-032 046

(68) S1A-001 049

(73) *The Guardian*, 6/12/06

(74) S2A-040 104

(75) S2B-023 012

(76) BBC News, 24/2/09

(77) BBC website, 4/11/2008

(78) J. D. Salinger, *The Catcher in the Rye*, p. 1

(79) S1B-064 104

(80) *Daily Telegraph*, 29/10/09

(81) *London Lite*, 16/4/07

(82) *London Paper*, 4/4/07

(83) *The Guardian*, 17/10/08

(84) *The Guardian*, 30/1/05

(85) *The Guardian*, 3/3/01

(86) S1B-014 132

(87) S1A-002 024

(88) *The Times*, 23/7/03

(89) *The Guardian*. 28/12/08

(90) *The Guardian*, 17/6/08

(91) S1B-052 082

(92) *Sunday Times*, 14/5/06

(93) *The Independent*, 19/9/03

(94) S2B-026 025

(95) S1A-080 062

(96) S1B-054 011

(97) S2A-059 003

(98) S2B-045 32

(99) Cassell's *Atlas of World History*, 1997

(105) S1A-001 071

(106) S1A-003 039

(107) W1B-027 008

(108) W1B-026 110

(109) S1A-040 249

(110) S1B-059 084

(111) *The Guardian*, 20/11/06

(112) BBC News, 10/12/03

(113) *The Independent*, 10/11/99

(114) W2F-007 064

(115) S1A-008 266

(116) S1A-002 149

(117) W2B-009 059

(118) *The Times*, 18/11/09

(119) S2B-023 085

(120) *Daily Telegraph*, 21/10/09

(121) *Daily Telegraph*, 18/1/10

(122) S2B-043 054

(123) *Daily Telegraph*, 21/1/06

(124) S2A-022 009

(125) BBC News, 20/7/00

(126) S1B-029 068

(127) S1A-049 025

(128) BBC News, 29/10/09

(129) W2A-016 118

(130) S1B-011 042

(131) S1A-088 019

(132) S2A-048 086

(133) W2E-009 006

(134) S1A-066 238

(135) S1A-034 123

(136) S2B-042 125

(137) BBC News, 18/11/09

(138) S1A-059 086

(139) W2B-037 091

(140) S1A-005 210

(141) S1A-056 286

(142) S1A-001 037

(143) W2F-017 065

(144) S2B-001 037

(145) S1B-045 074

(146) S2A-062 005

(147) S1A-003 114

(148) S1A-052 055

(149) S2B-025 016

(150) *The Guardian*, 16/5/08

(151) S1A-028 135

(152) *Daily Telegraph*, 11/11/09

(153) S1B-071 225

(155) S1B-058 004

(156) *The Times*, 24/5/09

(157) S1B-014 066

(158) *The Times*, 11/6/08

(159) S1B-021 136

(161) S2B-029 148

(162) S1A-010 251

(163) S1B-034 068

(164) S1B-040 004

(166) S2B-025 054

(167) W2D-019 013

(168) W2F-006 173

(169) S2B-024 009

(171) W2A-011 074

(172) *The Guardian*, 24/2/09

(173) S1A-081 311

(174) S1A-093 024

(175) S1B-011 121

(176) S1A-024 053

(177) S2A-042 075

(178) S1A-006 0316

(179) S1A-002 035

(180) S1B-051 058

(181) *New York Times*, 17/4/07

(182) W2F-009 044

(183) S1A-028 238

(184) S2A-008 191

(185) S1A-096 103

(186) *LA Times*, 23/12/86

(196) W2B-004 122

(197) S1A-046 100

(198) S1A-056 162

(199) S1A-049 260

(200) S1A-080 055

(201) *The Times*, 1/7/06

(202) S1A-022 227

(203) S1A-050 190

(204) S1A-055 033

(205) S1A-009 054

(206) S1A-011 256

(207) S2B-027 026

(208) W1A-003 042

(209) S1A-054 116
(210) S1A-041 181
(211) S1A-001 050
(212) *The Independent*, 11/10/09
(213) S1A-005 041
(214) W2B-003 039
(215) W2F-020 106
(216) S1B-021 154
(217) S1A-058 056
(218) W2B-002 012
(219) S2A-042 048
(220) S2B-036 026
(221) S2A-007 085
(222) W2D-014 063
(223) S1A-070 238
(224) S2B-030 001
(225) W2B-005 021
(226) S1A-076 069
(227) S1A-050 003
(228) S2A-055 084
(229) W2C-015 091
(230) W2F-004 172
(231) S2B-027 015
(232) W2B-009 042
(233) W2A-009 020
(234) S1A-012 151
(235) W2F-007 132
(236) W2B-035 048
(237) W1A-004 028
(238) W2B-017 005
(239) W2B-007 094
(240) S2B-020 113
(241) W2F-010 069
(242) W2C-009 090
(243) S1B-021 154
(244) S1A-047 079
(245) W2F-008 041
(246) S1A-025 071
(247) *The Guardian*, 3/5/03
(248) *The Guardian*, 5/9/04
(249) S1A-056 284

(250) W2C-020 036
(251) S1A-023 272
(252) S1A-053 013
(253) S2A-050 111
(254) S1A-022 295
(255) BBC News, 4/1/05
(256) S1A-036 148
(257) S1A-047 217
(258) S1A-074 024
(259) S2A-001 072
(260) S2A-002 019
(261) S2A-037 051
(262) S2A-016 049
(263) S1A-032 090
(264) BBC News, 9/5/02
(265) S2A-015 103
(266) *The Times*, 3/4/08
(267) W2A-003 055
(268) S1B-049 016
(269) *The Guardian*, 30/9/05
(270) *The Guardian*, 28/9/08
(271) W1B-017 016
(272) W2B-025 058
(273) W2D-020 103
(274) *The Guardian*, 30/4/06
(275) S1A-004 114
(276) S1A-060 073
(277) *Daily Telegraph*, 18/12/08
(278) BBC News, 23/10/03
(279) W2F-017 011
(280) S1A-017 379
(281) W1A-004 074
(283) S1A-005 157
(284) S2A-035 057
(285) W2B-006 106
(286) *The Independent*, 17/10/02
(287) W1B-009 175
(288) W2D-013 093
(289) S2B-047 035
(290) S1A-081 274
(291) S1A-004 007

(292) S1B-053 072

(293) S2B-033 046

(294) W2D-005 025

Table 5.10

(a) *The Guardian*, 19/4/08

(b) S1A-088 181

(d) S2A-068 073

(e) *The Guardian*, 26/1/09

(f) S1A-008 111

(g) The *Guardian*, 4/6//09

(h) S2B-032 045

(i) S2B-026 014

(j) *The Guardian*, 2/10/09

(k) BBC News, 7/11/99

(n) *The Guardian*, 9/6/09

(o) *Daily Telegraph*, 27/1/09

(p) *The Guardian*, 4/3/08

(q) *The Independent*, 7/3/02

Table 5.11

(a) S1A-090 231

(b) S2A-034 097

(c) BBC News, 22/9/03

(d) S1A-017 090

(e) S2A-017 157

(f) *The Daily Telegraph*, 11/5/01

(g) S2A-012 100

Chapter 6

· · · · · · · · · ·

(1) S1A-007 193

(3) S1A-018 003

(4) BBC News, 31/05/02

(5) BBC News, 19/9/07

(6) BBC News, 6/08/08

(7) S1A-019 307

(8) S1A-008 215

(9) S1A-006 174

(10) S1A-024 032

(11) W2A-016 011

(12) S1A-009 218

(13) S1A-066 100

(14) *Daily Telegraph*, 25/10/08

(15) *Daily Telegraph*, 22/9/03

(16) W1B-013 081

(17) S1A-020 018

(18) S1A-028 167

(19) S1A-070 057

(20) *The Independent*, 14/3/03

(21) S1A-004 046

(22) S1B-011 033

(23) S1B-072 244

(24) W2B-029 015

(25) S1A-044 104

(26) S1B-004 037

(27) S1A-019 153

(28) *The Independent*, 23/5/09

(29) *Daily Telegraph*, 18/2/08

(30) S1A-053 064

(31) S1B-048 134

(32) S1A-068 100

(33) *Daily Telegraph*, 13/09/08

(35) W1B-029 098

(36) S1A-010 278

(37) S1A-079 116

(38) *Daily Telegraph*, 23/8/07

(39) S1A-032 130

(40) S1A-008 106

(41) *Daily Telegraph*, 29/5/08

(42) S1B-069 110

(44) *The Times*, 21/8/06

(45) S1A-081 184

(46) S1A-014 088

(47) W1B-006 043

(48) W2F-014 003

(49) W2F-006 188

(50) W1B-020 020

(51) S1A-052 044

(52) S2A-062 112

(53) www.soap-news.com

(54) S1A-032 084

(55) S1A-022 243

(56) W2F-004 033

(57) S1B-079 075

(58) S1B-007 060

(59) *The Guardian*, 18/9/06

(60) W1B-006 107

(61) W1B-026 147

(62) W1B-004 004

(63) W1B-021 040

(64) S2B-030 052

(65) S1A-027 038

(66) S1A-007 103

(67) S1A-073 077

(68) S1A-083 067

(69) S1A-038 114

(70) S1A-086 152

(71) S1B-001 007

(72) S1A-007 078

(73) S2B-002 105

(74) S1A-006 323

(75) S1A-006 079

Chapter 7
. . . .

(1) W1B-028 117

(3) S1A-037 178

(4) W1A-018 094

(5) W2F-011 007

(6) W2F-005 015

(7) W1A-012 046

(8) *The Times*, 20/6/09

(13) S1A-001 048

(14) S1A-005 196

(17) S1A-015 145

(18) S1B-063 180

(19) S1A-009 003

(20) S1A-027 034

(21) W2B-030 022

(22) S1A-010 117

(23) W1A-018 094

(24) W2F002 082

(25) *The Guardian*, 20/7/09

(26) *The Guardian*, 27/8/98

(27) W1B-011 013

(28) BBC News, 8/9/08

(29) *The Guardian*, 28/7/09

(30) *The Times*, 23/2/09

(31) S1A-002 005

(33) S1B-053 002

(34) *The Independent*, 29/8/05

(35) S1A-082 033

(36) *The Guardian*, 16/9/09

(38) BBC News, 15/1/09

(40) BBC News, 9/9/04

(42) *The Independent*, 22/6/09

(43) BBC News, 23/2/09

(44) BBC News, 5/9/05

(46) S1B-053 035

(47) W2B-017 012

(48) BBC News, 19/11/09

(49) *The Irish Times*, 7/9/2010

(50) S1B-060 052

(51) S1B-028 016

(52) *The Independent*, 22/6/93

(53) W2F-011 007

(54) S2A-023 036

(55) W1B-016 062

(56) S1B-036 067

(57) S1A-052 052

(58) S1A-085 158

(59) S1B-005 060

(60) S1A-041 179

(61) S1B-026 015

(62) S2B-025 075

(63) S1A-001 030

(64) S1A-084 121

(65) S2A-054 098

(66) *The Independent*, 18/4/03

(67) W2D-001 016

(68) W1A-004 009

(69) S2A-022 078

(70) W1B-013 007

(71) W2E-003 075

(72) *Daily Telegraph*, 8/5/07

(73) W2A-003 058

(74) S1A-004 123

(75) W2A-003 058

(76) S1A-004 123

(77) W2C-007 070

(78) *The Independent*, 3/4/93

(79) S1A-008 266

(80) W2B-039 037

(81) S1B-029 172

(83) S1A-068 064

(84) W1B-011 051

(85) S2A-019 029

(86) W2C-002 015

(87) *The Daily Telegraph*, 11/3/09

(88) S1B-007 229

(89) *The Independent*, 27/1/09

(90) W1A-018 035

(91) *The Times*, 4/9/05

(92) BBC News, 11/10/02

(93) W2F-015 118

(94) *The Daily Telegraph*, 22/9/08

(95) S1A-058 210

(97) *Times Higher Education*,
9/7/09

(99) *The Guardian*, 10/2/07

(103) *The Guardian*, 16/5/09

(104) W2C-003 105

(105) *The Independent*, 12/1/05

(106) *The Daily Telegraph*, 22/8/08

Table 7.11

(a) S1A-017 376

(b) S1A-028 007

(c) W2D-011 019

(d) *New York Times*, 20/11/07

(e) *New York Times*, 28/4/10

Chapter 8
· · · · · · · · · ·

(1) S2B-029 145

(3) S2A-038 050

(4) W2E-004 064

(5) BBC News, 28/2/08

(6) S1B-069 002

(12) *The Guardian*, 12/7/05

(13) *The Guardian*, 27/10/06

(14) *New York Times*, 22/8/00

(15) W2D-009 103

(16) *The Independent*, 10/7/00

(17) S1A-064 077

(18) S1A-001 118

(19) *The Independent*, 22/6/04

(20) *The Guardian*, 10/3/09

(21) S2A-047 045

(23) BBC News, 9/2/06

(24) *Daily Telegraph*, 4/6/09

(26) *Daily Telegraph*, 26/5/04

(27) W2E-007 050

(33) *The Guardian*, 13/11/08

(34) *The Times*, 18/6/09

(35) *Daily Telegraph*, 6/10/05

(38) BBC News, 3/3/00

(40) W1A-018 096

(43) S1B-003 125

(45) S1A-024 53

(46) W2C-003 097

(47) S1A-060 012

(48) S1B-051 013

(49) W2A-032050

(50) W2D-001 053

(51) S1A-093 202

(52) S1A-014 062

(53) *Daily Telegraph*, 11/1/10

(55) *The Guardian*, 13/10/06

(57) *The Times*, 6/7/08

(58) S1A-036 093

(59) S1B-043 126

(60) S1A-043 211

(61) S1A-028 151

(62) W2C-020 096

(64) S1A-022 236

(65) S1B-022 222

(66) W1A-010 128

(67) W2C-002 086

(68) S1A-040 322

(69) *The Guardian*, 18/6/08

(71) W2C-006 041

(76) *The Times*, 20/11/07

(79) S1B-046 064

(80) BBC News, 22/11/06

(88) *The Guardian*, 10/11/06

(89) BBC News, 18/1/09

(93) *The Times*, 29/11/08

(94) *New York Times*, 17/7/09

(96) W2F-013 055

(98) W2C-011 018

(99) *Washington Post*, 9/12/07

(100) S2B-015 069

(102) W2E-010 050

(104) W1A-010 039

(105) W2D-017 103

(106) BBC News, 30/12/08

(107) S2A-026 065

(108) *The Guardian*, 28/11/09

(109) S1A-040 407

(110) S1A-051 118

(111) *New York Times*, 17/08/09

(114) *The Times*, 18/1/08

(117) *LA Times*, 6/10/07

(120) W1B-028 140

(122) W2F-002 006

(123) *The Independent*, 18/6/04

(126) *The Independent*, 16/01/07

(127) S2B-023 073

(128) S1B-035 095

(129) W2C-007 070

(130) S1A-002 028

(131) S1A-028 082

(152) *The Independent*, 7/1/89

(153) W1B-012 026

(154) S2A-054 219

(155) *New York Times*, 25/8/95

(156) W1B-017 017

(157) W2B-003 101

Chapter 9
· · · · · · · · · ·

(2) S2A-050 104

(4) S1A-042 343

(5) W2D-005 028

(6) W1B-003 187

(7) S1A-038 107

(8) S1A-031 023

(9) S1A-001 074

(10) S1B-053 075

(11) W2C-003 029

(12) S1A-083 237

(13) S1A-042 342

(14) S1A-032 237

(16) *The Times*, 16/07/07

(17) S2A-002 006

(18) S2A-017 030

(19) S2A-019 007

(20) S2A-011 127

(21) S1A-092 342

(22) W1B-022 020

(23) *Daily Telegraph*, 21/07/07

(24) *Daily Telegraph*, 7/06/06

(25) S1A-006 107

(26) S1B-077 074

(27) W2A-001 019

(28) W2C-004 003

(29) W2F-019 064

(30) W2F-016 059

(31) W2A-031 075

(32) S2A-022063

(33) Harold Pinter, *The Dumb Waiter*

(34) W2D-009 074

(35) W1B-014 090

(36) *The Guardian*, 11/04/09

(37) headline, *The Independent*, 19/3/06

(38) S1A-099 245

(39) W2E-006 015

(41) S1B-075 011

(42) W2B-012 055

(43) W2B-005 022

(44) S1A-057 002

(45) *The Guardian*, 5/11/00

(46) S1A-001 003

(47) S2A-055 098

(48) S1A-048 345

(49) *The Guardian*, 25/10/05

(50) *The Times*, 10/4/07

(51) *Daily Telegraph*, 25/9/01

(52) S2A-055 098

(53) *The Independent*, 26/6/09

(54) S1A-038 261

(55) W2F-003 135

(59) *The Guardian*, 21/8/00

(60) W2A-030 042

(61) W2F-018 148

(62) W2A-030 044

(63) S2B-016 085

(64) W1B-005 022

(66) S1B-053 105

(68) S1B-053 105

(70) BBC News, 8/5/09

(72) W2C-004 007

(73) W2F-009 113

(74) W1A-001 009

(75) W1B-001 155

(76) W2C-019 094

(77) S1A-074 362

(78) S1A-074 197

(79) W1B-014 092

(80) W1B-001 054

(81) http://ehealthforum.com

(84) S2B-015 063

(88) from Walker 2008; see References

(89) S1A-040 334

(90) W2E-005 012

(91) W2C-007 069

(93) W2C-011 076

(94) S2B-018 101

(95) S2B-015 060

(96) W1B-005 018

(98) S2B-027 161

(99) S1A-013 096

(100) W1B-022 027

(101) W1A-004 071

(102) W1B-021 047

(103) W2C-011 036

(104) W2C-011 091

(105) W2C-013 039

(106) S1B-032 091

(107) W2E-002 052

(108) S1B-044 113

(109) S1A-007 020

(110) S1A-049 278

(111) W1B-005 105

(112) S2A-059 114

(113) S1A-014 078

(114) S1A-041 124

(115) W2F-017 053

(117) S2B-043 055

(118) W2B-002 035

(119) W1A-001 088

(121) S1B-043048

(123) W1B-014 008

(124) S1B-064 128

(125) S1B-042 067

(126) S2A-067 08

(128) *The Guardian*, 3/12/06

(130) S1A-020 277

(131) S2B-026 095

(132) S1B-077 178

(133) S1A-034 069

(134) S2B-007 109

(135) S2B-008 007

(138) *The Independent*, 18/6/94

(141) W2B-023 032

(143) S2A-020 120

(144) S1A-001 083

(145) S2A-019 063

(147) S1A-013 228

(148) S1A-011 008

(149) S1A-003 160

(153) W1A-019 090

(155) W1B-011 009

(156) W2F-020 159

(157) W2F-013 114

(159) S1A-032 063

(160) W2F-020 130

(162) S2B-021 020

(163) S2B-035 031

(164) W1B-001 199

(165) S1A-059 059

(166) W1B-009 099

(167) W1B-013 055

(168) S1A-096 161

(169) S1A-092 027

(170) S2A-055 056

(174) S1A-007 224

(175) S1A-039 355

(176) W1B-004 084

(177) S1B-012 195

(198) S2B-020 037

(199) S1B-049 039

(200) S2A-061 110

(201) S1A-019 106

(202) S1A-061 261

(203) S1A-006 230

(205) Mrs Alfred Gatty, *Parables from nature*. T. Nelson & Sons, no date http://digital.library.upenn.edu/ women/gatty/parables/parables. html

(206) W2A-037 011

Chapter 10
. . . .

(1) S1A-031 116

(2) S1B-056 089

(3) S1A-075 140

(4) W2D-004 075

(5) W2F-002 050

(6) S1A-082 023

(7) S1B-003 092

(8) S1A-035 135

(9) W2A-011 028

(10) W1B-006 098

(13) W2F-010 079

(14) W2D-012 010

(15) W1B-014 047

(16) W2C-004 111

(17) S1A-074 375

(18) W2D-019 035

(19) S1A-057 078

(20) S2A-059 045

(21) S2A-039 038

(27) W1B-009 074

(28) S2B-024 053

(29) S1A-087 234

(30) *The Independent*, 4/7/09

(31) W1B-016 053

(32) S1A-083 131

(33) S2A-011 082

(34) S1B-054 071

(35) S1B-003 185

(36) *The Times*, 28/4/07

(37) W2D-010 060

(38) S1A-041 207

(39) S1A-038 058

(40) S1A-081 326

(41) S2B-005 056

(42) *The Times*, 12/7/03

(43) *New York Times*, 27/10/96

(44) *Daily Telegraph*, 18/7/09

(45) S2A-054 097

(46) S1B-052 096

(47) W2A-018 082

(48) W1B-028 046

(49) W1B-015 024

(50) W1B-027 122

(51) S2A-031 052

(52) W2D-008 049

(53) W2D-008 079

(54) W2D-008 040

(55) S1A-022 157

(56) *Daily Telegraph*, 2/12/06

(57) S1A-008 208

(58) S1B-053 105

(59) S1A-006 316

(60) S2A-054 204

(61) S1B-013 138

(62) W2E-006 095

(63) W1B-004 122

(64) S1A-070 073

(65) S1B-020 203

(66) S1A-007 262

(67) W2B-034 045

(68) S2A-011 091

(69) S2A-033029

(70) W2A-005 075

(71) S1B-041 150

(72) W2A-006 017

(76) W1B-016 063

(77) W1B-021 136

(78) S1B-031 098

(79) S1B-021 123

(80) S1B-027 036

(81) W2A-016 022

(82) S1A-021 075

(83) W2B-029 117

(84) S1A-005 189

(85) *The Times*, 21/12/07

(86) W2D-020 059

(87) *Daily Telegraph*, 8/4/05

(88) S1A-076 193

(89) W1B-002 140

(90) S1A-070 019

(91) S1A-074 004

(92) W1B-009 123

(93) S1B-079 175

(94) S1A-017 059

(95) W1B-025 048

(96) S1A-032 282

(97) S1A-036 090

(98) W1B-008 093

(99) S1A-047 059

(100) S2B-022 095

(101) S1B-053 065

(102) W1B-025 020

(103) W2D-004 051

(104) *The Times*, 22/11/08

(105) S2A-039 027

(106) W2F-008 071

(107) W2F-019 115

(108) S1B-025 078

(109) S1A-046 063

(110) S2B-038 106

(111) S1A-020 169

(112) S1A-052 043

(113) W1B-010 135

(114) W2A-005 108

(115) S2A-065 059

(116) S2B-022 116

(117) W2A-017 004

(118) thomson.co.uk

(119) S1A-065 202

(120) W1B-007 070

(121) S1A-057 064

(122) *Daily Telegraph*, 12/3/05

(123) S1A-025 097

(124) *The Times*, 1/3/09

(125) *The Times*, 3/12/09

(126) S1A-065 120

(127) S1A-027 113

(128) S1A-098 277

(129) S1A-053 010

(130) S2A-008 012

(131) S1B-060018

(132) W1B-013 122

(133) S1A-048 114

(134) S1B-079 187

(135) *Daily Telegraph*, 31/3/08

(136) *The Independent*, 9/5/06

(137) *The Guardian*, 20/8/09

(138) *Chicago Sun Times*, no date

(139) *Washington Post*, 10/6/09

(140) S1B-036 009

(141) S1A-030 020

(142) S1A-078 245

(145) S1A-067 009

(146) S1A-044 325

(147) S1A-026 329

(148) S1A-019 318

(149) BBC News, 30/1/99

(150) BBC News, 15/2/08

(151) BBC News, 1/6/09

(152) *The Independent*, 16/08/07

(153) S1B-078 131

(154) S2A-043 043

(155) W2C-018 046

(156) W1B-009 105

(157) *The Times*, 22/2/09

(158) *The Times*, 18/3/07

(159) W2D-009 152

(160) S1A-030 282

(161) S1A-080 078

(162) S1A-017 035

(163) *Daily Telegraph*, 1/01/09

(164) *The Guardian*, 14/7/08

(165) BBC News, 29/07/05

(166) *Daily Telegraph*, 5/9/08

(167) W2F-011 067

(168) BBC News, 24/8/05

(169) S1A-073 328

(170) *The Guardian*, 23/10/09

(171) S2B-012 010

(172) W2C-007 051

(173) W2E-001 029

(174) S2B-045 110

(175) *The Independent*, 13/1/99

(176) S2A-064 015

(177) W2B-014 009

(178) *The Guardian*, 13/09/08

(179) S2A-034 069

(180) W2F-015 121

(181) W2A-016 037

(182) S1B-034 113

(183) W2B-033 082

(184) S2B-007 027

(185) W2A-033 051

(186) W2A-017 045

(187) S1B-054 054

(188) W2D-018 036

(189) W1A-007 020

(190) S1A-030 050

(191) S1A-038 211

(192) *The Independent*, 8/7/08

(193) *The Guardian*, 21/10/04

(194) S1A-006 295

(195) S2A-018 048

(196) S1A-036 124

(197) S2B-011 036

(198) *Daily Telegraph*, 20/04/08

(199) *The Guardian*, 10/9/06

(200) S1A-068 035

(201) S1A-042 036

(204) S1A-020 268

(205) S1A-042 181

(206) W2F-009 113

(207) S1A-064 062

(208) W2D-010 060

(209) S2A-039 044

(210) S1B-030 086

(211) S1A-008 123

(212) W2A-017 025

(213) W2F-008 155

(214) W1A-009 056

(215) S1A-001 110

(216) W2B-033 094

(217) S1B-020 053

(218) S1A-003 073

(219) S1A-003 155

(220) S1A-052 026

(221) S1B-062 092

(222) S1A-007 154

(223) http://www.trfanatic.com

(224) W1B-004 048

(225) S2A-054 052

(226) W2D-020 017

(227) S2A-015 026

Chapter 11

· · · · · · · · · ·

(1) S1B-041 174

(3) S1A-043 098

(4) S1A-013 086/7

(6) W2F-005 025-027

(7) W2F-005 027

(8) S1A-057 131

(9) S1A-019 203

(10) S1B-005 125

(11) *Daily Telegraph*, 26/11/08

(12) W2E-005 010

(13) *The Guardian*, 1/9/08

(16) headline, *New York Times*, 14/2/09

(18) *Daily Telegraph*, 16/7/06

(21) W2F-010 024

(22) S1A-023 024

(25) W2A-002 066

(26) S1B-037 068

(27) S1A-057 114

(28) W2B-011 001

(33) W2C-005 035

(36) W2D-016 016

(38) W2C-001 034

(39) W1B-020 049

(40) W2D-016 015

(41) S1A-087 169

(44) W2B-019 003/4

(45) S1A-089 214

(47) S1A-071 342

(48) S1B-055 048

(50) S1B-056 089

(51) W1B-009 081

(52) S2A-059 128

(53) W1B-009 053

(54) S2A-004 063

(55) S2A-030 136

(56) S1B-077 169

(57) S2A-021 217

(58) *The Guardian*, 15/10/07

(59) *Daily Telegraph*, 1/06/03

(60) W1A-010 026

(61) S2B-005 070

(62) *Daily Telegraph*, 2/11/09

(64) W2C-007 072

(65) W2B-001 017

(68) *The Guardian*, 30/10/09

(69) S1A-092 342

(70) S2A-001 190

(71) S1B-038 086

(72) W2A-016 042

(73) W2B-037 170

(74) W2B-031 059

(75) W2B-031 040

(76) W2B-031 039

(83) S2A-014 196

(84) S1B-048 194

(85) W2F-013 045

(86) W2B-002 011

(87) S1B-050 005

(88) S1B-054 033

(98) *The Guardian*, 30/08/07

(99) S1A-022 236

(100) W1B-007 006

(101) *The Guardian*, 9/11/08

(102) S1A-009 024

(103) S1A-076 098

(107) S1A-004 004

References

Aarts, Bas (1992) *Small clauses in English: the non-verbal types*. Berlin and New York: Mouton de Gruyter.

Aarts, Bas (2007) *Syntactic gradience: the nature of grammatical indeterminacy*. Oxford: Oxford University Press.

Aarts, Bas (2008) *English syntax and argumentation*. Third edition. Basingstoke: Palgrave Macmillan.

Aarts, Bas, Joanne Close, Geoffrey Leech, and Sean Wallis (eds) (forthcoming) *Current change in the English verb phrase*. Cambridge: Cambridge University Press.

Aarts, Bas, David Denison, Evelien Keizer, and Gergana Popova (eds) (2004) *Fuzzy grammar: a reader*. Oxford: Oxford University Press.

Aarts, Bas, and Liliane Haegeman (2006) English word classes and phrases. In: Bas Aarts and April McMahon (eds) (2006) *The handbook of English linguistics*. Malden, MA, and Oxford: Blackwell Publishers. 117–145.

Aarts, Bas, and April McMahon (eds) (2006) *The handbook of English linguistics*. Malden, MA, and Oxford: Blackwell Publishers.

Aarts, Bas, and Charles F. Meyer (1995) Introduction: theoretical and descriptive approaches to the study of the verb in English. In: Bas Aarts and Charles F. Meyer (eds) (1995) *The verb in contemporary English: theory and description*. Cambridge: Cambridge University Press.

Aarts, Flor, and Jan Aarts (1982) *English syntactic structures*. Oxford: Pergamon Press.

Adams, Valerie (2001) *Complex words in English*. Harlow: Pearson Education.

Austin, J. L. (1962/1975) *How to do things with words*. Oxford: Clarendon Press.

Bauer, Laurie (1983) *English word-formation*. Cambridge: Cambridge University Press.

Bauer, Laurie (1998) When is a sequence of two nouns a compound in English? *English Language and Linguistics* 2, 65–86.

Bauer, Laurie (2003) *Introducing linguistic morphology*. Second edition. Edinburgh: Edinburgh University Press.

Bauer, Laurie (2004) *A glossary of morphology*. Edinburgh: Edinburgh University Press.

Bauer, Laurie (2006) Compounds and minor word-formation types. In: Bas Aarts and April McMahon (eds) (2006) *The handbook of English linguistics*. Malden, MA, and Oxford: Blackwell Publishers. 483–506.

Biber, Douglas, Stig Johansson, Geoffrey Leech, Susan Conrad, and Edward Finegan (1999) *Longman grammar of spoken and written English*. London and New York: Longman.

Binnick, Robert (2006) Aspect and aspectuality. In: Bas Aarts and April McMahon (eds) (2006) *The handbook of English linguistics*. Malden, MA, and Oxford: Blackwell Publishers. 244–268.

Birner, Betty J., and Gregory Ward (1998) *Information status and noncanonical word order in English*. Studies in Language Companion Series 40. Amsterdam: John Benjamins.

Birner, Betty J., and Gregory Ward (2006) Information structure. In: Bas Aarts and April McMahon (eds) (2006) *The handbook of English linguistics*. Malden, MA, and Oxford: Blackwell Publishers. 291–317.

Blevins, James P. (2006) English inflection and derivation. In: Bas Aarts and April McMahon (eds) (2006) *The handbook of English linguistics*. Malden, MA, and Oxford: Blackwell Publishers. 507–536.

Booij, Geert (2007) *The grammar of words: an introduction to linguistic morphology*. Second edition. Oxford: Oxford University Press.

Bullokar, W. (1586) *Pamphlet for grammar*. London: Henry Denham.

Carstairs-McCarthy, Andrew (2002) *An introduction to English morphology*. Edinburgh: Edinburgh University Press.

Coates, Jennifer (1983) *The semantics of the modal auxiliaries*. London: Croom Helm.

Collins, Peter (1991) *Cleft and pseudo-cleft constructions in English*. London: Routledge.

Collins, Peter (2006) Clause types. In: Bas Aarts and April McMahon (eds) (2006) *The handbook of English linguistics*. Malden, MA, and Oxford: Blackwell Publishers. 180–197.

Collins, Peter (2009) *Modals and quasi-modals in English*. Language and Computers: Studies in Practical Linguistics 67. Amsterdam: Rodopi.

Comrie, Bernard (1976) *Aspect*. Cambridge: Cambridge University Press.

Comrie, Bernard (1985) *Tense*. Cambridge: Cambridge University Press.

Crystal, David (2003) *The Cambridge encyclopedia of the English language*. Second edition. Cambridge: Cambridge University Press.

Crystal, David (2006) *The fight for English: how language pundits ate, shot, and left*. Oxford: Oxford University Press.

Curme, George O. (1947) *English grammar*. New York: Barnes & Noble, Inc.

Declerck, Renaat (1991) *Tense in English: its structure and use in discourse*. London: Routledge.

Depraetere, Ilse, and Susan Reed (2006) Mood and modality in English. In: Bas Aarts and April McMahon (eds) (2006) *The handbook of English linguistics*. Malden, MA, and Oxford: Blackwell Publishers. 269–290.

Fries, C. C. (1952) *The structure of English: an introduction to the construction of English sentences*. New York: Harcourt, Brace & Company.

Givón, Talmy (1993) *English grammar: a function-based introduction*. Two volumes. Amsterdam and Philadelphia: John Benjamins.

Huddleston, Rodney (1984) *Introduction to the grammar of English*. Cambridge: Cambridge University Press.

Huddleston, Rodney, and Geoffrey K. Pullum *et al.* (2002) *The Cambridge grammar of the English language*. Cambridge: Cambridge University Press.

Huddleston, Rodney, and Geoffrey K. Pullum (2006) Coordination and subordination. In: Bas Aarts and April McMahon (eds) (2006) *The handbook of English linguistics*. Malden, MA, and Oxford: Blackwell Publishers. 198–219.

Jespersen, Otto (1909–1949) *A modern English grammar on historical principles*. Seven volumes. Copenhagen: Munksgard.

Johnson, Samuel (1755) *A dictionary of the English language*. London: J. and P. Knapton, T. and T. Longman, C. Hitch and L. Hawes, A. Millar and R. and J. Dodsley.

Katamba, Francis, and John T. Stonham (2006) *Morphology*. Second edition. Basingstoke: Palgrave Macmillan.

Kruisinga, Etsko (1932) *A handbook of present-day English*. Groningen: P. Noordhoff.

Lambrecht, Knud (1994) *Information structure and language form*. Cambridge: Cambridge University Press.

Leech, Geoffrey N. (1969) *A linguistic guide to English poetry*. London: Longman.

Leech, Geoffrey N. (1983) *Principles of pragmatics*. Harlow: Longman.

Leech, Geoffrey N. (2004) *Meaning and the English verb*. Third edition. Harlow: Pearson Longman.

Leech, Geoffrey, Marianne Hundt, Christian Mair, and Nicholas Smith (2009) *Change in contemporary English: a grammatical study*. Cambridge: Cambridge University Press.

Leitner, Gerhard (ed.) (1986) *The English reference grammar: language and linguistics, writers and readers*. Tübingen: Max Niemeyer Verlag.

Levinson, S. (1983) *Pragmatics*. Cambridge: Cambridge University Press.

Linn, Andrew (2006) English grammar writing. In: Bas Aarts and April McMahon (eds) (2006) *The handbook of English linguistics*. Malden, MA, and Oxford: Blackwell Publishers. 72–92.

Long, R. B. (1961) *The sentence and its parts: a grammar of contemporary English*. Chicago: University of Chicago Press.

Lumsden, Michael (1988) *Existential sentences: their structure and meaning*. London: Croom Helm.

Mair, Christian, and Geoffrey Leech (2006) Current changes in English syntax. In: Bas Aarts and April McMahon (eds) (2006) *The handbook of English linguistics*. Malden, MA, and Oxford: Blackwell Publishers. 318–342.

Marchand, Hans (1969) *The categories and types of present-day English word-formation: a synchronic-diachronic approach*. Second edition. München: Beck'sche Verlagsbuchhandlung.

McCawley, James (1998) *The syntactic phenomena of English*. Second edition. Chicago: University of Chicago Press.

Michael, Ian (1970) *English grammatical categories and the tradition to 1800.*
    Cambridge: Cambridge University Press.

Michaelis, Laura A. (2006) Tense in English. In: Bas Aarts and April McMahon (eds)
    (2006) *The handbook of English linguistics.* Malden, MA, and Oxford: Blackwell
    Publishers. 220–243.

Minkova, Donka, and Robert Stockwell (2009) *English words: history and structure.*
    Second edition. Cambridge: Cambridge University Press.

Murray, Lindley (1795) *English grammar, adapted to the different classes of learners.*
    With an appendix, containing rules and observations for promoting perspicuity in
    speaking and writing. York: Wilson, Spence and Mawman.

Nelson, Gerald, Sean Wallis, and Bas Aarts (2002) *Exploring natural language: the*
    British component of the International Corpus of English. Varieties of English
    around the World series. Amsterdam: John Benjamins.

Palmer, Frank (1987) *The English verb.* Second edition. London: Longman.

Palmer, Frank (1990) *Modality and the English modals.* Second edition. London:
    Longman.

Palmer, H. E. (1924) *A grammar of spoken English, on a strictly phonetic basis.*
    Cambridge: W. Heffer & Sons Ltd.

Peters, Pam (2004) *The Cambridge guide to English usage.* Cambridge: Cambridge
    University Press.

Peters, Pam (2006) English usage: prescription and description. In: Bas Aarts and April
    McMahon (eds) (2006) *The handbook of English linguistics.* Malden, MA, and
    Oxford: Blackwell Publishers. 759–780.

Plag, Ingo (2003) *Word-formation in English.* Cambridge: Cambridge University Press.

Poutsma, Hendrik (1914–1929) *A grammar of late Modern English.* Groningen:
    P. Noordhoff.

Priestley, Joseph (1761) *The rudiments of English grammar.* London: Griffiths.

Quirk, Randolph, Sidney Greenbaum, Geoffrey Leech, and Jan Svartvik (1985)
    A comprehensive grammar of the English language. London: Longman.

Saeed, John (2009) *Semantics.* Third edition. Oxford: Wiley-Blackwell.

Salkie, Raphael (2010) *Will*: tense or modal or both? *English Language and Linguistics*
    14.2, 187–21.

Searle, J. (1969) *Speech acts: an essay in the philosophy of language.* Cambridge:
    Cambridge University Press.

Spencer, Andrew (1991) *Morphological theory.* Oxford: Blackwell.

Spinillo, Mariangela (2004) Reconceptualising the English determiner class. PhD
    thesis, English Department, University College London.

Stockwell, Robert P., Paul Schachter, and Barbara H. Partee (1973) *The major syntactic*
    structures of English. New York etc.: Holt, Rinehart & Winston.

Taglicht, Josef (1984) *Message and emphasis.* London: Longman.

Taylor, John (2003) *Linguistic categorization*. Third edition. Oxford: Oxford University Press.

Wales, Katie (1996) *Personal pronouns in present-day English*. Cambridge: Cambridge University Press.

Walker, Jim (2008) The strange phenomenon of the footballer's perfect. In: Geneviève Girard-Gillet (ed.) (2008) *Étrange/Étranger: études de linguistique anglaise*. C.I.E.R.E.C. Travaux 137, Publications de l'Université de Saint-Étienne. 21–32.

Warner, Anthony (1993) *English auxiliaries: structure and history*. Cambridge: Cambridge University Press.

Zandvoort, Reinard W. (1945) *A handbook of English grammar*. Several editions. Groningen: Wolters-Noordhoff.

Subject Index

Locators rendered in **bold** refer to tables.

386   **Subject Index**

Lexical Index